Disability in International Human Rights Law

Disability in International Human Rights Law

GAUTHIER DE BECO

OXFORD
UNIVERSITY PRESS

OXFORD
UNIVERSITY PRESS

Great Clarendon Street, Oxford, OX2 6DP,
United Kingdom

Oxford University Press is a department of the University of Oxford.
It furthers the University's objective of excellence in research, scholarship,
and education by publishing worldwide. Oxford is a registered trade mark of
Oxford University Press in the UK and in certain other countries

First Edition published in 2021

Impression: 1

Published in the United States of America by Oxford University Press
198 Madison Avenue, New York, NY 10016, United States of America

British Library Cataloguing in Publication Data

Data available

Library of Congress Control Number: 2021935954

ISBN 978–0–19–882450–3

DOI: 10.1093/oso/9780198824503.001.0001

Printed and bound by
CPI Group (UK) Ltd, Croydon, CR0 4YY

Preface

This book touches on the 'myth systems' of law and public policy. Every first-year law student is taught that because we are human, we have human rights. Yet even a cursory glance at societies in the past five or so decades since the human rights revolution shows that this is not so. Something indelibly etched into the human condition has carved out concentric circles of exclusion. It is as if we need to define our collective selves by whom we exclude.

So it was with disability and human rights. Human rights are supposed to be universal – yet it took an inordinately long time to bring persons with disabilities within its embrace. It was as if the 'all' in 'human rights for all' just didn't include persons with disabilities.

Think about that more deeply – our theory of justice which was largely expressed in human rights did not contemplate justice for persons with disabilities. What accounted for this invisibility – not just in society but in the very normative ideals that were supposed to govern society? Is it that human rights – like liberty – had to work itself pure from generation to generation? Did we have to wait for economic development to reach a certain point so that genuine equality for all could be acknowledged? Was it that the contradiction between universal rights and the exclusion of 15% of the world's population was simply no longer tolerable? Did it come down to all of the above co-mingled with the clarion calls of person with disabilities themselves including several outstanding advocates?

These are profound questions that help explain the march of ideas and especially the adoption of the Convention on the Rights of Persons with Disabilities. And it maybe points the way for the inclusion other contemporary outliers like older persons and indigenous persons who are still waiting for a full human rights framing.

This book is for anyone interested in the above questions and more. The advent of the human rights framing of disability has brought many innovations, and this book explores their value across the broader human rights spectrum. It points to a new and deeper theory of equality. It points to fresh ways of understanding economic and social rights – empowering and not entrapping – and civil and political rights – fostering participation in society. It points to radically new ways of imagining and operationalizing services – and therefore points the way for a more personalized social protection model for all in the 21st century. And it points the value of inclusion and belonging as core animating values – a new kind of active citizenship for all. And it gets us to address deeper questions – like why certain other groups still seem to be excluded from the embrace of human rights.

Human rights is a mirror that forces us to face contradictions, to openly acknowledge them and to rectify them. We need this mirror more than ever in the 21st century. This book keeps that flame alive and informs a new generation of advocates, activists and others who will no longer tolerate 'myth systems'.

Professor Gerard Quinn
UN Special Rapporteur on the Rights of Persons with Disabilities
2 February 2021
Galway, Ireland

Acknowledgement

This book is the culmination of a long journey. It is only later in my academic career that I developed a keen interest in disability and started to apply to it my knowledge acquired in the field of international human rights law. The project to write a monograph on the topic slowly matured while I was teaching, writing and speaking about the rights of disabled people. My expertise in both disability and international human rights law gave me a unique background that made me well-placed to undertake this project. It is thus the fruit of many years of research and work with colleagues and friends around the world.

I am grateful to all those who inspired me through conversations, collaboration and exchange of ideas, starting with Gerard Quinn and Theresia Degener, who are not by chance the authors of the UN study that laid the groundwork for the adoption of the UN Convention on the Rights of Persons with Disabilities, and continuing with Anna Lawson, Luke Clements, Michael Stein, Jerome Bickenbach, Colm O'Cinneide and Jonas Ruskus. There are many more I should mention, including disabled people and their families I have met in several countries especially through Inclusion Europe. A number of people have very kindly given their time and effort to provide feedback on one or more draft chapters. I would like thank for this particularly Janet Lord, Andrea Broderick, Lucy Series, Einat Albit, Jonathan Wolff, Sarah Arduin, Kimberlee Brownlee.

I wish furthermore to express my gratitude to the two institutions where I was based during the writing of this book, namely the University of Leeds and the University of Huddersfield. They have provided me with a motivating working environment and the resources needed in order to complete my project.

I am also grateful to the three reviewers for their comments on my book proposal as well as Merel Alstein and Jack McNichol at Oxford University Press and Mark Ajin for the book's production.

My gratitude goes finally to my family, including my wonderful aunt Wivine de Beco, whose proofreading has been so invaluable, and my two children Pierre-Adrien and Victoria de Beco, who are a permanent source of joy and encouragement.

Contents

II. STANDARDS: HUMAN RIGHTS FOR DISABLED PEOPLE AND BEYOND

III. IMPLEMENTATION: FROM RIGHTS TO REALITY

Introduction: The Book

For a long time, the issue of disability was considered to fall outside the domain of human rights. Although the focus on this issue has gradually increased in the field of anti-discrimination law, it is still relatively low in the field of international human rights law. This lack of awareness reached a tipping point in 2006 with the adoption of the Convention on the Rights of Persons with Disabilities (CRPD).[1] Disabled people have finally obtained their rightful place in international human rights law thanks to their own efforts at political mobilisation.

The CRPD has not just laid down all the rights of disabled people but also shed new light on the notion of human rights. Its significance for the whole field of international human rights law however remains quite uncharted. Without fully understanding the challenges posed by disability to international human rights law, not only the opportunity to capitalise on the adoption of the Convention is missed but also potential contradictions amongst international instruments threaten to keep hindering its implementation. Despite the attention that this Convention has attracted in recent years, there is still a long road ahead in order to deliver on its ambitions.

In 2002, Bengt Lindqvist, the Special Rapporteur on Disability of the Commission for Social Development, declared:

> Disability is a human rights issue! I repeat: disability is a human rights issue. Those of us who happen to have a disability are fed up being treated by the society and our fellow citizens as if we did not exist or as if we were aliens from outer space. We are human beings with equal value, claiming equal rights.[2]

Taking this claim as point of departure, the book explores ways of integrating disability into field of international human rights law. It examines how the CRPD has transformed the very notion of human rights through its consideration for distinct forms of embodiment and how this consideration can spill over in the entire field. By grounding the issue of disability more deeply in the canon of human rights, the ultimate objective is that the issue is no longer addressed by a limited number of

[1] Convention on the Rights of Persons with Disabilities 2006, 46 ILM 443.

[2] Bengt Lindqvist, 19th Congress of Rehabilitation International, Rio de Janeiro, 25–30 August 2000 (cited in G. Quinn and T. Degener, *The Current Use and Future Potential of United Nations Human Rights Instruments in the Context of Disability* (Geneva: UN, 2002) 13).

Disability in International Human Rights Law. Gauthier de Beco, Oxford University Press. © Gauthier de Beco 2021.
DOI: 10.1093/oso/9780198824503.003.0001

specialists but is fully taken into account by all human rights experts. While the Convention has been a milestone for protecting the rights of disabled people, the latter remain largely invisible in the international framework of human rights. This book defines what is needed in order to make disability an integral part of international human rights law.

Literature

Academic scholarship relating to the topic has very much expanded since the CRPD's arrival. However, it continues to address issues related to disability separately from other issues pertaining to human rights, and therefore remains foremost located within the field of disability law.

On the side of disability, the emphasis lies on the Convention particularly in the light of its negotiation process. Several scholars have examined particular rights as well as the requirements for the fulfilment of the legal obligations pertaining to them. They have also shown how the Convention exceeds and even collides with the provisions of other human rights treaties. Despite all examination, there has been as yet no inquiry into what the Convention rights imply for the whole domain of human rights.

On the side of human rights, literature in the field of international human rights law has begun to focus more seriously on the issue of disability. It has given the rights of disabled people greater importance although still less so than those of other marginalised groups. If disability is considered in greater detail, it has usually been with regard to the prohibition of discrimination with some reference to the new elements in the CRPD. Those concerned with broader human rights issues generally treat disability as an afterthought if they have treated it at all

The last ten years a series of works concerning the CRPD has seen the light of day. This includes the volumes of Arnardóttir and Quinn (published by Martinus Nijhoff Publishers in 2012), Anderson and Philips (published by the Netherlands Institute of Human Rights in 2012), Sabatello and Schulze (published by the University of Pennsylvania Press in 2013), Blanck and Flynn (published by Routledge in 2016) and O'Mahony and Quinn (published by Clarus Press in 2015).[3] Bantekas, Anastasiou and Stein have written a commentary on the Convention (published by Oxford University Press in 2018) which contains an

[3] O. Arnardóttir and G. Quinn (eds), *The UN Convention on the Rights of Persons with Disabilities. European and Scandinavian Perspectives* (London/Boston: Martinus Nijhoff Publishers, 2009); J. Anderson and J. Philips (eds), *Disability and Universal Human Rights: Legal, Ethical, and Conceptual. Implications of the Convention on the Rights of Persons with Disabilities* (Utrecht: Netherlands Institute of Human Rights, 2012); M. Sabatello and M. Schulze (eds), *Human Rights & Disability Advocacy* (Philadelphia: University of Pennsylvania Press, 2013); P. Blanck and E. Flynn (eds), *Routledge Handbook of Disability Law and Human Rights* (Abingdon: Routledge, 2016); C. O'Mahony and G. Quinn (eds), *Disability Law and Policy. An Analysis of the UN Convention* (Dublin: Clarus Press, 2017).

article-by-article examination.[4] Waddington and Lawson have furthermore considered the role of domestic courts in a volume which covers several jurisdictions (published by Oxford University Press in 2018).[5] While such volumes offer helpful guidance in the implementation of the CRPD, they do not actually aim to research disability as an integral part of international human rights law.

Some scholars have provided in-depth discussions on specific issues or rights protected by the CRPD, including the present author. There are monographs on disability strategies by Flynn (published by Cambridge University Press in 2011), the right to legal capacity both by Gooding (published by Cambridge University Press in 2017) and by Arstein-Kerslake (published by Cambridge University Press in 2017) and the right to work by Harpur (published by Cambridge University Press in 2019).[6] There are also volumes on independent mechanisms by de Beco (published by Martinus Nijhoff Publishers in 2013), on the right to work by Heymann, Stein and Moreno (published by Oxford University Press in 2014) and on the right to inclusive education by de Beco, Quinlivan and Lord (published by Cambridge University Press in 2018).[7] Broderick and Ferri have issued a handbook with cases and materials on the CRPD (published by Cambridge University Press in 2019).[8] A greater understanding of the rights of disabled people is indeed possible through a reading of the above-mentioned publications.

The works most relevant to the present book already from a few years ago are probably Kanter's monograph on *The Development of Disability Rights under International Law* (published by Routledge in 2015) and Broderick's monograph on *The Long and Winding Road to Equality and Inclusion for Persons with Disabilities* (published by Intersentia in 2015).[9] Both of them not only consider the CRPD's objectives including its understanding of disability but also focus on a number of

[4] I. Bantekas, D. Anastasiou and M. Stein (eds), *Commentary on the UN Convention on the Rights of Persons with Disabilities* (New York: Oxford University Press, 2018).

[5] L. Waddington and A. Lawson (eds), *The UN Convention on the Rights of Persons with Disabilities in Practice: A Comparative Analysis of the Role of Courts* (Oxford: Oxford University Press, 2018).

[6] E. Flynn, *From Rhetoric to Action: Implementing the UN Convention on the Rights of Persons with Disabilities* (Cambridge: Cambridge University Press, 2011); P. Gooding, *A New Era for Mental Health Law and Policy: Supported Decision-Making and the UN Convention on the Rights of Persons with Disabilities* (Cambridge: Cambridge University Press, 2017); A. Arstein-Kerslake, *Restoring Voice to People with Cognitive Disabilities. Realizing the Right to Equal Recognition Before the Law* (Cambridge: Cambridge University Press, 2017); P. Harpur, *Ableism at Work: Disablement and Hierarchies of Impairment* (Cambridge: Cambridge University Press, 2019).

[7] G. de Beco (ed), *Article 33 of the UN Convention on the Rights of Persons with Disabilities: National Structures for the Implementation and Monitoring of the Convention* (Leiden/Boston: Martinus Nijhoff Publishers, 2013); J. Heymann, M. Stein and G. Moreno (eds), *Disability and Equity at Work* (New York: Oxford University Press, 2014); G. de Beco, J. Lord and S. Quinlivan (eds), *The Right to Inclusive Education in International Human Rights Law* (Cambridge: Cambridge University Press, 2019).

[8] A. Broderick and D. Ferri, *International and European Disability Law and Policy: Text, Cases and Materials* (Cambridge: Cambridge University Press, 2019).

[9] A. Kanter, *The Development of Disability Rights under International Law. From Charity to Human Rights* (Abingdon: Routledge, 2015); A. Broderick, *The Long and Winding Road to Equality and Inclusion for Persons with Disabilities. The United Nations Convention on the Rights of Persons with Disabilities* (Mortsel: Intersentia, 2015).

Convention rights. What they fail to do is to harvest the gains that can be derived from this Convention from the perspective of international human rights law, with the result that they remain more or less confined to the field of disability law. There are no works that seek to study the issue of disability within the broader framework of international human rights.

Also worth mentioning is the significant number of articles on the CRPD the totality of which cannot be listed in this introduction. A closer look at these shows a gradually evolving perspective on the Convention. While earlier articles underline the Convention's actual benefits for disabled people in the wake of its entry into force,[10] more recent articles either emphasise the shift in thinking regarding what the Convention has come to represent in the field or provide a critical account of its fundamental premises which may include downright criticism.[11] Other articles express particular views on CRPD rights, some of which will play a central role in setting out the argument defended in the present book (in particular in Part II).[12]

Aims and Method

The unique feature of this book lies in its objective of developing a theoretical framework which explicitly integrates disability into international human rights law. In order to meet this aim, it provides a thorough examination of the innovations the CRPD has introduced in the field as well as a critical evaluation of its repercussions

[10] R. Kayess and P. French, 'Out of Darkness into Light? Introducing the Convention on the Rights of Persons with Disabilities' (2008) 8 *Human Rights Law Review* 1; A. Dhanda, 'Constructing a New Human Rights Lexicon: Convention on the Rights of Persons with Disabilities' (2008) 5 *International Journal on Human Rights* 43; P. Bartlett, 'The United Nations Convention on the Rights of Persons with Disabilities and Mental Health Law' (2012) 75 *Modern Law Review* 752–78; P. Harpur, 'Embracing the New Disability Rights Paradigm: The Importance of the Convention on the Rights of Persons with Disabilities' (2012) 27 *Disability & Society* 1.

[11] F. Mégret, 'The Disabilities Convention: Human Rights of Persons with Disabilities or Disability Rights' (2008) 30 *Human Rights Quarterly* 494; F. Mégret, 'The Disabilities Convention: Towards a Holistic Concept of Rights' (2008) 12 *International Journal of Human Rights* 261; K. Johnson, 'The UN Convention on the Rights of Persons with Disabilities: A Framework for Ethical and Inclusive Practice?' (2013) 7 *Ethics & Social Welfare* 218; S. Arduin, 'Taking Metaregulation to the United Nations Human Rights Treaty Regime: The Case of the Convention on the Rights of Persons with Disabilities' (2019) 41 *Law & Policy* 411; B. Byrne, 'Dis-Equality: Exploring the Juxtaposition of Disability and Equality' (2018) 6 *Social Inclusion* 9; G. de Beco, 'The Indivisibility of Human Rights and the Convention on the Rights of Persons with Disabilities' (2019) 68 *International & Comparative Law Quarterly* 141; J. Grue, 'Inclusive Marginalisation? A Critical Analysis of the Concept of Disability, Its Framings and Their Implications in the United Nations Convention on the Rights of Persons with Disabilities' (2019) 37 *Nordic Journal of Human Rights* 3.

[12] A. Dhanda, 'Universal Legal Capacity as a Universal Human Right' in M. Dudley, D. Silove and F. Gale (eds), *Mental Health and Human Rights: Vision, Praxis and Courage* (Oxford: Oxford University Press, 2012) 177; B. Byrne, 'Hidden Contradictions and Conditionality: Conceptualisations of Inclusive Education in International Human Rights Law' (2013) 28 *Disability & Society* 332; E. Albin, 'Universalising the Right to Work of Persons with Disabilities: An Equality and Dignity Based Approach' in V. Mantouvalou (ed), *The Right to Work. Legal and Philosophical Perspectives* (Oxford: Hart Publishing, 2015) 61.

on the concept of human rights. While the book does revolve around the CRPD, it pays as much attention to the international instruments and explores how both the Convention is intricately bound up with these instruments. It does so both by studying the relationship between the Convention rights and those protected by other human rights treaties and by examining the cross-pollination between these rights and the overall objectives of the UN. The book thus explores how disability can be integrated into international human rights law in a way that yields benefits for all individuals. This integration is anchored in the idea of the disabled subject—coined in Chapter 4—which proceeds from the fact that all individuals encounter disability-related issues in one or the other way in the course of their lives. Through its acknowledgement of disability as a universal experience, the disabled subject is a construct helping to move away from the traditional legal subject that is defined in international human rights law as a fixed and distant figure. It paves the way towards the adoption of a universal approach which provides the basis for an explicit integration of disability into the field of international human rights law. While the first part of the book sets out how this disabled subject assumes importance and how it relinquishes any group-based approach, the second part of the book shows what are the implications of bringing the disabled subject to bear upon a number of rights and what are the lessons of the Convention for the implementation of human rights treaties. Behind the book lies the postulate that the consideration of disability can advance the field of international human rights law itself.

By exploring what the CRPD rights imply for the whole domain of human rights, the present book provides an agenda-setting analysis for all human rights experts by inviting them to appreciate the benefits of placing disabled people at the heart of international human rights law. It explores how the Convention enriches the notion of human rights and reveals its capacity to act as a catalyst for uniting the human rights community.

In addition to the above-mentioned publications, the book relies on the general literature in the field of international human rights law. It draws upon the preparatory works of the CRPD as well as the recommendations of treaty bodies. The latter include not only the CRPD Committee, which has already issued seven general comments to date,[13] but also the other treaty bodies so as to reveal how all human rights treaties are interlinked.

In order to highlight the actual conditions in which disabled people live, this book draws upon the reports of UN agencies, starting with the one published by the World Health Organisation (WHO) and the World Bank published in 2011.[14] Other agencies that have shaped the rights of disabled people include the Office of the UN High Commissioner for Human Rights (OHCHR) and the United Nations

[13] They are available here: https://www.ohchr.org/EN/HRBodies/CRPD/Pages/GC.aspx.

[14] World Health Organization (WHO) and World Bank, *World Report on Disability* (Geneva: WHO, 2011).

Children's Fund (UNICEF) as well as the International Labour Organisation (ILO). The book also leans on evidence from disabled people's organisations (DPOs) on the challenges experienced by disabled people. While it does not emphasise the role of the courts as such, it makes references to case law where relevant, including that of the European Court of Human Rights.

The method used in the present book is first and foremost doctrinal. It is however impossible to assess the CRPD's normative underpinnings without bringing to bear concepts proper to a number of related disciplines. Among the latter are not only the burgeoning field of disability studies, which has informed current views of disability, but also the more traditional legal and political theory, which will provide assistance in developing the purported theoretical framework.

Throughout its various chapters, the book concentrates on two transversal themes. First, it deals with the indivisibility of human rights, which is at the core of the CRPD much more so than in any other human rights treaty. Bridging civil and political and economic and social rights as it does, the Convention questions some of the dichotomies of international human rights law, such as its division into two sets of rights. Second, the book pays special attention to the question of intersectionality, which likewise is a prominent feature of the Convention. The question of intersectionality is essential in understanding disability because it further attests to the heterogeneity of disabled people. By factoring in characteristics other than disability the road also remains open for establishing deeper connections with the other human rights treaties. The two transversal themes will perform an essential function both in the conceptual part of the book and in the analysis of particular rights the choice of which shows how the Convention inter-mixes both sets of rights.

In contrast to most academic scholarship relating to the topic, the book targets not so much students, although they could find it useful at an advanced level but rather a broad range of stakeholders. The latter include not only human rights experts, both within and outside academia, but also international organisations, NGOs, national human rights institutions, public administrations, lawyers and consultants not to mention DPOs themselves. This book will appeal to both those with a particular interest in the rights of disabled people, even if only superficial, and those willing to make human rights more of a reality for vulnerable groups generally.

The world since starting this book has experienced high levels of anxiety following the outbreak of the Covid-19 pandemic. The crisis has led to extreme forms of hardship particularly for disabled people, who are more likely to live in institutions where rates of infection are higher and who are often the first ones to be negatively affected.[15] This book was in its final stages when the crisis started, so it

[15] UN, *A Disability-Inclusive Response to Covid-19*, May 2020, https://www.un.org/sites/un2.un.org/files/sg_policy_brief_on_persons_with_disabilities_final.pdf.

was impossible to change course in order to properly address all the implications emanating from it. It is quite clear though that any progress towards giving effect to the CRPD has been temporarily halted due to the consequent worsening of their lives. Much of society will have to be rebuilt, and it is hoped that the insights provided in this book will be of use to all those pushing in that direction.

As far as terminology is concerned, both 'disabled people' or 'persons with disabilities' are widely accepted terms often used interchangeably. The first term, 'disabled people', stresses that disability is a product of societal organisation as underscored by the social model of disability; the second term, 'persons with disabilities', which is the one used in the CRPD, highlights that the people in question are 'persons first'. While both terms have their value, the book will always refer to 'disabled people'. The reason for this, as will be explained, is that it employs a social model lens on disability even if it concedes that the Convention has not adopted this model entirely. The book uses this term in order to draw attention to the social dimension of disability that this term brings to mind.

Structure

The book itself is divided into three parts: Part I is about concepts (I. Concepts: The Integration of Disability into International Human Rights Law), Part II concerns standards (II. Standards: Human Rights for Disabled People and Beyond) and Part III deals with implementation (III. Implementation: From Rights to Reality). This division is not only one that is normally used in the field of international human rights law but also one that by itself reflects the CRPD's main innovative features. While any chapter can be read individually, the chapters within the three parts (Chapters 1–4, Chapters 5–8 and Chapters 9–10) follow a similar internal pattern and provide a consistent and coherent argumentation when taken together, as can been seen from the sub-headings.

Part I addresses the general background of disability in international human rights law. It examines not only the evolution that the CRPD represents but also what its approach to disability reveals about the notion of human rights. It further highlights how this Convention elevates the very concept of human rights by appreciating the entire range of human differences. Bringing in the idea of the disabled subject, it argues in favour of the adoption of a universal approach that regards disability as a universal experience.

Chapter 1 starts by outlining the steps towards the adoption of a human rights treaty for disabled people. Chapter 2 explores not only the shift in focus with regard to disability and the social model's impact on the CRPD's drafters but also the extent to which disability has been brought into the mainstream. Chapter 3 goes on to discuss theories of justice, including social contract theory, which several disability scholars have criticised with regard to disability, as well as capability and recognition theories, both of which can prove useful in order to facilitate the inclusion of disabled people. Chapter 4 investigates how international human rights falsely dressed up the legal subject and how the CRPD has retrieved it from its disembodied conception before calling upon vulnerability theory to show its relevance for advancing the idea of the disabled subject.

Part II offers an analysis of particular rights which together not only provide an overall snapshot of the rights of disabled people but also reflect upon the new emphasis that the Convention places on all human rights. It examines the four rights for this purpose: the right to legal capacity; the right to inclusive education; the right to work and; the right to political participation. While the said rights have roots that predate the CRPD, they bring to the fore elements which are left aside by previous human rights treaties and which offer a fresh perspective on the field of international human rights law.

Chapter 5 analyses the right to legal capacity by focusing on the need to provide support for the exercise of legal capacity particularly by the strengthening of social relationships. Chapter 6 investigates the right to inclusive education that results from the incorporation of the goal of inclusive education into international human rights law. Chapter 7 examines the right to work including the aim to ensure equal employment opportunities for disabled people through the transformation of the labour market. Chapter 8 analyses the right to political participation by stressing the importance of fostering inclusion into political life to achieve political participation at large.

Part III turns to the implementation of human rights treaties by addressing two inter-related issues which are crucial to its achievement, namely participation and monitoring. It not only surveys the involvement of civil society organisations but also delves into the functioning of national human rights institutions (NHRIs). It thereby shows the essential role of both issues (participation and monitoring) in translating rights into reality.

Chapter 9 addresses the participation of disabled people, which reached a peak in the CRPD's negotiation process, and the manner in which the Convention has strengthened 'participatory rights' in general. Chapter 10 examines the role of independent mechanisms, including the requirements of independence and pluralism as well as the reference to the Paris Principles' consequence for NHRIs.

The book finishes first with a short summary of all the chapters. It further explains the manner in which the CRPD has moved away from the non-discrimination norm while it absorbed it and what further action is needed in order to make disability an integral part of international human rights law.

I

CONCEPTS: THE INTEGRATION OF DISABILITY INTO INTERNATIONAL HUMAN RIGHTS LAW

1

Historical Background: Towards a Human Rights Treaty for Disabled People

This chapter follows the path towards the enactment of the CRPD (1.1 The Adoption of the CRPD). It looks at the preceding international instruments on disability as well as the steps taken to elaborate a legally binding international instrument. It goes on to evaluate the way in which the Convention distinguishes itself from other human rights treaties (1.2 Disabled People and Human Rights Treaties). It not only discusses the role of the prohibition of discrimination with regard to disabled people as well as its potential to address their marginalisation but also analyses any resemblances between the CRPD and the Convention on the Rights of the Child (CRC). It moreover examines how the CRPD has improved human rights protection generally by advancing the principle of substantive equality.

1.1 The Adoption of the CRPD

The present book takes as a starting point the International Year of Disabled Persons in 1981.[1] The International Year of Disabled Persons led to subsequent events that facilitated the drafting of the CRPD, and its overall purpose gave direction to all the rights of disabled people as we know them today. The International Year of Disabled Persons was preceded by the adoption of a number of other non-legal binding international instruments on disability. These international instruments, which include the Declaration on the Rights of Mentally Retarded Persons and the Declaration on the Rights of Disabled Persons, adopted in 1971 and 1975, respectively,[2] recognised human rights for disabled people. Nonetheless, they persisted both in granting disabled people a lower social status and in depicting them as dependent and inferior.[3] Such international instruments were relying on the dominant medical model of disability (explained in Chapter 2).[4] The shift in focus,

[1] GA, *International Year of Disabled Persons*, 8 December 1981, A/RES/36/77.

[2] GA, *Declaration on the Rights of Mentally Retarded Persons*, 20 December 1971, A/RES/26/2856; GA, *Declaration on the Rights of Disabled Persons*, 9 December 1975, A/RES/3447 (XXX).

[3] A. Kanter, *The Development of Disability Rights under International Law. From Charity to Human Rights* (Abingdon: Routledge, 2015) 31–2.

[4] M. Stein, 'Disability Human Rights' (2007) 95 *California Law Review* 75, 88.

Disability in International Human Rights Law. Gauthier de Beco, Oxford University Press. © Gauthier de Beco 2021.
DOI: 10.1093/oso/9780198824503.003.0002

which was necessary to enable disabled people to be treated with equal consideration and to be recognised as subjects of rights, had yet to come.

The Resolution declaring 1981 the International Year of Disabled Persons was the first step towards such a shift in focus. Its theme, as expressed by the General Assembly, namely '[f]ull participation and equality',[5] still represents the primary goal of international human rights law with regard to disability. The Resolution stressed 'the continuing need to promote the realization of the right of disabled persons to participate fully in the social life and development of their societies and to enjoy living conditions equal to those of other citizens'.[6] This International Year of Disabled Persons was an initial response to the marginalised position of disabled people around the world. It encouraged steps taken towards developing what would become the World Programme of Action for Persons with Disabilities in 1982. Despite its emphasis on the prevention of disability and efforts towards rehabilitation,[7] the World Programme of Action for Persons with Disabilities would represent another milestone in the affirmation of the human rights of disabled people. Distancing itself from the medical model of disability,[8] the Programme stressed the importance of 'activities related to equalization of opportunities for disabled persons' and enumerated a series of measures in order to achieve it.[9] The World Programme of Action for Persons with Disabilities also required that States regularly report on its implementation to the UN Secretary General. It is noteworthy that this international instrument is still in action, and therefore works in parallel with the CRPD. The UN subsequently launched the International Decade of Disabled Persons, which took place from 1983 to 1992.[10] The Principles for Protection of Persons with Mental Illness and the Improvement of Mental Health Care further provided for standards to protect people with a mental health condition regardless of whether they lived in institutions.[11] The aforementioned international instruments thus paved the way for the human rights treaty that would later become the CRPD. They are proof that seeing disability as a human rights issue had started to gain ground before its adoption.

The Vienna Declaration and Programme of Action (VDPA), adopted in 1993,[12] paid particular attention to disabled people. This attention was significant, not only because this is a generic human rights document but also given the importance it would acquire in the coming decades. The VDPA spelled out what was the new

[5] GA, *International Year of Disabled Persons*, Preamble.

[6] Ibid.

[7] Ibid, paras 3, 10, 15, 16 and 17.

[8] A. Rimmerman, *Disability and Community Living Policies* (Cambridge: Cambridge University Press, 2017) 32.

[9] GA, *World Programme of Action for Persons with Disabilities*, 3 December 1982, A/RES/37/52.

[10] GA, *International Decade of Disabled Persons*, 23 November 1984, A/RES/39/26.

[11] GA, *Principles for Protection of Persons with Mental Illness and the Improvement of Mental Health Care*, 17 December 1991, A/RES/46/119.

[12] World Conference on Human Rights, *Vienna Declaration and Programme of Action*, 25 June 1993, A/Conf.157/23.

vision of human rights at the international level. It famously proclaimed that '[a]ll human rights are universal, indivisible and interdependent and interrelated'.[13] Reaffirming 'that all human rights and fundamental freedoms are universal and thus unreservedly include persons with disabilities', the VDPA declared that '[t]he place of disabled persons is everywhere'.[14] It further considered that '[p]ersons with disabilities should be guaranteed equal opportunity through the elimination of all socially determined barriers, be they physical, financial, social or psychological, which exclude or restrict full participation in society'.[15] This recommendation was a predictive sign of how international human rights law would articulate the rights of disabled people in the future. It already reflected the idea that these rights entail the removal of obstacles created by society.

This being said, prior to the CRPD, none of the existing human rights treaties referred to disability, with one notable exception. The CRC, adopted in 1989,[16] not only listed disability in its general non-discrimination clause, unlike these human rights treaties, but also devoted a separate article to disabled children.[17] Article 23 of the CRC provides that disabled children must 'enjoy a full and decent life, in conditions which ensure dignity, promote self-reliance and facilitate the child's active participation in the community'.[18] The CRC can be seen as the 'cousin' of the CRPD, as both human rights treaties share resemblances, including their focus on disabled children, as explained further below. Considering that the former treaty chronologically precedes the latter treaty, it is possible that more lessons can be learned from the CRC that can benefit the CRPD than the other way around.[19] However, the CRC has a number of limitations with regard to disability, such as its focus on 'special care' for disabled children, which should be 'subject to available resources ... appropriate to the child's condition' and for which 'assistance ... shall be provided free of charge, whenever possible'.[20] This wording implies that disability remains a question of welfare and that the need to protect the rights of disabled people is subordinate to the protection afforded to others.

While neither the Convention on the Elimination of All Forms of Discrimination against Women (CEDAW) nor the International Covenant on Economic, Social and Cultural Rights (ICESCR) make explicit reference to disability,[21]

[13] Ibid, para 5.
[14] Ibid, paras 63–4.
[15] Ibid, para 64.
[16] Convention on the Rights of the Child 1989, 1577 *UNTS* 3 (CRC).
[17] Articles 2 and 23, CRC.
[18] Article 23(1), CRC.
[19] See, however, R. Sandland, 'Lessons for Children's Rights from Disability Rights' in E. Brems, E. Desmet and W. Vandenhole (eds), *Children's Rights Law in the Global Human Rights Landscape: Isolation, Inspiration, Integration?* (Abingdon: Routledge, 2017) 109.
[20] Article 23(2) and (3), CRC.
[21] Convention on the Elimination of All Forms of Discrimination against Women 1979, 1249 *UNTS* 13 (CEDAW); International Covenant on Economic, Social and Cultural Rights 1966, 993 UNTS 3 (ICESCR).

both the Committee on the Elimination of Discrimination against Women (CEDAW Committee) and the Committee on Economic, Social and Cultural Rights (CESCR Committee) issued general recommendations/general comments in relation to disabled people. In its General Recommendation on the situation of disabled women, the CEDAW Committee asked States Parties to provide information regarding disabled women in its reports on the implementation of CEDAW,[22] although it later on highlighted their particular needs in the context of health.[23] The Committee on Economic, Social and Cultural Rights (CESCR) (CESCR Committee) carried out a more in-depth examination of the rights of disabled people in its General Comment on the situation of disabled people.[24] It thereby set out one of the first key sets of recommendations on the issue. In that General Comment, it not only urged States Parties to the ICESCR to take steps so that disabled people can 'overcome any disadvantages, in terms of the enjoyment of the rights specified in the Covenant, flowing from their disability' but also provided a definition of discrimination on the basis of disability that included a failure to provide reasonable accommodation.[25] The CESCR Committee was therefore the first treaty body to recognise that such failure amounted to a form of discrimination on the basis of disability. The Committee further clarified that disability was covered by 'other status' in the general non-discrimination clause of the ICESCR,[26] a clarification which has not been provided as yet by the Human Rights Committee in relation to the general non-discrimination clause of the International Covenant on Civil and Political Rights (ICCPR).[27]

In the late 1980s, two countries, namely Italy and Sweden, proposed to begin to negotiate a human rights treaty for disabled people, but their respective proposals were dismissed by the General Assembly.[28] The time was not ripe for such a human rights treaty, especially since the CRC was being drafted at that point. The

[22] CEDAW Committee, *General Recommendation No 18: Disabled Women*, 30 January 1991, A/46/38.

[23] CEDAW Committee, *General Recommendation No 24: Women and Health*, 5 February 1999, A/54/38. The Beijing Declaration Platform for Action also paid particular attention to disabled women (Fourth World Conference on Women, *Beijing Declaration and Platform for Action*, 15 September 1995, A/CONF.177/20, paras 60(a), 81(a), 106(c), 124(m), 175(d), 178(j), 195(a) and 206(k)).

[24] CESCR Committee, *General Comment No 5: Persons with Disabilities*, 9 December 1994, E/1995/22.

[25] Ibid, paras 5 and 9.

[26] Ibid, para 5. The CESCR defined discrimination on the basis of disability as 'any distinction, exclusion, restriction or preference, or denial of reasonable accommodation based on disability which has the effect of nullifying or impairing the recognition, enjoyment or exercise of economic, social or cultural rights' (Ibid, para 15).

[27] International Covenant on Civil and Political Rights 1966, 999 UNTS 171 (ICCPR). On this issue see F. Mégret, 'The Disabilities Convention: Human Rights of Persons with Disabilities or Disability Rights' (2008) 30 *Human Rights Quarterly* 494, 502; M. Jones and L. Basser Mark, 'Law and the Social Construction of Disability' in M. Jones and L. Basser Mark (eds), *Disability, Divers-Ability and Legal Change* (The Hague: Martinus Nijhoff Publishers, 1999) 3, 21.

[28] G. Quinn, 'Disability and Human Rights: A New Field in the United Nations' in K. Krause and M. Scheinin (eds), *International Protection of Human Rights: A Textbook* (Turku: Åbo Akademi University-Institute for Human Rights, 2009) 24, 252.

disability rights movement was perhaps also not ready to assist in elaborating a legally binding international instrument. Instead, the General Assembly adopted the Standard Rules for the Equalisation of Opportunities for Persons with Disabilities (Standard Rules) in 1993.[29]

The Standard Rules were the first international instrument to promote the participation of disabled people in society. They are still the most important international instrument on disability that was adopted prior to the CRPD. The terminology used in the Standard Rules reflects a remarkable change in approach to dealing with disability, as they focus on participation, equality and non-discrimination. The Standard Rules enunciate with considerable precision the measures necessary to include disabled people in various areas of life, including education, employment, social security, family life and recreation. They also promote the involvement of disabled people's organisations (DPOs) in the adoption of policies relating to disability.[30] Despite their non-binding nature and continued medicalised perspective,[31] the Standard Rules remain a point of reference for the human rights of disabled people. They have been a source of inspiration both for international monitoring mechanisms, including the treaty bodies, and for domestic actors, including the CRPD's drafters themselves. Importantly, the Standard Rules foresee the appointment of a Special Rapporteur on Disability who has to report to the Commission for Social Development.[32] Disabled people slowly started to find their rightful place in international human rights law.

Following the adoption of the Standard Rules, different voices called, once more, for the adoption of a legally binding international instrument on disability. A Consultative UN Expert Group met at the University of California, Berkeley, and recommended the negotiation of such an international instrument.[33] Meanwhile, the Durban Declaration and Programme of Action had invited the UN to elaborate 'an integral and comprehensive international convention to protect and promote the rights and dignity of disabled people'.[34]

The Office of the High Commissioner for Human Rights (OHCHR) subsequently commissioned a study on the protection of disabled people within the international human rights system by two prominent disability rights lawyers.[35] The study examined the utility of existing human rights treaties for disabled people

[29] GA, *Standard Rules for the Equalisation of Opportunities for Persons with Disabilities*, 20 December 1993, A/RES/48/96.

[30] Rule 14(2), Standard Rules.

[31] R. Kayess and P. French, 'Out of Darkness into Light? Introducing the Convention on the Rights of Persons with Disabilities' (2008) 8 *Human Rights Law Review* 1, 16.

[32] Rule 6(2), Standard Rules.

[33] Quinn, 'Disability and Human Rights', 253.

[34] *Report of the World Conference against Racism, Racial Discrimination, Xenophobia and Related Intolerance Durban*, 31 August–8 September 2001, A/Conf.189.12, para 180. It also encouraged stakeholders 'to address the situation of persons with disabilities who are subject to racism' (Ibid, para 57).

[35] G. Quinn and T. Degener, *The Current Use and Future Potential of United Nations Human Rights Instruments in the Context of Disability* (Geneva: UN, 2002).

and the extent to which the international monitoring mechanisms were considering them in their work. Noting that both the treaty bodies and NGOs were paying little attention to such people, the study set out a series of potential remedies for this gap. Recognising that 'a convention would mark a huge step forward and should not undermine but underpin the protections provided in the existing six human rights treaties',[36] this study eventually proved to be a decisive step towards the drafting of the new human rights treaty starting a few years later. In the end, the CRPD would go much further than that, as it would not just 'underpin' but strengthen the international human rights system, as is argued in the present book.

In 2001, the Mexican government put forward a proposal to the General Assembly to start the process of negotiating a 'comprehensive and integral international convention to promote and protect the rights and dignity of persons with disabilities'.[37] The General Assembly, this time, mandated an Ad Hoc Committee to elaborate a draft for such a convention. The drafting took place over eight sessions, from July 2002 to August 2006, and, after its redaction by a Working Group, the Convention was negotiated twice by the Ad Hoc Committee in New York (since the Economic and Social Council (ECOSOC) acted as its secretariat and not as usual the OHCHR). A significant feature of the negotiation process was the active participation of disabled people through the International Disability Causus (IDC). While the number of DPOs involved was initially restricted, the IDC grew expansively during the various sessions of the Ad Hoc Committee, where disabled people acted as experts alongside governmental delegations.[38] This negotiation process created a real momentum for civil society, and even a sense of ownership on the part of disabled people, that would persist after the entry into force of the Convention. Several other actors played an important role, such as national human rights institutions (NHRIs), academics as well as the European Union, not to mention the Chair of the Ad Hoc Committee during the last four sessions: Ambassador Don MacKay, from New Zealand.

After the Ad Hoc Committee had finished its work, the CRPD was adopted by the General Assembly on 13 December 2006,[39] thereby creating the first legally binding international instrument on disability. An Optional Protocol was added to allow individuals, or groups of individuals, to lodge complaints on alleged violations of the Convention. The 'comprehensive and integral international convention to promote and protect the rights and dignity of persons with disabilities' had, at last, been born. The CRPD entered into force on 3 May 2008, after its 20th

[36] Ibid, 297.

[37] GA, *Comprehensive and Integral International Convention to Promote and Protect the Rights and Dignity of Persons with Disabilities*, 26 February 2002, A/RES/56/168.

[38] S. Tromel, 'Personal Perspective on the Drafting History of the United Nations Convention on the Rights of Persons with Disabilities' in G. Quinn and L. Waddington (eds), *European Yearbook of Disability Law* (Antwerp: Intersentia, 2009) 115, 117–18.

[39] GA, *Convention on the Rights of Persons with Disabilities*, 13 December 2006, A/RES/61/106.

ratification. By January 2021, there were 182 ratifications for the Convention and 97 ratifications for the Optional Protocol.[40] The CRPD introduced a high number of innovations that opened up new horizons in the field of international human rights law, a point that will be elaborated on throughout this book.

The CRPD itself is divided into three parts. The first part consists of transversal provisions (Articles 1–9). This part includes: the general principles of the Convention (Article 3); the general obligations imposed upon States Parties (Article 4); the right to equality and non-discrimination (Article 5); a separate article on disabled women (Article 6); a separate article on disabled children (Article 7); as well as provisions on awareness-raising (Article 8) and accessibility (Article 9). It is worth stressing that Article 4(3) of the CRPD provides that '[i]n the development and implementation of legislation and policies', States Parties should 'closely consult with and actively involve persons with disabilities'.[41] Importantly, the CRPD also provides that States Parties must 'take all appropriate steps to ensure that reasonable accommodation is provided', an obligation which applies to all the rights protected by the Convention.[42] The second part of the CRPD sets out an exhaustive catalogue of civil, political, economic, social and cultural rights (Articles 10–30). This includes: the right to life (Article 10); the right to equal recognition before the law (Article 12); the right to access to justice (Article 13); the right to liberty and security (Article 14); freedom from torture or cruel, inhuman or degrading treatment or punishment (Article 15); freedom from exploitation, violence and abuse (Article 16); the right to live independently and be included in the community (Article 19); freedom of expression and opinion and access to information (Article 21); the right to privacy (Article 22), respect for home and the family (Article 23); the right to education (Article 24); the right to health (Article 25); the right to habilitation and rehabilitation (Article 26); the right to work (Article 27); the right to social protection (Article 28); and participation in cultural life, recreation, leisure and sport (Article 30). Although all of those rights are equally important for disabled people, several of these rights will the subject of in-depth discussions in Part II for the purposes of the argument made by the book. The third part deals with implementation and monitoring (Articles 31–40). After addressing data collection (Article 31) and international co-operation (Article 32), it prescribes the creation of national mechanisms for implementation and monitoring (Article 33) and establishes the Committee on the Rights of Persons with Disabilities as well as a Conference of States Parties (Article 40). It is particularly interesting to note here that the Ad Hoc Committee decided to provide for both

[40] See https://treaties.un.org/Pages/ViewDetails.aspx?src=TREATY&mtdsg_no=IV-15&chapter=4&clang=_en and https://treaties.un.org/Pages/ViewDetails.aspx?src=TREATY&mtdsg_no=IV-15-a&chapter=4&clang=_en.

[41] Article 4(3), CRPD.

[42] Article 5(3), CRPD.

national and international monitoring mechanisms.[43] Despite some innovative aspects, the international monitoring mechanisms are nonetheless essentially the same as those foreseen by other human rights treaties.[44] One of the reasons is that the CRPD was being negotiated in the middle of discussions on reforming the treaty body system,[45] and not much time was devoted to this aspect of the Convention.

1.2 Disabled People and Human Rights Treaties

Going back to the evolution of international human rights law, the CRPD has followed the move to adopt human rights treaties on specific issues of concern. While disability initially was not seen as a human rights issue, this evolution has allowed to give shape to the rights of disabled people. These rights were initially considered through the general non-discrimination clauses of the ICCPR and ICESCR.[46] Both Covenants prohibit discrimination in the enjoyment of the rights protected by them on the basis of a non-exhaustive number of grounds.[47] The ICCPR even includes an autonomous provision, which extends such prohibition to all rights, including economic and social rights,[48] as recognised by the Human Rights Committee.[49] It is also worth noting that the prohibition of discrimination creates not only negative obligations but also positive obligations, including 'positive action', which aims to remedy past disadvantages.[50] In the absence of a legally binding international instrument on disability, disabled people therefore were – implicitly – protected by the general non-discrimination clauses of the foregoing Covenants.[51]

After the adoption of the ICCPR and ICESCR, States opted for the crafting of a number of group-specific human rights treaties. International human rights law

[43] G. de Beco, 'Article 33(2) of the UN Convention on the Rights of Persons with Disabilities. Another Role for National Human Rights Institutions?' (2011) 29 *Netherlands Quarterly of Human Rights* 84.

[44] M. Stein and J. Lord, 'Monitoring the Convention on the Rights of Persons with Disabilities: Innovations, Lost Opportunities, and Future Potential' (2010) 32 *Human Rights Quarterly* 689.

[45] OHCHR, *Concept Paper on the High Commissioner's Proposal for a Unified Standing Treaty Body*, 22 March 2006, HRI/MC/2006/2.

[46] The two Covenants together with the Universal Declaration on Human Rights (UDHR) form the International Bill of Human Rights.

[47] Article 2(1), ICCPR; Article 2(2), ICESCR.

[48] Article 26, ICCPR.

[49] Human Rights Committee, *General Comment No 18: Non-discrimination*, 10 November 1989, HRI/GEN/1/Rev.6 at 146, para 12; Human Rights Committee, *Broeks v The Netherlands*, 9 April 1987, CCPR/C/29/D/172/1984, para 12.3; Human rights Committee, *Zwaan de Vries v The Netherlands*, 9 April 1987, CCPR/C/29/D/182/1984, para 12.3.

[50] O. De Schutter, 'Chapter Seven. Positive Action' in D. Schiek, L. Waddington and M. Bell (eds), *Cases, Materials and Text on National, Supranational and International Non-Discrimination Law: Ius Commune Casebooks for the Common Law of Europe* (Oxford: Hart, 2007) 757, 759–61.

[51] B. Saul, D. Kinley and J. Mowbray, *The International Covenant on Economic, Social and Cultural Rights. Commentary, Cases, and Materials* (Oxford: Oxford University Press, 2014) 1010–11.

thus gradually evolved towards the direction of explicit recognition of rights for a number of historically marginalised groups of people. The necessity for doing so stemmed from the fact that the two Covenants do not focus on such groups (although the rights enshrined in those Covenants are universal). The International Convention on the Elimination of All Forms of Racial Discrimination (ICERD) – actually predating the ICCPR and ICESCR[52] – the CEDAW, the CRC and, ultimately, the CRPD were adopted in order to improve human rights protection for these groups.

The prohibition of discrimination has had the role of reaching out to a number of marginalised groups of people and served as a springboard for the adoption of the group-specific human rights treaties that have broadened this prohibition. These group-specific treaties, however, have done so inconsistently. The ICERD and CEDAW, which came first, elaborate on race and gender discrimination in provisions addressing civil and political rights and economic and social rights even though CEDAW provides for 'temporary special measures' to achieve *de facto* equality for women.[53] The CRC and CRPD, which came later, provide for a whole series of rights relating specifically to children and disabled people. The fact that these international instruments go much further than merely prohibiting discrimination is what makes them proper human rights treaties, as their very names indicate.

The CRPD has borrowed extensively from and expanded particularly on the CRC. The CRC is indeed the human rights treaty that is the closest to the CRPD, which is why it is has been described earlier as being the 'cousin' of the CRPD. At the same time, the CRC itself draws particular attention to disabled children not only through its separate article on disabled children but also through its reference to disability in its general non-discrimination clause. Both human rights treaties (the CRC and CRPD), like the UDHR but unlike the ICCPR or ICESCR, moreover set out a full catalogue of civil, political, economic, social and cultural rights. The CRC thereby successfully bridged civil and political, and economic and social rights for the first time in a human rights treaty,[54] a move that has been replicated subsequently in the CRPD. The CRPD's Preamble further reaffirms 'the universality, indivisibility, interdependence and interrelatedness of all human rights'[55] (a reaffirmation which is not to be found in the CRC though), thereby echoing the VDPA.[56]

[52] International Convention on the Elimination of All Forms of Racial Discrimination 1965, 660 UNTS 195 (ICERD).

[53] Article 4(1), CEDAW.

[54] R. Brett, 'Rights of the Child' in Krause and Scheinin, *International Protection of Human Rights*, 227, 229.

[55] Preamble(c), CRPD. The CRC's Preamble does not include such a clause.

[56] World Conference on Human Rights, *Vienna Declaration and Programme of Action*, para 5.

The CRPD still perpetuates the distinction between civil and political and economic and social rights. As the ICESCR,[57] it provides that '[w]ith regard to economic, social and cultural rights, each State Party undertakes to take measures to the maximum of its available resources ... with a view to achieving progressively the full realization of these rights'.[58] A number of Convention rights are therefore subject to the duty of progressive realisation. The CRPD nonetheless specifies that this duty must give priority to 'those obligations contained in the ... Convention that are immediately applicable according to international law'.[59] Such is the case with regard to the 'minimum core obligation to ensure the satisfaction of, at the very least, minimum essential levels of each of the [economic, social and cultural] rights' in the view of the ICESCR Committee.[60] As is the case with the ICESCR,[61] the CRPD rights also create immediate obligations, which include the prohibition of discrimination.

The CRPD is in continuity with the CRC, which, likewise, has a provision on economic and social rights that set a precedent for the Convention's drafters.[62] It has been noted, however, that it is difficult to accurately define the content of this category with regard to most of the CRC rights,[63] with the CRC Committee admitting that there is 'no simple or authoritative division of human rights in general or of Convention rights into the two categories'.[64] In fact, the CRPD has exacerbated the issue. It is impractical to try and determine which of the CRPD rights merely belong to economic and social rights, as the latter rights are intertwined with civil and political rights. The CRPD has actually blurred the distinction between the two sets of rights to the point where making such a distinction would deprive the Convention rights of real meaning.[65] Even though the proposal to provide for the notion of progressive realisation was not disputed, an attempt to establish a list of all economic and social rights failed during the negotiation process.[66]

57 Article 2(1), ICESCR.

58 Article 4(2), CRPD.

59 Ibid.

60 CESCR Committee, *General Comment No 3: The Nature of State Parties Obligations (Art. 2, par. 1)*, 14 December 1990, E/1991/23, para 10.

61 CESCR Committee, *General Comment No 20: Non-Discrimination in Economic, Social and Cultural Rights (Art. 2, par. 2)*, 29 May 2009, E/C.12/GC/20, para 7; 'Maastricht Guidelines on Violations of Economic, Social and Cultural Rights' (1998) 20 *Human Rights Quarterly* 691, para 11.

62 Article 4 of the CRC provides that '[w]ith regard to economic, social and cultural rights, States Parties shall undertake all ... measures to the maximum extent of their available resources ... for the implementation of the rights recognized in the present Convention'.

63 M. Rishmawi, *A Commentary on the United Nations Convention on the Rights of the Child, Article 4: The Nature of States Parties' Obligations* (Leiden: Martinus Nijhoff, 2006) 16.

64 CRC Committee, *General Comment No 5: General measures of implementation of the Convention on the Rights of the Child*, 27 November 2003, CRC/GC/2003/5, para 6.

65 G. de Beco, 'The Indivisibility of Human Rights and the Convention on the Rights of Persons with Disabilities' (2019) 68 *International & Comparative Law Quarterly* 141, 153–4.

66 B. Flóvenz, 'The Implementation of the UN Convention and the Development of Economic and Social Rights as Human Rights' in O. Arnardóttir and G. Quinn (eds), *The UN Convention on the Rights of Persons with Disabilities. European and Scandinavian Perspectives* (London/Boston: Martinus Nijhoff Publishers, 2009) 265–6.

Unable to resolve the problem, the Convention's drafters simply decided that this Convention should follow the precedent set by the CRC.

Further similarities exist between the two human rights treaties. The CRC has four general principles, including the 'best interest' of the child, that were established by the CRC Committee.[67] The CRPD also contains a series of general principles, which are not only more numerous but are also contained in the CRPD itself.[68] While the large number of general principles enumerated in the Convention has been criticised,[69] there is a benefit in having them codified so as to avoid any misinterpretation and guarantee their widest possible application. The CRC is furthermore the most ratified human rights treaty within the UN with ratifications in all countries except for one,[70] while the CRPD likewise was ratified extremely rapidly reaching 182 States Parties at the time of writing.[71] In view of this, it is not surprising that the CRC Committee supported the adoption of the new human rights treaty in its General Comment on the situation of disabled children.[72] This General Comment was issued very soon after the CRPD was adopted (and elaborated by the CRC Committee at the same time as the CRPD was being drafted), and remains a point of reference in advancing the rights of disabled children generally.

The CRPD and CRC moreover stand out in insofar as they consider characteristics other than those associated with the categories they aim to protect. Both human rights treaties prohibit discrimination on the basis of multiple grounds, that is, beyond the grounds that characterise those who fall within their remit (namely age and disability),[73] unlike the ICERD and CEDAW.[74] While the CRPD prohibits discrimination 'on all grounds',[75] the CRC does so on the basis of a non-exhaustive number of grounds.[76] The CRPD's Preamble also refers to an exhaustive number of grounds and even refers to 'multiple or aggravated forms of discrimination'.[77] Like the ICCPR and ICESCR, the CRPD and CRC, through their general non-discrimination clause, therefore, protect people against so-called 'intersectional

[67] Article 3, CRC. The three other ones are: non-discrimination (Article 2); the right to life, survival and development (Article 6) and; respect for the views of the child (Article 12).

[68] Article 3, CRPD.

[69] L. Lundy and B. Byrne, 'The Four General Principles of the United Nations Convention on the Rights of the Child: the Potential Added Value of the Approach in other Areas of Human Rights Law' in Brems, Desmet and Vandenhole, *Children's Rights Law*, 52, 64–6.

[70] All States except the US ratified the CRC. See https://treaties.un.org/Pages/ViewDetails.aspx?src=IND&mtdsg_no=IV-11&chapter=4&clang=_en.

[71] See https://treaties.un.org/Pages/ViewDetails.aspx?src=TREATY&mtdsg_no=IV-15&chapter=4&clang=_en.

[72] CRC Committee, *General Comment No 9: the Rights of Children with Disabilities*, 27 February 2007, CRC/C/GC/9, para 2.

[73] Article 2(1), CRC; Article 5(2), CRPD.

[74] Article 1, ICERD; Article 1, CEDAW.

[75] Article 5(2), CRPD.

[76] Article 2(1), CRC.

[77] Preamble(p), CRPD.

discrimination'. Such discrimination occurs when people are discriminated against on the basis of several different grounds which, taken together, result in a level of prejudice that is higher than if these different grounds were taken separately. Coined for the first time by Crenshaw with regard to gender and race,[78] the theory of intersectionality highlights the fact that when certain different grounds intersect they can create specific disadvantages that are greater than simply the sum of their parts.[79]

The CRPD is concerned with specific groups of disabled people. Not only does it have a separate article on disabled women and children but also a large number of provisions relating to both gender and age. The CRPD's Preamble further stresses the need to incorporate a 'gender perspective' into the entire Convention.[80] The Convention has thus adopted a 'twin-track' approach to the issue of gender and age (although it does not provide for an 'age perspective' in its Preamble). It is remarkable how much the CRPD draws attention to intersectionality seeing that so little consideration has been given to the issue with regard to disability in the past. It can even be argued that this Convention is the human rights treaty that takes this issue into account more than any other human rights treaty to date. While the CRC also includes a separate article on disabled children, the CRPD goes a step further by addressing matters specifically relating to gender and age throughout its provisions and by requiring explicit consideration for each specific group in its implementation generally.

Since the CRPD deals with specific groups of disabled people, there can be an added-value in applying it along with the other human rights treaties. It is therefore possible to draw upon these human rights treaties in order to achieve further protection for those who come within their remit besides that of the CRPD (such as disabled women and children who are also especially protected by CEDAW and the CRC).[81] In order to enhance human rights protection for them, it is important to examine how different characteristics can intersect. This is necessary given that the human rights treaties other than the CRC have neglected disabled people, although the treaty bodies have sought to fill the gap.

The CRPD is part of a movement that seeks to gradually expand the notion of equality through the explicit recognition of human rights for a number of historically marginalised groups of people. The general non-discrimination clauses of both

[78] K. Crenshaw, 'Demarginalising the Intersection of Race and Sex: A Black Feminist Critique of Antidiscrimination Doctrine, Feminist Theory and Antiracist Politics' (1989) 4 *University of Chicago Legal Forum. Feminism in the Law: Theory, Practice and Criticism* 139; K. Crenshaw, 'Mapping the Margins: Intersectionality, Identity Politics, and Violence against Women of Color' (1991) 43 *Stanford Law Review* 1241.

[79] I. Solanke, 'Putting Race and Gender Together: A New Approach to Intersectionality' (2009) 72 *Modern Law Review* 723, 731.

[80] Preamble(s), CRPD.

[81] R. de Silva de Alwis, 'Mining the Intersections: Advancing the Rights of Women and Children with Disabilities within an Interrelated Web of Human Rights' (2009) 18 *Pacific Rim Law & Policy Journal* 293, 294–5.

the ICCPR and the ICESCR were not sufficient to provide adequate protection for disabled people notwithstanding their universal nature.[82] By proclaiming a full catalogue of rights tailored to their specific situation, the Convention has firmly embraced the principle of substantive equality which stresses the requirement of achieving *de facto* equality. Unlike the two Covenants, the CRPD adopts a broad approach to dealing with disability by applying the entire range of human rights to disabled people. It therefore represents a further move away from the principle of formal equality, which only aims to ensure that all individuals are treated equally throughout the law. This is precisely how to interpret the term 'on an equal basis with others', which is repeated multiple times in the Convention. It does not mean that disabled people have more or fewer rights than others but rather that steps must be taken so that they can enjoy their rights in the real world.[83]

The CRPD acknowledges that a different type of treatment may be necessary to include disabled people. Disabled people face obstacles that are not only due to biological factors but also to disadvantage caused by social structures.[84] Disability requires that society itself be changed assuming that there is a real willingness to accommodate human differences. 'Blindness to differences' creates a requirement of assimilation for those who are disadvantaged, as they are obliged to '[come] into the game after it is already begun'.[85] They have no choice then but to fit into the pre-existing environment. By uncovering the existence of detrimental power relationships between individuals, the CRPD, in fact, pursues the achievement of transformative equality,[86] which advances the principle of substantive equality by calling for the actual removal of the underlying structures of disadvantage that have the effect of sustaining inequality.[87] The CRPD Committee, for its part, considers this Convention to be a further expansion of this principle of substantive equality evolving towards the concept of 'inclusive equality', which is based on the dimensions of distribution, recognition, participation and accommodation.[88]

Consideration of disability therefore demands a deeper understanding of the principle of substantive equality. Disability poses a real challenge to equality as it can be the most obvious manifestation of human variation. Contrary to what is

[82] C. O'Cinneide, 'Extracting Protection for the Rights of Persons with Disabilities' in Arnardóttir and Quinn, *The UN Convention on the Rights of Persons with Disabilities*, 136, 172–3.

[83] CRPD Committee, *General Comment on Equality and Non-discrimination*, 9 March 2018, CRPD/C/GC/6, para 17.

[84] O. Arnardóttir, 'A Future of Multidimensional Disadvantage Equality?' in Arnardóttir and Quinn, *The UN Convention on the Rights of Persons with Disabilities*, 41, 54.

[85] I. Young, *Justice and the Politics of Difference* (Princeton: Princeton University Press, 1990) 164.

[86] J. Goldschmidt, 'New Perspectives on Equality: Towards Transformative Justice through the Disability Convention?' (2017) 35 *Nordic Journal of Human Rights* 1, 5.

[87] A. Broderick, *The United Nations Convention on the Rights of Persons with Disabilities* (Cambridge-Antwerp: Intersentia, 2015) 36–8.

[88] CRPD Committee, *General Comment on Equality and Non-discrimination*, para 11. As will be seen in Chapter 3, these four dimensions were proposed by Fredman in relation to the principle of substantive equality.

required with regard to other characteristics, the accommodation of human differences with regard to disability calls for the adoption of measures that go beyond just remedying past disadvantage. While other historically marginalised groups have wrongly been considered to lack certain capacities,[89] disabled people may in fact be restricted in their capacities if nothing is done to meet their individual needs and allow them to develop their potential. This is the reason why the CRPD does not require States Parties to take '*temporary* special measures', as done by CEDAW, to be halted 'when the objectives of equality of opportunity and treatment have been achieved'.[90] Rather, the CRPD merely prescribes 'specific measures . . . to . . . achieve *de facto* equality'.[91] Since disabled people could rely permanently on these 'specific measures', the Convention does not impose any time limit to their adoption.

However, the promotion of transformative equality and of 'inclusive equality' may contradict the very notion of equality. Such a notion generally revolves around society's dominant model and leads to endorsing this model by asking that individuals specifically conform themselves to it.[92] The consequence is that equal treatment, in fact, could not make enough room for the real complexity of human diversity.[93] This is the problem of the so-called 'difference dilemma'. On the one hand, focusing on human differences can produce stigma by creating a number of distinctions; on the other, failure to do so ignores the fact that society has established certain norms that have the effect of hindering inclusion.[94] A way out of this dilemma is hard to find, since it is practically impossible to consider every single individual as different in order to avoid such distinctions. The real accommodation of human differences sometimes entails extensive forms of unequal treatment that can be difficult to reconcile with the very notion of equality. If the purpose is to foster respect for human diversity in such a way, it is possible that the principle of equality is not always be the best way forward.[95]

Such opposing ways of understanding the principle of substantive equality reflect the tension created by inherent and inescapable differences amongst all individuals, which disability exposes to the full light of day. As will be seen in Chapter 4, there has been a tendency to regard the legal subject as somehow 'disembodied' in international human rights law, thus ignoring the particular needs of disabled people. A broadening of the concept of human rights to include disabled people requires that greater emphasis be placed on distinct forms of embodiment so as to

[89] Jones and Basser Mark, 'Law and the Social Construction of Disability', 5.

[90] Article 4(1), CEDAW (emphasis added).

[91] Article 5(4), CRPD.

[92] H. Collins, 'Social Inclusion: A Better Approach to Equality Issues?' (2005) 14 *Transnational Law and Contemporary Problems* 897, 910–11.

[93] S. Fredman, 'Substantive Equality Revisited' (2016) 14 *International Journal of Constitutional Law* 712, 722–3.

[94] M. Minow, *Making All the Difference. Inclusion, Exclusion, and American Law* (Ithaca: Cornell University Press, 1990) 20–3.

[95] Collins, 'Social Inclusion', 910.

transcend the general confines of the group concerned. The concept of disability itself does not leave any alternative given its sweeping scope. Through its concern for the varied needs of disabled people, the CRPD in a way solves the 'difference dilemma'. The Convention both acknowledges that disability is part of human diversity and provides for the utmost individualisation of measures for achieving its implementation.

The CRPD further expands the prohibition of discrimination in another specific way. It establishes a duty to provide reasonable accommodation to a disabled people,[96] that is, an accommodation that does not impose 'a disproportionate or undue burden'.[97] It recognises that failure to do so is a form of discrimination.[98] This duty, therefore, is of immediate application. It was originally enshrined in anti-discrimination law, including the Americans with Disabilities Act (ADA) and EU Directive 2000/78/EC.[99] The provision of reasonable accommodation has not only found its way into the general obligations but is also repeated in several articles of the CRPD.[100] It applies across both civil and political and economic and social rights, as had been already confirmed by the CESCR Committee.[101] It is an 'individualized reactive duty', which is triggered as soon as requested by any disabled person.[102] The European Court of Human Rights (ECtHR) has ruled that the lack of reasonable accommodation constitutes a violation of the European Convention of Human Rights.[103]

The duty to provide reasonable accommodation further distorts the nature of legal obligations attached to the different sets of rights. As explained by Quinn, economic and social rights in the CRPD now 'reflect a blending of the principle of non-discrimination (immediately achievable) with obligations that are more progressive in character'.[104] Reasonable accommodation has infiltrated and narrowed the sphere of progressive realisation. States Parties must take steps to enable disabled people to exercise their human rights. They are obliged to do so straight away, thereby differentiating the provision of reasonable accommodation from the notion of progressive realisation. Each right under the Convention imposes

96 Article 5(3), CRPD.

97 Article 2, CRPD.

98 Ibid. Article 2 of the Convention defines reasonable accommodation as 'necessary and appropriate modifications and adjustments not imposing a disproportionate or undue burden, where needed in a particular case, to ensure to persons with disabilities the enjoyment or exercise on an equal basis with others of all human rights and fundamental freedoms'.

99 Title I, Americans with Disabilities Act (ADA), 42 U.S.C § 12111(9); Article 5, Directive 2000/78/EC Establishing a General Framework for Equal Treatment in Employment and Occupation, 2000 O.J. (L 303).

100 Articles 13(1) (access to justice), 14(2) (right to liberty and security of the person), 24(2)(c) (right to education) and 27(1)(i) (right to work), CRPD.

101 CESCR Committee, *General Comment No 5: Persons with Disabilities*, para 15.

102 CRPD Committee, *General Comment on Equality and Non-discrimination*, para 24(b).

103 ECtHR, *Çam v Turkey*, 23 February 2016, App No 51500/08, paras 64 and 69; ECtHR, *Enver Şahin v Turkey*, 30 January 2018, App No 23065/12, paras 67 and 27.

104 Quinn, 'Disability and Human Rights', 266.

an *immediate* obligation to make particular adjustments to a disabled person's environment. Having migrated from the field of anti-discrimination law to that of international human rights law, the provision of reasonable accommodation has become an inherent feature of the human rights of disabled people.

Despite its potential usefulness, the provision of reasonable accommodation may not put an end to the marginalisation of disabled people as it leaves disabling structures intact and does not deal with the root causes of their exclusion. The duty to provide reasonable accommodation is not only reactive to personal demand but also concerned with single individuals, thereby showing a lack of aspiration to remove obstacles for all disabled people.[105] This duty can indeed lead to bringing changes in the environment for the sake of this or that individual, but it does not question the nature of the environment itself. Since it calls for a calculation of cost-effectiveness, the provision of reasonable accommodation is more likely to result in 'inclusive marginalisation'.[106] Relying essentially on judicial litigation, its fulfilment furthermore requires that people first qualify as disabled, and that has been the focus of jurisprudence on the matter.[107] Anti-discrimination law adopts a group-based approach which revolves around identity in order to determine to whom it will offer its protection and whom will be excluded from it.[108] It does not espouse fully the social model of disability, as it does not have the ambition to alleviate the barriers embedded in society.[109] Although it can contribute to *de facto* equality for some disabled people, it does not aim to make society inclusive overall.

The CRPD moreover adds a number of '*sui generis* entitlements',[110] which go a step further towards achieving substantive equality. These '*sui generis* entitlements' highlight aspects that were not anticipated in previous human rights treaties, in that they pertain to the particular needs of disabled people. An example is the right to independent living, which calls for 'a range of in-, residential and other community support services, including personal assistance'.[111] Another one is the right to inclusive education, which presupposes that '[e]ffective individualized support measures are provided in environments that maximize academic and social development'.[112] The CRPD therefore obliges States Parties to create an environment

[105] B. Byrne, 'Dis-Equality: Exploring the Juxtaposition of Disability and Equality' (2018) 6 *Social Inclusion* 9, 15.

[106] J. Grue, 'Inclusive Marginalisation? A Critical Analysis of the Concept of Disability, Its Framings and Their Implications in the United Nations Convention on the Rights of Persons with Disabilities' (2019) 37 *Nordic Journal of Human Rights* 3, 17.

[107] Jones and Basser Marks, 'Law and the Social Construction of Disability', 18–19.

[108] A. Satz, 'Disability, Vulnerability, and the Limits of Antidiscrimination' (2008) 83 *Washington Law Review* 513, 535.

[109] P. Harpur, *Ableism at Work: Disablement and Hierarchies of Impairment* (Cambridge: Cambridge University Press, 2019) 29.

[110] Mégret, 'The Disabilities Convention: Human Rights of Persons with Disabilities or Disability Rights', 506.

[111] Article 19(b), CRPD.

[112] Article 24(2)(e), CRPD.

in which disabled people can enjoy their rights. Inclusion expands the notion of equality by prescribing the transformation of social institutions.[113] As will be explained in the next chapter, such an understanding of the principle of equality is closely related to the social model of disability, which does not locate disability in the individual as such but in society itself.

This leads to the ultimate question of whether the Convention has established new rights. It was stressed time and again that this was not the aim during its negotiation process, a move that somewhat eased the mind of recalcitrant governmental delegations.[114] If the question has to be answered, this book concludes that the Convention indeed has not produced any new rights. It sees the rights protected by the CRPD as a particular expression of human rights, though it acknowledges that this has implications which reach far beyond the Convention. Group-specific human rights treaties arguably do nothing but extend existing legal obligations. As indicated by Jones, 'they aim only to narrow the gap' for historically marginalised groups of people.[115] According to Mégret, 'certain groups do need separate restatements of how rights apply to them, either because they have specific needs to enjoy their rights, different versions of the same rights, or possibly even slightly different rights'.[116] While such a view carries the risk of confusing human rights that are universal with their realisation for a particular group of people, the purpose is still not to create a different regime for those who are disabled. An alternative and more insightful response would be that the question does not really matter. What does matter is to define exactly how to make all human rights more of a reality for disabled people.

A step further is to look at the issue the other way around by asking what international human rights law, in turn, has gained from the adoption of the CRPD. The CRPD takes stock of the persisting marginalisation of disabled people in order to enhance protection for them. While recommending the adoption of a new human rights treaty, Quinn and Degener defended the view that such a treaty would help to make the question of disability more central to the international framework of human rights.[117] By so doing, the Convention would offer important lessons to the field of international human rights law itself.

It has been argued that human rights 'are aimed at changing the status quo within social institutions by rendering possible the inclusion of those historically

[113] H. Collins, 'Discrimination, Equality and Social Inclusion' (2003) 66 *Modern Law Review* 16, 25.

[114] Tromel, 'Personal Perspective on the Drafting History', 118–19.

[115] P. Jones, 'Collective and Group-Specific: Can the Rights of Ethno-Cultural Minorities be Human Rights?' in G. Pentassuglia (ed), *Ethno-Cultural Diversity and Human Rights. Critiques and Challenges* (Leiden/Boston: Martinus Nijhoff Publishers, 2018) 27, 47.

[116] Mégret, 'The Disabilities Convention: Human Rights of Persons with Disabilities or Disability Rights', 497.

[117] Quinn and Degener, *The Current Use and Future Potential of United Nations Human Rights Instruments in the Context of Disability*, 295.

excluded'.[118] Whether this has always been the case is questionable; nevertheless, the CRPD emphasises the importance of doing just that. The Convention has done more than re-affirming human rights, which as yet have been unable to satisfactorily cater for human differences.[119] It has enriched the notion of human rights. In order to understand how the CRPD has achieved this and what disability involves for this notion, it is crucial that disability be seen as an integral part of international human rights law. This is why this book examines not only how the CRPD relates to other human rights treaties but also what the Convention rights imply for the whole domain of human rights.

[118] C. Sheppard, 'Constitutional Equality and Shifting Conceptions of the Role of the State: Obstacles and Possibilities' (2006) 33 *Supreme Court Law Review* 251, 265.

[119] Mégret, 'The Disabilities Convention: Human Rights of Persons with Disabilities or Disability Rights', 515–16.

2

Conceptual Background: Disability in the Field of International Human Rights Law

This chapter starts by outlining the existing models of disability and by relating these models to the Convention (2.1. Disability and the CRPD). The aim is not to advance debates about the models themselves but to examine the extent to which these models have influenced the CRPD's own understanding of disability. The focus lies especially on the social model of disability, which has transformed the view of disability around the world. This is followed by an investigation of the way in which this understanding of disability bears upon the entire field of international human rights law (2.2. Disability and the International Human Rights Law System). The chapter further examines the mainstreaming of disability and its consideration by the treaty bodies as well as its consequences for the field as a whole. It finally looks beyond international human rights law by evaluating how disability is addressed by UN agencies.

2.1 Disability and the CRPD

2.1.1 Different Models of Disability

There are several models of disability. These models have, over time, been succeeded by other models of disability or have been refined in order to respond to criticisms. The three main models of disability which are discussed here are: (1) the religious model, which is now more or less outdated; (2) the individual model, which is still dominant; and (3) the social model, which is the most recent model of disability.

Fist, the religious model of disability, which is also called the ancient-symbolic or, sometimes, moral model of disability, considers disability as a divine phenomenon. Disability is essentially a punishment for wrongful acts, past or present, by persons, their family or their community.[1] The Greeks, for instance, saw disability as a divine wrath leading, in most cases, to infanticide ('exposure to the Gods').[2]

[1] A. Rimmerman, *Social Inclusion of People with Disabilities. National and International Perspectives* (Cambridge: Cambridge University Press, 2013) 24.

[2] H.-J. Stiker, *A History of Disability*, Trans. W. Sayers (Ann Arbor: University of Michigan Press, 1999) 39–40.

Disability in International Human Rights Law. Gauthier de Beco, Oxford University Press. © Gauthier de Beco 2021.
DOI: 10.1093/oso/9780198824503.003.0003

According to the symbolic model, disability is a sin, and it calls for redemption to be healed, although it can sometimes also be seen as a blessing. Because this model makes disabled people the subject of pity, they are generally regarded as outcasts. The religious model is now almost completely abandoned, although there is a lingering perception in some communities and professional circles that disability is nothing but a curse.

Second, the individual model of disability views disability as a problem that lies with the individual. It conceives of disability as a failure of the body due to the loss or dysfunction of a limb, organ or any body part.[3] Disability, therefore, is established through the presence of impairment.[4] This impairment needs to be diagnosed and repaired in order to allow the body to function again, hence the important role played by the various areas of medicine. Relying upon the work of Foucault, Tremain argues that the notion of impairments is used as an objective justification for the adoption of different forms of social regulation.[5] The purpose is to ensure that disabled people can be normalised or, where that is not possible, locked out. The result is the frequent placement of disabled persons in institutions, a trend which started in the 19th century. It even led to their murdering with the rise of the eugenics movement, which reached its peak in Nazi Germany in the 20th century.[6] The individual model of disability continues to exist to this day and serves as a basis for domestic legislation, especially in welfare states, where disabled persons are segregated or receive compensation in the form of allowances.

Third, the social model of disability sees disability as a product of societal organisation. Originating in the United Kingdom, it was coined as a reaction to the individual model by the Union of the Physically Impaired against Segregation (UPIAS) in the following terms: 'Disability is something imposed on top of our impairments, by the way we are unnecessarily isolated and excluded from full participation in society'.[7] The social model therefore relates to obstacles encountered by disabled people – physical, attitudinal and legal obstacles, among others.[8] According to the social model disability is distinct from impairment.[9] It is a consequence of how society is actually organised. This view of disability was subsequently taken up

[3] L. Schur, D. Kruse and P. Blanck, *People with Disabilities. Sidelined or Mainstreamed?* (New York: Cambridge University Press, 2013) 9; Rimmerman, *Social Inclusion of People with Disabilities*, 26.

[4] Shur, Kruse and Blanck, *People with Disabilities*, 9.

[5] S. Tremain, 'Foucault, Governmentality and Critical Disability Theory' in S. Tremain (ed), *Foucault and the Government of Disability* (Ann Arbor: The University of Michigan Press, 2005) 1, 10–11.

[6] H. Friedlander, 'The Exclusion and Murder of the Disabled' in R. Gellately and N. Stoltzfus (eds), *Social Outsiders in Nazi Germany* (Princeton: Princeton University Press 2001) 145, 153–7.

[7] *The Union of the Physically Impaired Against Segregation and The Disability Alliance Discuss Fundamental Principles of Disability* (London: UPIAS/The Disability Alliance, 1976), http://disability-studies.leeds.ac.uk/files/library/UPIAS-fundamental-principles.pdf.

[8] C. Barnes and G. Mercer, *Exploring Disability* (Cambridge: Polity Press, 2nd edn, 2010) 29–31.

[9] T. Shakespeare, 'The Social Model of Disability' in L. Davis (ed) *The Disability Studies Reader* (London: Routledge, 4th edn, 2013) 214, 215–16.

and theorised by several scholars who introduced the social model by contending that disability is about institutionalised forms of social oppression against disabled people.[10] In the British context, these scholars have used a materialist lens, in particular, to explain the exclusion of disabled people in the advent of capitalism.[11] The social model of disability calls for the removal of whatever barriers that prevent disabled people from participating in society. This model has had a significant influence in developing the modern concept of disability, and it has contributed to shaping the new field of disability studies. Over time it has resonated in fact much further than the United Kingdom. The social model has offered disabled people a new mobilising force to transform their lives and empowered them to ask for changes in society.[12]

Despite its major success, the social model of disability faced criticism early on. The main contention was that its protagonists neglected the existence of impairments. The social model would deny the effects of impairments that disabled people may encounter, regardless of how society is actually organised.[13] It also would discount the entangled relationship between disability and impairment.[14] It has further been pointed out that this model still relies upon the notion of impairments as one of the primary conditions for being as disabled.[15] It would limit its own reach by alleging that disability is only about how society treats those who do have such impairments. While this is not the place to fuel such controversy and contribute to the abundant literature on the matter, its critics have generally claimed that the social model provides a false account of disability.

The reality is that disability as a protected ground is distinct from other characteristics. Impairments can create real restrictions in terms of inclusion in society, above and beyond the way in which society is actually organised. Although the restrictions that arise as a result of impairments will vary depending on the

[10] M. Oliver, *Understanding Disability. From Theory to Practice* (New York: Palgrave Macmillan, 2nd edn, 2009) 42–6; J. Campbell and M. Oliver, *Disability Politics: Understanding our Past, Changing our Future* (London: Routledge, 1996) 20–1; V. Finkelstein, *Attitudes and Disabled People: Issues for Discussion* (New York: World Rehabilitation Fund, 1980).

[11] D. Goodley, *Dis/ability Studies: Theorising Disablism and Ableism* (London: Routledge, 2014) 51–3.

[12] R. Traustadóttir, 'Disability Studies, the Social Model and Legal Developments' in O. Arnardóttir and G. Quinn (eds), *The UN Convention on the Rights of Persons with Disabilities. European and Scandinavian Perspectives* (London/Boston: Martinus Nijhoff Publishers, 2009) 3, 10.

[13] T. Shakespeare, *Disability Rights and Wrongs Revisited* (London/New York: Routledge, 2nd edn, 2014) 21–3 and 77; L. Terzi, 'The Social Model of Disability: A Philosophical Critique' (2004) 21 *Journal of Applied Philosophy* 141, 152; J. Morris, 'Impairment and Disability: Constructing an Ethics of Care that Promotes Human Rights' (2001) 16 *Hypatia* 1, 14; L. Barclay, 'Natural Deficiency or Social Oppression? The Capabilities Approach to Justice for People with Disabilities' (2012) 9 *Journal of Moral Philosophy* 500, 520.

[14] D. Anastasiou and J. Kauffman, 'The Social Model of Disability: Dichotomy between Impairment and Disability' (2013) 38 *Journal of Medicine and Philosophy* 441, 449–50; M. Corker and S. French, 'Reclaiming Discourse in Disability Studies' in M. Corker and S. French (eds), *Disability Discourse* (Buckingham: Open University Press, 1999) 1, 6; Shakespeare, 'The Social Model of Disability'; 218–19; Tremain, 'Foucault, Governmentality and Critical Disability Theory', 11.

[15] S. Tremain, 'On the Subject of Impairment' in Corker and French, *Disability Discourse*, 41–2.

environment in which disabled people live, there will remain functional limitations that affect the lives of some of them, regardless of that environment. While gender and race can also be associated with restrictions on participation, disability is different in the sense that the very occurrence of impairment in itself can give rise to inherent limitations.[16] Nonetheless, the fact remains that appropriate responses must be made in order to ensure the full participation of disabled people, rather than causing even more restrictions by failing to acknowledge their particular needs.

By the same token, the concept of impairment itself has evolved in light of the social context.[17] Changes in the workplace have gradually increased reliance on cognitive skills. Certain disabilities have been discovered only lately, in particular learning disabilities (such as dyslexia and attention hyperactive deficit disorder), because of the importance attributed to reading and mathematical skills.[18] In addition, any impairment will in practice have different consequences depending on the way of life and the kind of activities someone is used to or has chosen to do.[19] The way in which individuals cope with the impairment will furthermore depend on personal experience and social relationships. There is therefore no rigid distinction between the bodily and societal aspects of disability. It is unproductive to attempt to include disabled people by placing undue emphasis on one over the other or by dissociating the different kinds of barriers from their lived experience.[20]

On the other hand, there are limitations to the extent to which social changes can achieve inclusion. Constraints to social changes actually do exist, as it is not possible to organise society in a way that takes account of everyone's physical and mental characteristics.[21] Social institutions are not utterly flexible. While modifying the environmentto the greatest possible extent will have advantages for disabled people, it might cost too much or, at least, not be cost-effective for society as a whole.[22] This applies in particular to intellectual disabilities, to which the social model is not as readily applicable as it is to physical disabilities.[23] No longer using certain social institutions, such as contracts, might help address barriers stemming

[16] A. Silver, 'An Essay on Modeling: The Social Model of Disability' in C. Ralston and J. Ho (eds), *Philosophical Reflections on Disability* (New York: Springer, 2012) 1, 32.

[17] S. Vehmas and P. Mäkelä, 'The Ontology of Disability and Impairment: A Discussion of the Natural and Social Features' in K. Kristiansen, S. Vehmas and T. Shakespeare (eds), *Arguing about Disability: Philosophical Perspectives* (London: Routledge, 2009) 42, 44.

[18] J. Herring, *Vulnerable Adults and The Law* (Oxford: Oxford University Press, 2016) 28.

[19] E. Barnes, *The Minority Body. A Theory of Disability* (Oxford: Oxford University Press, 2016) 112.

[20] L. Terzi, *Justice and Equality in Education: A Capability Perspective on Disability and Special Educational Needs* (London/New York: Continuum, 2008) 37–41.

[21] L. Barclay, 'Disability, Respect and Justice' (2010) 27 *Journal of Applied Philosophy* 154, 161–3; T. Shakespeare, *Disability Rights and Wrongs Revisited*, 219–20.

[22] J. Wolff, 'Disability among Equals' in K. Brownlee and A. Cureton (eds), *Disability and Disadvantage* (Oxford: Oxford University Press, 2009) 112, 128.

[23] A. Chappell, D. Goodley and R. Lawthom, 'Making Connections: The Relevance of the Social Model of Disability for People with Learning Difficulties' (2001) 29 *British Journal of Learning Disabilities* 45, 46.

from deficits in mental capacity, but would hinder society's proper functioning.[24] These social institutions need to stay in order to maintain stable and continuing social relationships. The expectations set by the social model could be unrealistic, as a truly barrier-free world will never actually come to be despite the best efforts made to bring it about.

The protagonists of the social model of disability have reacted to such criticism. They have pointed out that their intention was only to provide a 'tool' to combat social oppression against disabled people.[25] If the social model has shed light on major misunderstandings about disability, it was not intended to lay out solutions to the problem it had identified. By seeing disability as a social construct, this model has rather served as a catalyst for political mobilisation. While it provided new insights into approaching disability, it has never had the ambition to offer a comprehensive theory. In order to push forward the debate on the issue, some scholars have pleaded in favour of a social relational approach to disability, which was a reaction to the criticism of the social model.[26] It has also been remarked that there are actually different versions of the social model.[27] This debate, which is not over yet, has extended the field of disability studies and resulted in much inquiry into how disability is understood by the CRPD itself.

There are other models of disability. Such models can be seen as further expressions of the social understanding of disability. The cultural model of disability lays emphasis on the different communities of disabled people, thereby counterbalancing the unique focus on the individual by the individualmodel and on society by the social model.[28] The minority group model of disability, which was born in the US, considers disabled people as a minority group alongside other marginalised groups of people.[29] This model is in fact the American variant of the social model, albeit with special consideration for the common identity of disabled people. The Nordic relational model of disability concentrates on the relationship between the individual and the environment, without however separating the concept of

[24] J. Wolff, 'Cognitive Disability in a Society of Equals' (2009) 40 *Metaphilosophy* 402, 413 and 407.

[25] M. Oliver, 'The Social Model of Disability: Thirty Years On' (2013) 28 *Disability & Society* 1024, 1026; M. Oliver and C. Barnes, *New Politics of Disablement* (London: Palgrave Macmillan, 2nd edn, 2012) 10.

[26] C. Thomas, 'Rescuing a Social Relational Understanding of Disability' (2004) 6 *Scandinavian Journal of Disability Research* 22, 29; C. Thomas, 'Developing the Social Relational in the Social Model of Disability: a Theoretical Agenda' in C. Barnes and G. Mercer (eds), *Implementing the Social Model of Disability: Theory and Practice* (Leeds: the Disability Press, 2004) 32, 43–4.

[27] M. Priestley, 'Constructions and Creations: Idealism, Materialism and Disability Theory' (1998) 13 *Disability & Society* 75, 86–90.

[28] S. Snyder and D. Mitchell, *Cultural Locations of Disability* (Chicago: University of Chicago Press, 2006) 9–10; R. Garland Thomson, 'The Case for Conserving Disability' (2012) 9 *Bioethical Enquiry* 339, 342.

[29] H. Hahn, 'Antidiscrimination Law and Social Research on Disability: The Minority Group Perspective' (1996) 4 *Behavioural Sciences and the Law* 41; R. Admundson, 'Disability, Handicap and the Environment' (1992) 23 *Journal of Social Philosophy* 105; H. Hahn, 'The Politics of Physical Differences: Disability and Discrimination' (1988) 44 *Journal of Social Issues* 39.

disability from the notion of impairments.[30] Finally, the bio-psychosocial model, which underlies the International Classification of Functioning, Disability and Health (ICF) of the World Health Organisation (WHO), embodies a mixture of both the social model and the individual model by distinguishing between impairments, activity limitations and participation restrictions.[31] Although it factors in societal organisation, it has likewise been criticised for not placing enough emphasis on the relationship between both the individual and the environment.[32]

2.1.2 The Social Model and the CRPD

Several scholars expressed the view that the CRPD has adopted the social model of disability.[33] The way in which the Convention itself understands disability attests to this view. Article 1 of the Convention provides that disabled people 'include those who have long-term physical, mental, intellectual or sensory impairments which in interaction with various barriers may hinder their full and effective participation in society on an equal basis with others'. This is however not really a definition of the concept of disability, something which the CRPD's drafters chose to avoid. As will be explained in Chapter 4, it is more a way of establishing the scope of the Convention.

Through underscoring the 'various barriers' encountered by disabled people, the Convention distances itself from the individualmodel of disability. Its Preamble further recognises 'that disability results from the interaction between persons with impairments and attitudinal and environmental barriers that hinders their full and effective participation in society on an equal basis with others'.[34] This wording confirms that the Convention is consonant with the view of disability rooted in the social model, although the Preamble strictly speaking is not legally binding.[35] Significantly, the Preamble further adds that disability is 'an evolving concept', thereby avoiding a definite understanding of the concept in question.[36]

[30] Traustadóttir, 'Disability Studies', 12–14.

[31] J. Bickenbach et al, 'Models of Disablement, Universalism and the International Classification of Impairments, Disabilities and Handicaps' (1999) 48 *Social Science & Medicine* 1173, 1183–4.

[32] Barnes and Mercer, *Exploring Disability*, 38–40.

[33] R. Kayess and P. French, 'Out of Darkness into Light? Introducing the Convention on the Rights of Persons with Disabilities' (2008) 8 *Human Rights Law Review* 1, 21; P. Bartlett, 'The United Nations Convention on the Rights of Persons with Disabilities and Mental Health Law' (2012) 75 *Modern Law Review* 752, 758–61; P. Harpur, 'Embracing the New Disability Rights Paradigm: The Importance of the Convention on the Rights of Persons with Disabilities' (2012) 27 *Disability & Society* 1, 3–4.

[34] Preamble(e), CRPD.

[35] It is worth noting though that wording differs slightly from that in Article 1. In this Preamble, the 'interaction' is with the 'persons with impairments' and not just the 'impairments'. While in essence the meaning remains the same, it would perhaps have been better had this 'interaction' in Article 1 been similarly coupled with impairments, as this stresses a reaction to a particular characteristic rather than to a one associated with a particular group.

[36] It also refers to 'attitudinal and environmental barriers' instead of 'various barriers' (as in Article 1 of the Convention), which is consonant with the social model of disability.

The aforementioned provisions signal the impact that the social model of disability has had on the drafters of the CRPD. This model has given shape to the underlying philosophy of the Convention, which regards disability primarily as a problem within society. The social model has been the founding and animating spirit of the disability rights movement that led to the adoption of the CRPD in 2006. 'Full and effective participation and inclusion in society' is indeed one of the general principles that should guide the Convention's implementation.[37] The CRPD aims not only to preserve the dignity of disabled people but also to foster their participation in society by abolishing the different mechanisms that sustain their marginalisation.

Having said that, a closer look reveals that the CRPD does not purely adopt the approach taken by the social model of disability. By requiring 'acceptance of persons with disabilities as part of human diversity',[38] it goes further than this model, and therefore avoids some of the pitfalls mentioned earlier. Degener argues in favour of a 'human rights model of disability', which would be 'an improvement of the social model of disability and ... a tool to implement the CRPD'.[39] In this way, a new model of disability emerged out the controversy surrounding the social model itself.

Though the social model constituted an important source of inspiration for the negotiators, it is true that the CRPD did not merely absorb the view that disability is a social construct. It is revealing in this regard that it guarantees a right to habilitation and rehabilitation in order to achieve the inclusion of disabled people.[40] As will be seen throughout this book, the Convention acknowledges both the actual existence of barriers and the inherent effects of the impairments, both of which need to be considered together if its objectives are to be attained. It has thus brought to life a more expansive understanding of disability.

The CRPD actually applies all people with impairments who, in '*interaction* with various barriers', are hindered in 'their full and effective participation in society'.[41] The Convention relates the impairments to those barriers, and all its rights hinge on the removal of these barriers.[42] This means that these impairments are very much considered in the steps to be taken towards this end. The CRPD has built

[37] Article 3(c), CRPD.

[38] Article 3(d), CRPD.

[39] T. Degener, 'A Human Rights Model of Disability' in P. Blanck and E. Flynn (eds), *Routledge Handbook of Disability Law and Human Rights* (Abingdon: Routledge, 2016) 31, 33. Arlene Kanter also considers the human rights model of disability to be a variant of the social model of disability. See A. Kanter, 'The Relationship between Disability Studies and Law' in A. Kanter and B. Ferri (eds), *Righting Educational Wrongs* (Syracuse: Syracuse University Press, 2013) 1, 12–13. During a conversation, Arlene Kanter however told the author that she no longer defended her view about the human rights model of disability but considered that this model was just part of the social model of disability.

[40] Article 26, CRPD.

[41] Article 1, CRPD (emphasis added).

[42] Degener, 'A Human Rights Model of Disability', 39–40; Bartlett, 'The United Nations Convention on the Rights of Persons with Disabilities', 759.

upon the social model in order to protect the rights of disabled people.[43] It has a more pragmatic view of disability that takes into account both the internal and the external factors of disability and the extent to which their interplay may impede the enjoyment of human right. This view is more congruent with the aforementioned relational approach to disability. The Convention leans on the idea that disability is about a 'misfit' between certain individuals and the environment in which they find themselves.[44]

While acknowledging that the social model of disability has not exactly found its way into international human rights law – which in any event would be impracticable – this discussion must rest on a broader perspective. Notwithstanding its criticism, the social model remains a powerful tool for disabled people to protest against the obstacles created by society. It serves as an important reminder that disability is, at least partly if not most of the time, about societal organisation, something which has been ignored for a long time. As indicated by Hirschmann, it 'tells a vital part of the story', especially since disabled people remain excluded from many areas of life.[45]

The social model of disability highlights the need for the removal of the various barriers that hinder participation in society. To that extent, it can give shape to the different aspects of domestic policies in accordance with the CRPD. The latter requires that States Parties adopt measures in order to dismantle such barriers, and these measures will only be successful if they seek to modify the environment itself. The social model points to the necessity of the actual reconstruction of social institutions in a way that reduces the continuing disadvantage experienced by those with impairments. As argued by Collins, it is precisely through working on these social institutions that society will ultimately bring about inclusion for all.[46]

For this reason, the present book does not apply a 'human rights model of disability'. Rather, it adopts a social model lens on disability, which does not contradict this 'human rights model' but lays more emphasis on disability's social dimension. However, it does not use the social model as a model per se but as guidance for ensuring that the CRPD's implementation takes place in conformity with the very idea that gave momentum to its enactment. The book therefore connects with the view that disability is first and foremost located in society. Integrating the social model of disability into the inquiry will not only assure that the book faithful to the underlying philosophy of the CRPD but also contribute to a better engagement with a tool that has bolstered the disability rights movement. This model can serve

[43] A. Kanter, *The Development of Disability Rights under International Law. From Charity to Human Rights* (Abingdon: Routledge, 2015) 8.

[44] R. Garland-Thomson, 'Misfits: A Feminist Materialist Disability Concept' (2011) 26 *Hypatia* 591, 599–600.

[45] N. Hirschmann, 'Disabling Barriers, Enabling Freedom' in B. Arneil and J. Hirschmann (eds), *Disability and Political Theory* (Cambridge: Cambridge University Press, 2017) 99, 100–1.

[46] H. Collins, 'Discrimination, Equality and Social Inclusion' (2003) 66 *Modern Law Review* 16, 24–5.

the achievement of the Convention's objectives both by encouraging the questioning of misapprehensions about disabled people and by urging States Parties to have more regard for the external factors of disability. This does not mean that there are not internal factors that need to be considered if these objectives are ever to be achieved. On the contrary, the book views that the States Parties must consider any consequences of impairment as stemming from *both* the individual and society.

Although it is valid to state that the CRPD Convention has not wholly adopted the social model of disability, it has in fact legally anchored this model in international human right law. As a human rights treaty, the Convention had to translate this model into a practical device. It was not meant to ensure a straightforward application of the social model, as envisioned by its protagonists. Its drafters leaned on that model as they laid down the requirement on States Parties to improve social institutions in order to remove the obstacles to participation in society. The CRPD aims to empower disabled people by offering them entitlements in order to do so. Whether in doing so this Convention adopts an individual or social model, a mix of both, or even any other model of disability, is of limited importance and, in the view of the present author, misleading. What matters in the end are the steps to be taken so that disabled people can enjoy their human rights and that their exclusion from many areas of life be avoided, no matter what are the actual causes. The CRPD tells us that it is perhaps time to drop the question of the strengths and weaknesses of the different models of disability but bear in mind the lessons drawn from them to date.

2.2 Disability and the International Human Rights System

2.2.1 International Human Rights Law

Before the adoption of the CRPD, disabled people received limited attention in international human rights law. As seen in Chapter X, disability was not seen as a human rights issue prior to the CRPD. Not only was disability not dealt with in the existing human rights treaties (except in the CRC), but also the human rights community showed scant regard for it. NGOs working on human rights indeed were practically absent from the negotiation process.[47] The Convention was mainly the result of efforts achieved by the newly formed disability rights movement.

The question to be answered here is whether and how the CRPD permeates the whole of international human rights law. This question is essentially related to the

[47] J. Lord, 'Disability Rights and the Human Rights Mainstream: Reluctant Gate-Crashers?' in B. Clifford (ed), *The International Struggle for New Human Rights* (Philadelphia: University of Pennsylvania Press, 2008) 83, 90.

mainstreaming of disability. In order to answer such question, it is necessary first to define what is understood by mainstreaming. While the term has been applied in relation to human rights generally and also to gender in particular, it can similarly be used with regard to disability. It has been noted that mainstreaming entails the risk that human rights become diluted though, because it can result in interpretations that diverge too much from those of the competent treaty bodies.[48] The mainstreaming of gender has also been criticised for resulting in nominal reforms, such as the participation of women in management and interventions in a limited number of areas of life.[49] It may therefore spread false hope by opting for a narrow perspective in promoting the equality of men and women.

According to Skarstad and Stein, who have studied the question with regard to disability, mainstreaming needs to be understood as 'a scheme in which the human rights of vulnerable groups are fully integrated across the human rights treaties as well as constituent policies and practices'.[50] It involves investigating whether all treaty bodies are drawing enough attention to disabled people, or whether disability continues to be an afterthought or ignored altogether. If disability were merely the CRPD Committee's concern, disability would never get into the mainstream, a point similarly been made about gender.[51] While disability is above all an issue to be addressed by this Committee, it is equally important that other treaty bodies do pay attention to disabled people so as to avoid its further neglect.

Related to this is the question of the way in which the treaty bodies consider disability. The answer has manifold implications, since States Parties must implement human rights treaties and since this implementation can have a knock on effect on national legislation. While it is true that this question principally relates to the CRPD,[52] the rights protected by human rights treaties other the Convention also touch upon different branches of law that may not directly address disability but can have significant effects on those who are disabled. Mainstreaming should aim at avoiding the further neglect of disability in the recommendations of the treaty bodies, which may be pulling in opposite directions. Such contradictions have occurred in a General Comment by the Human Rights Committee, which allows States Parties to detain disabled people 'for the purpose of protecting [them] from serious harm or preventing injury to others',[53] which is in contradiction with their right to legal capacity and right

[48] C. McCrudden, 'Mainstreaming Human Rights' in C. Harvey (ed), *Human Rights in the Community: Rights as Agents for Change* (Oxford: Hart Publishing 2005) 9, 16–17.

[49] H. Charlesworth, '*Not Waving but Drowning:* Gender Mainstreaming and Human Rights in the United Nations' (2005) 18 *Harvard Human Rights Journal* 1, 14–15.

[50] K. Skarstad and M. Stein, 'Mainstreaming Disability in the United Nations Treaty Bodies' (2018) 17 *Journal of Human Rights* 1, 2.

[51] R. Johnstone, 'Feminist Influences on the United Nations Human Rights Treaty Bodies' (2006) 28 *Human Rights Quarterly* 148, 181.

[52] J. Lord and M. Stein, 'The Domestic Incorporation of Human Rights Law and the United Nations Convention on the Rights of Persons with Disabilities' (2008) 83 *Washington University Law Review* 449, 469–70.

[53] Human Rights Committee, *General Comment No 35: Article 9 (Liberty and security of person)*, 16 December 2014, CCPR/C/GC/35, para 19.

to liberty and security under the CRPD.[54] It is important to ensure that the interpretation of human rights treaties remains coherent and to undertake efforts of harmonisation towards this end.[55] The treaty bodies must endeavour to align with each other and incorporate the CRPD Committee's views into their work so that all disabled people are protected throughout international human rights law.

The present inquiry goes even a step further. Not only does it examine whether and how disability is addressed by all treaty bodies but it also explores the extent to which its consideration can have a transformative effect on the entire field of international human rights law. This requires inquiring into what the CRPD's understanding of disability actually means for the field. As with gender,[56] such an inquiry should ask whether and how this understanding calls into question some of the assumptions that have shaped power relationships. The Convention thus challenges the formation of the notion of human rights. As argued by Kanter, it provides 'a new model for implementation of all human rights treaties',[57] and this new model needs to be considered in light of international human rights law as a whole.

This inquiry should nonetheless be preceded by a determination of just how far-reaching this mainstreaming really is. Having reviewed the concluding observations of the treaty bodies, Skarstad and Stein note that the average number of recommendations addressing disability was below 20% prior to the CRPD, but that this average has increased to 62% post the Convention.[58] Nonetheless, there remains a significant variation between the treaty bodies, with the CESCR Committee obtaining 69% average number of recommendations and the CERD Committee 26% in 2014.[59] The enactment of a human rights treaty for disabled people had the effect of rapidly turning people's attention to disabled people, although not evenly across the treaty bodies. The CEDAW Committee issued a few recommendations highlighting matters specifically relating to disability, and it mentioned disabled people alongside other marginalised groups of people.[60] It has also delivered a decision where it considered that the absence of sign language for a deaf woman in legal proceedings amounted to a violation of CEDAW.[61] The shift in focus from the CESCR Committee is remarkable, all the more so since the Committee was much less consistent with regard to disability in the CRPD's

[54] As indicated by the CRPD Committee, '[t]he denial of the legal capacity of persons with disabilities and their detention in institutions against their will, either without their consent or with the consent of a substitute decision-maker ... constitutes arbitrary deprivation of liberty and violates articles 12 and 14 of the Convention' (CRPD Committee, *General comment No 1. Article 12: Equal recognition before the law*, para 40).

[55] J. Tobin, 'Seeking to Persuade: A Constructive Approach to Human Rights Treaty Interpretation' (2010) 23 *Harvard Human Rights Journal* 1, 35.

[56] Charlesworth, '*Not Waving but Drowning*', 14–15.

[57] Kanter, *The Development of Disability Rights under International Law*, 11.

[58] Skarstad and Stein, 'Mainstreaming Disability in the United Nations Treaty Bodies', 7.

[59] Ibid, 8.

[60] Ibid, 12–13.

[61] CEDAW Committee, *R.P.B. v the Philippines*, 12 March 2014, CEDAW/C/57/D/34/2011, para 8.7.

absence, despite its General Comment on the situation of disabled women.[62] While the Human Rights Committee remains in the background with regard to disability, it did address it recently, albeit not always in line with the CRPD.[63]

The CRC requires a separate analysis, since it contains provisions on disability contrarily to the human rights treaties that were adopted before it.[64] This means that the CRC Committee has had to focus on disabled children when reviewing States Parties' reports on the Convention's implementation, which it had been doing prior the CRPD.[65] Slowly but surely, the CRC Committee has moved away from a individualmodel towards a social model of disability. This took place especially after it issued a general comment on the situation of disabled children, and it may in so doing have been influenced by the adoption of the CRPD a few months earlier.[66] The CRC Committee has subsequently made more recommendations on issues affecting the lives of disabled children.[67] It is probably the one treaty body that has gone the furthest in bringing disability into the mainstream.

Interestingly, the CRPD seems not to have had any impact on the International Convention for the Protection of All Persons from Enforced Disappearance (ICPPED) adopted only a few days after it.[68] The ICPPED does refer to 'persons with disabilities', but only insofar as to oblige States Parties to establish 'aggravating circumstances' if the victims of enforced disappearance are 'particularly vulnerable persons' such as disabled people.[69] While it mentions disabled people amongst others, it does nothing more than require an increase in the criminal sanctions imposed on the perpetrators. It is nonetheless uncertain whether the ICPPED could have given more consideration to disability given its own objectives.

Last but not least, there is limited attention paid to disabled people in academic literature on international human rights law. In the majority of textbooks, the question of disability is discussed briefly, if at all, and usually from the perspective of anti-discrimination law.[70] Disabled people are generally overlooked, while

[62] G. Quinn and T. Degener, *The Current Use and Future Potential of United Nations Human Rights Instruments in the Context of Disability* (Geneva: UN, 2002) 130–1.

[63] While emphasising the necessity to provide 'less restrictive alternatives to confinement' for disabled people, it permits their compulsory detention when they may pose a danger to themselves or to others (Human Rights Committee, *General Comment No 35: Article 9 (Liberty and security of person)*, 16 December 2014, CCPR/C/GC/35, para 19).

[64] Articles 2 and 23, CRC.

[65] Quinn and Degener, *The Current Use and Future Potential of United Nations Human Rights Instruments in the Context of Disability*, 216.

[66] CRC Committee, *General Comment No 9: the Rights of Children with Disabilities*, 27 February 2007, CRC/C/GC/9, para 2.

[67] Skarstad and Stein, 'Mainstreaming Disability in the United Nations Treaty Bodies', 15–16.

[68] International Convention for the Protection of All Persons from Enforced Disappearance 2006, 14 IHRR 582 (ICPPED).

[69] Article 7(2)(b), ICPPED.

[70] D. Moeckli et al (eds), *International Human Rights Law* (Oxford: Oxford University Press, 3rd edn, 2018); O. De Schutter, *International Human Rights Law* (Cambridge: Cambridge University Press, 2nd edn, 2014); J. Steiner and P. Alston, *International Human Rights in Context: Law, Politics, Morals* (Oxford: Oxford University Press, 3rd edn, 2007).

the CRPD is sometimes cursorily touched upon, or they are just mentioned in passing. Some exceptions are to be found, however, with entire chapters written on the topic and with discussions held in the background of the Convention's negotiation process.[71] These chapters discuss the rights of disabled people alongside those of women, children, racial minorities and so on. Bringing disability more to the fore in this academic literature would be highly desirable, and it is actually one of the aims of the present book. It is important that disability be seen as an integral part of international human rights law instead of as a question to be addressed by a restricted number of specialists. The field of international human rights law has undergone a kind of 'internal fragmentation', which may diminish the overall consistency of the field and result in losing the ties that bind the whole of this field.[72] Hence, in addition to analysing the CRPD's important function as a group-specific human rights treaty, there is a need to carefully examine the interconnections between disability and human rights treaties other than the CRPD itself.

2.2.2 Global Policy Making

The mainstreaming of disability goes beyond international human rights law, which alone cannot ensure that disabled people benefit from its full reach. It is therefore important to look into how far actors other than those who traditionally belong to the international human rights system are taking disability into consideration. While treaty bodies are essential to promote the rights of disabled people, this will not happen without concerted efforts at the wider international level.

Indeed, UN agencies have the capacity to give effect to human rights treaties.[73] They do more than just remind States of their international commitments, as they can advise on the practical steps States must take in order to implement human rights treaties. It is often these agencies that have the particular ability to provide the know-how required for such implementation. As their activities are relevant to human rights, it has even been argued that these agencies could actually be considered as part of the international human rights system.[74] If, on the other hand, the human rights treaties were to be considered in isolation by the treaty bodies, efforts will remain in vain, especially since the methods of enforcement of international

[71] J. Rehman, *International Human Right Law* (Essex: Pearson, 2nd edn, 2010); Krause and M. Scheinin (eds), *International Protection of Human Rights: A Textbook* (Turku: *Åbo Akademi University-Institute for Human Rights*, 2009).

[72] B. Çali, L. McGregor and I. Radačić, *ESIL Interest Group on Human Rights Launches Online Symposia on International Human Rights Law*, 16 June 2014, https://www.ejiltalk.org/esil-interest-group-on-human-rights-launches-online-symposia-on-international-human-rights-law.

[73] G. Oberleitner, 'A Decade of Mainstreaming Human Rights in the UN: Achievements, Failures, Challenges' (2008) 26 *Netherlands Quarterly of Human Rights* 359, 387–8.

[74] P. Hunt, 'Configuring the UN Human Rights System in the "Era of Implementation": Mainland and Archipelago' (2017) 39 *Human Rights Quarterly* 489, 527–8.

human rights law are in fact rather weak. These treaty bodies simply do not have the power, not to mention the resources, to take up the task on their own, as they are already struggling to fulfil their own mandate.

This observation also applies to disability. The CRPD's success depends on the contribution of many actors besides the treaty bodies (let alone the CRPD Committee). The arrival of the Convention is a positive contribution in terms of enhanced human rights protection. However, on its own it is insufficient to improve human rights protection for those who have been marginalised for long time such as disabled people.[75] In view of this, the UN agencies – which again could be considered as part of the international human rights system – have a crucial role to play in achieving the objectives of the CRPD. They, too, should actually operate in keeping with the Convention. These agencies have as much an obligation to comply with the Convention, as they have with regard to any human rights treaty that comes within the remit of the UN Charter.[76] Despite this obligation, no systematic review has been conducted of the extent to which disabled people are benefiting from their programmes to date. Disability has been regarded as an issue to be examined only by some specialists.[77] Disabled people are moreover noticeably absent in debates on development in the southern hemisphere.[78] This is in stark contrast to gender, the status of which sits high on the UN agenda.

The CRPD offers a legal basis for raising the profile of disability in global policy making. Article 32 of the Convention provides that States Parties must take steps to ensure that 'international cooperation, including international development programmes, is inclusive of and accessible to persons with disabilities'.[79] This means that the design of such programmes must be done not only in collaboration with disabled people's organisations (DPOs) but also with due consideration for the broad range of impairments.[80] In order to do so, the UN agencies should address the issue through a 'twin-track' approach, both by mainstreaming disability in all their activities and by adopting measures especially directed to disabled people.[81]

[75] R. Lang et al, 'Implementing the United Nations Convention on the Rights of Persons with Disabilities: Principles, Implications, Practice and Limitations' (2011) 5 *ALTER European Journal of Disability Research* 206, 211–12.

[76] M. Stein and P. Stein, 'Disability, Development, and Human Rights: A Mandate and Framework for International Financial Institutions' (2014) 47 *UC Davis Law Review* 1231, 1250–1.

[77] M. Kett, R. Land and J.-F. Trani, 'Disability, Development and the Dawning of a New Convention: A Cause for Optimism?' (2009) 21 *Journal of International Development* 649, 656.

[78] M. Keogh, 'Inclusive Development Aid' in Blanck and Flynn, *Routledge Handbook of Disability Law and Human Rights*, 228, 240.

[79] Article 32(1)(a), CRPD.

[80] OHCHR, *Study on international cooperation to support national efforts for the realization of the purposes and objectives of the Convention on the Rights of Persons with Disabilities*, 20 December 2010, A/HRC/16/38, para 10.

[81] Ibid, para 12. Twin-tracking can also refer to UN agencies' programmes directed solely at disabled people, as opposed to mainstreaming, which would relate to giving consideration to them throughout all the programmes (Stein and Stein, 'Disability, Development, and Human Rights', 1263).

This requires, for instance, no longer discounting their needs when providing financial support to new projects and infrastructure.[82]

Beyond international human rights law, Article 11 of the CPRD refers to 'all necessary measures to ensure the protection and safety of persons with disabilities in situations of risk, including situations of armed conflict, humanitarian emergencies and the occurrence of natural disasters'. It appears nonetheless that these measures are strongly based on the individualmodel of disability and essentially aim at providing assistance to disabled people in the context of warfare.[83] This narrow focus may partially be due to the inherent scope of international humanitarian law.

From an institutional perspective, disability falls within the competencies of the Division for Social Policy and Development (DESA), even if the OHCHR has acquired key responsibilities following the CRPD's entry into force. DESA is hosting the Conference of States Parties (COSP) and has the task of fostering awareness of disabled people across UN agencies.[84] Each of these agencies has to address disability within its own sphere of competences, while an Inter-Agency Support Group on the Convention on the Rights of Persons with Disabilities has been set up with a view to improving collaboration between them.[85] The question is still whether such mainstreaming is happening throughout global policy-making.

An overview of the activities of the UN agencies reveals that consideration for disabled people has increased but is still uneven. The World Health Organisation (WHO) has turned its attention to disability and, together with the World Bank, produced a seminal report on the issue, laying bare the dire situation of disabled people around the world.[86] It endeavours to design its programmes in keeping with CRPD in liaison with other UN agencies.[87] Another agency that has been keen to address disability is the UN Children's Fund (UNICEF). With a mandate very much linked to the CRC, UNICEF has complemented the efforts of treaty bodies by providing expertise on the content of particular children's rights, while encouraging the participation of the relevant stakeholders in its work.[88] Its examination of the rights of disabled children has been steady, as testified by an early report of UNICEF Innocenti Research Centre and a number of subsequent reports that are informed

[82] OHCHR, *Study on international cooperation to support national efforts*, paras 47–8.

[83] J. Lord, 'Persons with Disabilities in International Humanitarian Law – Paternalism, Protectionism or Rights?' in C. Schuland-Vials and M. Gill (eds), *Disability, Human Rights and the Limits of Humanitarianism* (Aldershot: Ashgate, 2014) 155, 168–71.

[84] J. Lord et al, *Disability and International Cooperation and Development: A Review of Policies and Practices* (Washington: World Bank, 2010) 6–7, http://siteresources.worldbank.org/DISABILITY/Resources/Publications-Reports/Disability_and_Intl_Cooperation.pdf.

[85] See https://www.un.org/development/desa/disabilities/about-us/inter-agency-support-group-for-the-convention-on-the-rights-of-persons-with-disabilities.html.

[86] World Health Organization (WHO) and World Bank, *World Report on Disability* (Geneva: WHO, 2011).

[87] Lord et al, *Disability and International Cooperation and Development*, 12.

[88] Oberleitner, 'A Decade of Mainstreaming Human Rights in the UN', 387.

by the CRPD.[89] The International Labour Organisation (ILO) helped raise awareness of the special situation of disabled people at an early stage by adopting several conventions on issues related to disability,[90] although the emphasis still lies mainly on the provision of rehabilitation (and less on inclusive employment). As a pivotal UN agency in the field of development, the UN Development Programme (UNDP) has been attentive to the needs of disabled people by integrating disability into its programmes, with the active involvement of DPO's.[91] It assists governments in implementing the CRPD, although its strategic position could allow it in fact to go much further.[92] By contrast, the International Monetary Fund (IMF) has shown manifest unwillingness to regard disability as part of its mandate.[93]

Recent changes in the field of development have triggered renewed attention to disabled people. The Millennium Development Goals (MDGs), adopted in 2000, provided for a series of targets in order to improve the living standards of the world population. They have nevertheless been criticised for largely ignoring the different forms of inequality which result in marginalisation.[94] They completely failed to address disability, despite its major relevance for the objective of reducing poverty.[95] The CRPD's adoption rectified this omission, urging more consideration of disability with regard to development. Disabled people are now included in the 2030 Agenda for Sustainable Development.[96] The Sustainable Development Goals (SDGs) – which succeeded the MDGs in 2015 – mention disabled people in severalof their targets.[97] The fact that this Agenda is more aligned with international human rights law has further facilitated cross-pollination with the CRPD. Although this is a positive outcome for the rights of disabled people, it has been a matter of regret that further consideration was not given to disability in the SDGs.[98]

[89] UNICEF Innocenti Research Centre, *Promoting the Rights of Children with Disabilities* (Geneva: UNICEF, 2007); UNICEF, *The Right of Children with Disabilities to Education: A Rights-based Approach to Inclusive Education. Position Paper* (Geneva: UNICEF, 2012); UNICEF, *The State of the World's Children 2013. Children with Disabilities* (Geneva: UNICEF, 2013).

[90] Convention concerning Vocational Rehabilitation and Employment (Disabled Persons), ILO Convention No 159, 20 June 1983; Convention concerning Employment Promotion and Protection against Unemployment, ILO Convention No 168, 21 June 1988.

[91] Lord et al, *Disability and International Cooperation and Development*, 7–8.

[92] UNDP Independent Evaluation Office, *Evaluation of Disability-Inclusive Development at UNDP* (New York: UN, 2016) 34–5, http://web.undp.org/evaluation/evaluations/thematic/disability.shtml.

[93] Stein and Stein, 'Disability, Development, and Human Rights', 1273–4.

[94] M. Darrow, 'Master or Servant? Development Goals and Human Rights' in M. Langford, A. Sumner and A. Yamin (eds), *The Millennium Development Goals and Human Rights. Past, Present and Future* (Cambridge: Cambridge University Press, 2013) 67, 75–7.

[95] D. Mulligan and K. Gooding, *The Millennium Development Goals and People with Disabilities* (UK: Sightsavers International, 2009).

[96] GA, *Transforming our World: The 2030 Agenda for Sustainable Development*, 21 October 2015, A/RES/70/1.

[97] See, inter alia, Goal 4 (Quality Education), Goal 8 (Decent work and economic growth), Goal 10 (Reduced Inequalities) and Goal 11 (Sustainable Cities and Communities).

[98] E. Lockwood and R. Tardi, 'The Inclusion of Persons with Disabilities in the Implementation of the 2030 Agenda for Sustainable Development' (2014) 57 *Development* 433, 434; C. Brolan, 'A Word of Caution: Human Rights, Disability, and Implementation of the Post-2015 Sustainable Development Goals' (2016) 5 *Laws* 1, 22.

On the other hand, the SDGs have remedied a serious shortcoming of the MDGs, a move which was probably encouraged by Article 32 of the CRPD. Convergence with the Convention's objectives was also made easier as DESA was the secretariat for the MDGs and, subsequently, for the SDGs.[99]

The disability rights movement has been able to capitalise on the adoption of the CRPD in order to increase awareness of disabled people in the field of development. International cooperation is now an important channel for bringing disability into the mainstream. It is crucial, however, that such mainstreaming takes place in conformity with international human rights law. It has been stated two decades ago that, though they overlapped, both the human rights agenda and the development agenda were not actually convergent.[100] This has led to the adoption of a human rights-based approach to development within the UN, the purpose of which was to integrate human rights fully into development programming.[101] The UN agencies also reached a Common Understanding on a Human Rights-Based Approach to Development Cooperation.[102] While the human rights community was absent in discussions leading to the MDGs, it actively participated in those leading to the SDGs.[103] In order to take stock of the CRPD, all the activities of UN Agencies that can affect disabled people's lives must be guided by the same human rights-based approach to development. This is why it is imperative not only to reconcile the implementation of the Convention with efforts to attain the SDGs, but also to ensure that the 2030 Agenda for Sustainable Development itself is pursued in conformity with the CRPD. The treaty bodies play an essential part in reaching out to the UN agencies and, thereby, in sustaining the role of these agencies themselves in implementing the Convention.

[99] M. Stein, C. McClain-Nhlapo and J. Lord, 'Education and HIV/AIDS. Disability Rights and Inclusive Development' in Langford, Sumner, and Yamin, *Millenium Development Goals and Human Rights*, 274, 278.

[100] P. Alston, 'Ships Passing in the Night: The Current State of the Human Rights and Development Debate Seen Through the Lens of the Millennium Development Goals' (2005) 27 *Human Rights Quarterly* 755.

[101] See OHCHR, *Frequently Asked Questions on a Human Rights-Based Approach to Development Cooperation* (New York/Geneva: UN, 2006).

[102] UN, *The Human Rights Based Approach to Development Cooperation: Towards a Common Understanding among UN Agencies, Stamford*, 5–7 May 2003.

[103] T. Winkler and Carmel Williams, 'The Sustainable Development Goals and Human Rights: a Critical Early Review' (2017) 21 *The International Journal of Human Rights* 1023, 1023.

3

Theoretical Background: The Inclusion of Disabled People

This chapter starts by challenging the view of independence in legal theory (3.1. Disability and the Autonomous Individual). It goes on to assess social contract theory, in particular Rawls's Theory of Justice, as well as criticisms of this theory put forward regarding disability. The aim is not only to expose the vacuum in political theory as well as the failure to offer disabled people equal moral consideration but also to examine what are the possible ways forward. The chapter therefore explores how theories of justice other than the social contract theory can be used in order to determine what is needed for including disabled people (3.2. The Inclusion of Disabled People). It discusses two such theories, namely capabilities and recognition theories, and investigates both their limits and their potential in making them of benefit to all disabled people. It also proposes a combination of those theories so as to gear them towards the objectives of the CRPD.

3.1 Disability and the Autonomous Individual

3.1.1 Independence

From a young age, individuals are encouraged to aspire to the ideal of independence. This ideal is however based on a wrong premise, since the reverse – dependency – is an inevitable and universal aspect of life. As a matter of fact, dependency is a constitutive part of the human condition.[1] Such dependency is unevenly acknowledged: that of children and of the elderly, as well as of those who are dependent for a limited time is commonly accepted. They have lost, or are about to gain or to regain, their independence, and share characteristics that society deems reflect 'normalcy'; other forms of dependency are considered to depart from it, and therefore are less well tolerated. These latter forms of dependency have generally been associated with disabled people. Consequently,

[1] M. Fineman, *The Autonomy Myth: A Theory of Dependency* (New York: The New Press, 2004) 34–5; F. Kittay, 'A Feminist Care Ethics, Dependence and Disability' (2007) 6 *Feminism and Philosophy* 3–7, 4–5.

Disability in International Human Rights Law. Gauthier de Beco, Oxford University Press. © Gauthier de Beco 2021.
DOI: 10.1093/oso/9780198824503.003.0004

for the two last centuries, society has been trying to bring these people back to 'normalcy'.[2]

The premise that one must be independent is built on the idea that individuals are able to distance themselves from society. As shown by Elias, both individuals and society are actually not separate entities.[3] Like the parts of the body and the body itself, the former constitute the latter and the latter is made up of the former. According to Elias, in order to better understand what both are and mean, we need to move from the '*homo clausus*' (closed person) to the '*homines aperti*' (open people).[4] People can only be understood in relation to each other. There is no society without individuals, as these individuals exist only through society, both of which ought to be considered jointly.

In view of this, a strict separation between the notions of dependency and of independence – and accordingly those of disability and of ability – does not make sense.[5] It is not a matter of 'either or'; rather, it is one of degree.[6] A strict separation between these notions categorises those who are more dependent than others as oddities, unless when this is regarded as part of the live course or as a temporary event. The result is that they, especially those with severe forms of impairments, are supposed to rely on others for whatever they do. Even for these individuals, however, dependency is never total, in the sense that they do not lack any form of human agency; rather, they have a number of limitations that will vary according to the circumstances.[7] This explains why it always remains difficult to strictly distinguish between 'disabled' and 'abled' (or, for that matter, between moderately and severely disabled).

The ideal of independence has led to the assumption that people are autonomous human beings. This assumption is a cornerstone of political liberalism.[8] It means that people are self-governing individuals who are able to define what is of value to them without external intervention. Those whose capacity for reason is reduced pose a serious challenge to such assumption, as this capacity for reason is seen as one of the most fundamental human attributes.[9] The assumption, of course, is especially prejudicial to people with cognitive impairments.

[2] H.-J. Stiker, *A History of Disability*, Trans. W. Sayers (Ann Arbor: University of Michigan Press, 1999) 134–38.

[3] N. Elias, *What is Sociology?* Trans. S. Mennell and G. Morrissey (New York: Columbia University Press, 1978) 112–13.

[4] Ibid, 124–5.

[5] J. Wolff, 'Disability among Equals' in K. Brownlee and A. Cureton (eds), *Disability and Disadvantage* (Oxford: Oxford University Press, 2009) 112, 126.

[6] J. Vorhaus, 'Disability, Dependency and Indebtedness' (2007) 4 *Journal of Philosophy of Education* 29, 35–6.

[7] O. O'Neill, *Towards Justice and Virtue: A Constructive Account of Practical Reasoning* (Cambridge: Cambridge University Press, 1996) 108–9.

[8] W. Kymlicka, *Liberalism, Community and Culture* (Oxford: Oxford University Press Clarendon, 1989) 9.

[9] L. Carlson and E. Kittay, 'Introduction: Rethinking Philosophical Presumptions in Light of Cognitive Disability' (2009) 40 *Metaphilosophy* 307, 307–8.

From an empirical perspective, it has been shown that people are actually not self-governing individuals. When it comes to decision making, all individuals call on each other on a daily basis.[10] Any choice is informed by reliance on others, and isolation, in fact, provides the greatest likelihood that any degree of independence will be unreachable. Decisions are not made *ex nihilo*, but depend on one's social relationships, which foster the values in which someone believes. Choices are made through such social relationships, which, in turn, may also potentially inhibit them. The belief that people can define what is of value to them by themselves, therefore, is a fiction. It has nonetheless shaped the concept of autonomy up until now.

The result is that a large proportion of disabled people do not fit in with current theories of justice. In order to reverse this, it is necessary to include those who seem to be dependent in a way that is outside the 'norm' into what would constitute the 'norm'. It does not mean that the ideal of independence must be necessarily rejected, but that there is a need to acknowledge dependency as part of the ontological characteristics of human beings.

There have been attempts to define the concept of autonomy in conjunction with the role of social relationships. As proposed by Mackenzie, relational autonomy recognises that one's level of autonomy is contingent upon the availability of support, on the one hand, and decreases with oppressive social institutions, on the other.[11] What counts is not the ability to decide by oneself only what is valuable but the real opportunity to rely on others in order to make such decisions. The formation of social relationships is therefore fundamental for the furtherance of autonomy. According to Mackenzie, society has the 'obligation not just to respect but also to promote autonomy'.[12] Seen in this light, autonomy and dependency are not that contradictory.[13] One could lack some forms of dependency, but still be able to seek support for the purpose of acting autonomously. Autonomy is not a question of presence or absence; rather, it is something that should be enabled through 'relations of support'.[14] It is a matter of interdependency. The chance of accessing a large network of people in order to seek and find support will allow individuals to make those decisions that govern their own lives more easily.

[10] L. Francis, 'Understanding Autonomy in Light of Intellectual Disability' in Brownlee and Cureton, *Disability and Disadvantage*, 206–8.

[11] C. Mackenzie, W. Rogers and S. Dodds, 'Introduction: What Is Vulnerability and Why Does It Matter for Moral Theory?' in C. Mackenzie, W. Rogers and S. Dodds (eds), *Vulnerability New Essays in Ethics and Feminist Philosophy* (Oxford: Oxford University Press, 2014) 1, 16–17; C. Mackenzie, 'The Importance of Relational Autonomy and Capabilities for an Ethics of Vulnerability' in Moackenzie, Roogers and Dodds, *Vulnerability New Essays in Ethics and Feminist Philosophy*, 30, 42–3.

[12] Mackenzie, 'The Importance of Relational Autonomy', 34.

[13] J. Scully, 'Disability and Vulnerability: On Bodies, Dependence, and Power' in Mackenzie, Rogers and Dodds, *Vulnerability New Essays in Ethics and Feminist Philosophy*, 204, 213–14.

[14] L. Davy, 'Philosophical Inclusive Design: Intellectual Disability and the Limits of Individual Autonomy in Moral and Political Theory' (2015) 30 *Hypatia* 132, 144.

Given that all people are dependent on others in different ways throughout their life course, acknowledging such interdependency will indeed be more in harmony with the human condition. Delineating certain forms of dependency from the boundaries of those that are seen as acceptable has pushed many individuals, such as those who are disabled, to the margins of society. The problem is heightened by the constant underscoring of a number of very severe impairments, thereby diminishing attention to more casual, and actually more numerous, impairments. Disability, seen in this light, is just one instance requiring a certain way of offering support.[15]

A more holistic approach to appreciating dependency requires a greater appreciation of the lived experience of disabled people. Different sorts of social arrangements are necessary to mitigate the internal and external factors of disability. In order to do so, Wolff argues that disabled people should benefit from 'personal enhancement', 'material enhancement' and 'status enhancement', which call for the provision of internal resources, external resources and social structures, respectively.[16] 'Personal enhancement' and 'material enhancement' are concerned with the individual, whereas 'status enhancement' concentrates on society. Amongst them, 'status enhancement' is to be favoured, because it reduces the risk of stigma and because it can be beneficial to all.[17] A strategy that targets social structures will treat disabled people more as equals than one that endeavours to make them conform better to the 'norm'. Wolff nonetheless stresses the importance of mixing the three kinds of enhancement.[18] Although 'status enhancement' must remain the primary target, there must be provision for other kinds of enhancement if disabled people are to participate in society.

It is worth delving further into the mutual strengthening of the internal and external factors of disability. As suggested by Dodds, the more social arrangements that are in place to control the external factors, the less likely the internal factors will engender any forms of dependency.[19] Expanding the reach of these social arrangements by themselves can help reduce such forms of dependency and avoid the necessity of making further additions. For instance, flexible working conditions and supportive networks will decrease the need for personal assistance. Social arrangements can aggravate the effects of impairments by increasing the obstacles to participation in society, but, by the same token, they may facilitate

[15] F. Kittay, 'The Ethics of Care, Dependence and Disability' (2011) 24 *Ratio Juris* 49, 53.

[16] Internal resources involve developing abilities and skills by training and medicine. External resources are either 'cash compensation' or 'targeted resource enhancement', which are provided through goods and services to be used either freely or conditionally, respectively. Social structures involve changing the environment as well as social attitudes (Wolff, 'Disability among Equals', 124).

[17] Ibid, 129–32.

[18] J. Wolff, 'Cognitive Disability in a Society of Equals' (2009) 40 *Metaphilosophy* 402, 413–14; J. Wolff, 'Disability, Status Enhancement, Personal Enhancement and Resource Allocation' (2009) 25 *Economics and Philosophy* 49, 51–5.

[19] S. Dodds, 'Dependence, Care, and Vulnerability' in Mackenzie, Rogers and Dodds, *Vulnerability New Essays in Ethics and Feminist Philosophy*, 181, 186–7.

such participation should they be designed so as to overcome the barriers encountered by disabled people.[20] In this way, both the internal factors and the external factors of disability could even become indistinguishable, insofar as many of these people are concerned. A society that creates conditions allowing for this to happen could minimise the notion of impairments and leads to greater tolerance of human differences. The improvement of social institutions has the advantage of bringing dependency back into the centre of our understanding of human beings. It facilitates a process of inclusiveness, thereby blurring even further the line between disabled and non-disabled.

3.1.2 Social Contract Theory

The question of disability has initiated a renewed debate about social contract theory. In his Theory of Justice, Rawls undertook to determine the way in which members of society form a social contract about the fundamental principles of justice that will govern them.[21] Behind a 'veil of ignorance', the parties agree on how the burdens and benefits of social cooperation will be distributed amongst themselves.[22] They are deprived of knowledge about their race, gender and social class as well as their natural endowments. In this 'original position', they define together the basic terms of social cooperation. The contractors thereby reach a reasonable agreement on 'the way in which the major social institutions distribute fundamental rights and duties and determine the division of advantages from social cooperation'.[23]

According to Rawls, the reasonable agreement leads to the formation of a social contract, whereby society's members agree on two fundamental principles of justice. The first principle is the Liberty Principle, which stipulates that '[e]ach person has an equal claim to a fully adequate scheme of equal basic rights and liberties, which scheme is compatible with the same scheme for all'.[24] The 'basic rights and liberties' have priority over the sharing of the burdens and benefits of social cooperation, and therefore cannot be traded off against other public goods. The second principle is divided into two parts: the Equal Opportunities Principle and the Difference Principle. It stipulates that '[s]ocial and economic inequalities are to satisfy two conditions: first, they are to be attached to positions and offices open to all under conditions of fair equality of opportunity; and second, they are to be to the greatest benefit of the least advantaged'.[25] Social cooperation has to provide

20 Mackenzie, 'The Importance of Relational Autonomy', 39; Scully, 'Disability and Vulnerability', 208–9.

21 J. Rawls, *A Theory of Justice* (Cambridge, MA: Harvard University Press, 2nd rev. edn, 1999) 102–5.

22 Ibid, 118–23.

23 Ibid, 6.

24 J. Rawls, *Political Liberalism* (New York: Columbia University Press, 1993) 5.

25 Ibid, 6. The just savings principle means that enough resources must be left for future generations.

similar economic opportunities to all, and should be especially beneficial for the most deprived of society by placing the 'least advantaged' in the most favourable position.

Thus, a society is just provided it is governed by rules that are agreed upon on the basis of mutual advantage. The condition, however, is that the contractors involved possess two moral powers: 'the capacity for a sense of justice and the capacity for a conception of the good'.[26] In the words of Rawls, the basic terms of social cooperation are defined 'between citizens regarded as free and equal, and as normal and fully cooperating members of society over a complete life'.[27] These citizens must be able to commit to reciprocity if they are to participate in the social contract.

There are two sorts of goods to be shared by society's members.[28] On the one hand, natural primary goods do not come under consideration. On the other hand, social primary goods must be distributed according to the two fundamental principles of justice described above. The reason is that the natural primary goods are 'simply natural facts ... [but] [w]hat is just and unjust is the way that institutions deal with these facts'.[29] Rawls works out his Theory of Justice in three further stages following the 'original position': the constitutional stage; the legislative stage and; the judicial and administrative stage.[30]

While this new social contractarian approach has had a huge influence in political theory, it has been criticised with regard to disability. To start with, disabled people may not possess the two moral powers ('the capacity for a sense of justice and the capacity for a conception of the good'). Although these two powers should not be applied too strictly, 'scattered individuals' fail to meet the condition according to Rawls.[31] As pointed out by Silver and Francis, such people are regarded as 'outliers', because they are supposedly incapable of agreeing on the two fundamental principles of justice.[32] The parties must be able to pursue their 'conception of the good' and, thereby, be able to act autonomously.[33] This again targets intellectually disabled people, as they may lack the cognitive skills required for adhering to the social contract.

The result is that those who depend on others to define what is of value to them have no say whatsoever about what will constitute the basic terms of social cooperation. Rawls confirms that he opts to 'leave aside permanent physical disabilities or mental disorders so severe as to prevent persons from being normal and fully

[26] Ibid, 19.
[27] Ibid, 20.
[28] Ibid, 54–5.
[29] Rawls, *A Theory of Justice*, 87.
[30] Ibid, 171–6.
[31] Ibid, 443.
[32] A. Silvers and L. Francis, 'Justice through Trust: Disability and the "Outlier Problem" in Social Contract Theory' (2005) 116 *Ethics* 40, 46.
[33] A. Silvers and L. Francis, 'Thinking About the Good: Reconfiguring Liberal Metaphysics (or Not) for People with Cognitive Disabilities' (2009) 40 *Metaphilosophy* 475, 481–2.

cooperating members of society in the usual sense'.[34] This excludes many disabled people from the 'original position', although the problem is not just related to them. Particularly staggering is that Rawls refers to 'physical disabilities' and assimilates them to 'mental disorders', as if both affect social cooperation in a similar way. The amalgamation of both 'mental disorders' and 'physical disabilities' indeed displays political theory's far-reaching disdain for those with impairments.[35] It shows the determination not to see disability, stemming from whichever kind of impairment, as a matter of justice.

This way of treating disabled people is indeed very problematic. Only those who display the two moral powers are allowed to participate in the social contract. Rawls simply plans addressing disability during the 'legislative stage'.[36] The 'original position' includes only those 'citizens who are normally active and fully cooperating members of society over a complete life'.[37] The result is that many disabled people are represented by trustees. However, there is no guarantee that these trustees will protect disabled people's interests, as they have their own interests to defend. It can also be asked how the trustees are able to determine the appropriateness of their undertakings without being aware of the disabilities of those whom they are representing.[38] Hence, they may ignore the particular needs of disabled people, whose disabilities they are not supposed to be aware of in this 'original position'. In the words of Anderson and Honneth, 'Rawls allows the veil of ignorance to fall a bit too low'.[39] The commitment to reciprocity raises a further concern for disabled people. The fact that the social contract has to be mutually advantageous means that the parties might be reluctant to enter into negotiation with those who they think would actually contribute less to society. These parties may not want to involve disabled people, since doing so might seem unfavourable to them.

There are two ways out of this problem: amending Rawls' Theory of Justice or turning to other options. Several scholars have made proposals to amend the social contract. Such proposals have the advantage of leaving this social contract intact, while guaranteeing that disabled people are still included. They will not be

[34] Rawls, *A Theory of Justice*, 234.

[35] B. Arneil, 'Disability, 'Self Image, and Modern Political Theory' (2009) 27 *Political Theory* 218, 223–4 and 226.

[36] Rawls, *Political Liberalism*, 184. However, Rawls makes it clear in later works that we do have moral duties towards those who are severely disabled (*J. Rawls, Justice as Fairness: A Restatement* (Cambridge, MA: Harvard University Press, 2001) 176 note 59).

[37] J. Rawls, 'Social Unity and Primary Goods' in S. Freeman (ed), *Collected Papers* (Cambridge, MA: Harvard University Press, 1999) 359, 368.

[38] H. Richardson, 'Rawlsian Social-Contract Theory and the Severely Disabled' (2006) 10 *The Journal of Ethics* 419, 433.

[39] J. Anderson and A. Honneth, 'Autonomy, Vulnerability, Recognition, and Justice' in J. Christman and J. Anderson (eds), *Autonomy and the Challenges to Liberalism: New Essays* (Cambridge: Cambridge University Press, 2005) 127, 141.

examined in depth in this chapter, given the large amount of literature devoted to this topic. The purpose here is only to highlight possible solutions and, above all, to make the case for looking out for alternatives to social contract theory.

Silvers and Francis envisage reaching a reasonable agreement not through the mechanism of representation but through a cultivation of trust.[40] They thereby seek to redefine the bargaining process which leads to the formation of the social contract. A variant of such a way out of the problem is to replace the commitment to reciprocity with the objective of living together peacefully.[41] Hartley suggests having a broader interpretation of the various kinds of contributions to society by differentiating the idea of reciprocity from that of mutual advantage.[42] Similarly, Becker considers that the notion of reciprocity should be regarded not as a 'tit-for-tat' exchange but as a form of 'generalized reciprocity'.[43] The common feature of these proposals is that the parties would regard those who contribute to social cooperation in different ways still as 'normal and fully cooperating members of society'. By contrast, Stark proposes to keep the normal and full cooperation assumption in the 'original position' but to abandon it in the constitutional stage.[44] Everyone will then be able to decide on the optimal allocation of social primary goods.

These solutions, albeit attractive, only provide partial remedies to the disregard of disabled people as parties to the social contract. The reason is that altering the bargaining process in such a way risks making the social contract itself more fragile. In the end, it might no longer secure the mutual consent that binds the parties together. It may also set requirements that certain disabled people in fact are not be able to fulfil or that include them only partially. As a result, they would remain 'outliers', albeit to a lesser degree. No matter how the problem is dealt with, the aforementioned proposals do not fill the gap that political theory has opened up for disabled people. A deeper question is why any form of contribution to social cooperation is required at all in order to offer such people a social status equal to that of others. The question concerns not only disabled people but also all those whose involvement may be seen as disadvantageous to the parties. While this conclusion could be debated and needs to be explored further, it demonstrates the significant difficulties that theories of justice have had in addressing disability generally.

[40] Silvers and Francis, 'Justice through Trust', 61–4.

[41] M. Sisson and M. DeNicola, 'Minimal Mutual Advantage: How the Social Contract Can do Justice to the Disabled (2015) 14 *European Journal of Political Theory* 161, 169–72.

[42] C. Hartley, 'Justice for the Disabled: A Contractualist Approach' (2009) 40 *Journal of Social Philosophy* 17, 25–7.

[43] L. Becker, 'Reciprocity, Justice and Disability' (2005) 116 *Ethics* 9, 34.

[44] C. Stark, 'How to Include the Severely Disabled in A Contractarian Theory of Justice' (2007) 15 *The Journal of Political Philosophy* 127, 138–40.

3.2 The Inclusion of Disabled People

3.2.1 Capabilities Theory

Initially elaborated by Sen and further developed by Nussbaum,[45] capabilities theory stipulates that society must be arranged so as to enhance people's own capabilities. Capabilities are opportunities to achieve a number of essential human functionings, so that individuals can have the kind of life they have reason to value. They create entitlements that must be fulfilled through the distribution of resources amongst members of society. While Sen is silent on what sort of capabilities must be strengthened and places particular emphasis on freedom, Nussbaum proposes a list of ten capabilities that are indispensable for having a 'life that is worthy of human dignity',[46] which she considers to be the object of an 'overlapping consensus'.[47] This list is not exhaustive, and therefore may evolve over time. She argues that people should be able to achieve a minimum 'threshold level of each capability' if they are to enjoy true human functioning.[48] Nussbaum thus adopts a normative conception of the capabilities, which she has applied, in particular, to disabled people. This is why Nussbaum's approach will be the main focus here.

In contrast to social contract theory, capabilities theory is not procedural but outcome-based. Both theories of justice have common grounds, since they are rooted in the tradition of political liberalism. Capabilities theory is nonetheless presented as an alternative to social contract theory. It aims to replace the reasonable agreement which is reached by mutual consent (which underlies the social contract) with entitlements to a number of capabilities for every single individual.

Capabilities theory turns out to be a useful conceptual lens for improving the life of disabled people. Instead of allocating a fixed amount of resources to them, the amount allocated varies according to the extent to which resources can be converted into essential human functionings.[49] As argued by Sen, disabled people often need more resources than others in order to fulfil such human functionings.[50] Applying Rawls' terminology, the capabilities theory recognises that one's 'natural

[45] A. Sen, *Development as Freedom* (New York: Knopf, 1999); A. Sen, *Inequality Reexamined* (Oxford: Clarendon Press, 1992); M. Nussbaum, *Creating Capabilities: The Human Development Approach* (Cambridge, MA: Belknap Press, 2011); M. Nussbaum, *Women and Human Development. The Capabilities Approach* (Cambridge: Cambridge University Press, 2000).

[46] M. Nussbaum, *Frontiers of Justice: Disability, Nationality, Species Membership* (Cambridge: MA: The Belknap Press, 2007) 77. These capabilities are: life; bodily health; bodily integrity; senses, imagination and thought; emotions; practical reason; affiliation; other species; play and; control over one's environment (Ibid, 77–9).

[47] Ibid, 136.

[48] Ibid, 72.

[49] E. Anderson, 'Justifying the Capabilities Approach to Justice' in H. Brighouse and I. Robeyns (eds), *Measuring Justice: Primary Goods and Capabilities* (Cambridge: Cambridge University Press, 2010) 81, 87–8.

[50] Sen, *Development as Freedom*, 88; Sen, *Inequalities Reexamined*, 20 and 28.

primary goods' will impact upon the possible use of 'social primary goods'. By prescribing the allocation of resources so that disabled people can enhance their capabilities, it is more sensitive to human differences. The theory looks into what the real opportunities are for disabled people, with due regard for their particular situation.

Nonetheless, capabilities theory has also faced criticism with regard to disability. Several scholars have been particularly critical of Nussbaum's approach. They have pointed out that some disabled people will not be able to reach her advocated minimum threshold level of designated capabilities,[51] especially those who are suffering from very profound disabilities.[52] The question is whether they still have entitlements in order to develop such capabilities. Giving an indication of the answer, Nussbaum affirms that a life lacking one of 'the actual features of a characteristic human form of life ... at any level, is not fully a human life, a life worthy of human dignity, even if the others are present'.[53] Conversely, those who might have the capacity to go beyond the minimum threshold level of the capabilities will not get the resources they would require in order to so.[54] Nussbaum sets the same outcome for everyone. She does not account for the fact that some individuals may be able to reach a higher level of such capabilities without additional resources while others may not.

Capability theory's outcome-based nature creates another issue. While Nussbaum's justification for the list of ten capabilities is debatable, the outright rejection of a social contract denies the human dignity of those who actually possess the two moral powers. These may include disabled people who happen to fulfil the condition and are willing to participate in the social contract. This is a considerable limitation since society's members are prevented from defining by themselves how the burdens and benefits of social cooperation are to be distributed amongst them.[55]

Besides this theoretical question, there is also a practical question. Nussbaum does not provide any way of resolving the trade-offs that must be made in order to strengthen everyone's capabilities. Scarcity of resources inevitably requires making hard choices between multiple requests by different groups of people. In order to facilitate decision-making in relation to this, Wolff and De-Shalit propose to identify the 'fertile functionings' and 'corrosive disadvantages' that have effects on several essential human functionings at the same time (positive effects as far as

[51] Silvers and Francis, 'Thinking About the Good', 484. L. Barclay, 'Natural Deficiency or Social Oppression? The Capabilities Approach to Justice for People with Disabilities' (2012) 9 *Journal of Moral Philosophy* 500, 514.

[52] M. Stein, 'Disability Human Rights' (2007) 95 *California Law Review* 75, 104–5.

[53] Nussbaum, *Frontiers of Justice*, 181.

[54] A. Silvers, 'A Diverse Theory of Justice for Disability' in Brownlee and Cureton, *Disability and Disadvantage* 181–84; Stein, 'Disability Human Rights', 107.

[55] C. Stark, 'Respecting Human Dignity: Contract Versus Capabilities' (2009) 40 *Metaphilosophy* 366, 374.

'fertile functionings' are concerned and negative effects as far as 'corrosive disadvantages' are concerned).[56] An example of 'fertile functioning' relating to disability would be affiliation given its manifold utility for disabled people.[57] This approach to enhancing capabilities may allow greater reliance on capability theory so as to facilitate their participation in society.

Another option is to mix the social contract and capabilities theories so as to get the best out of both. Richardson proposes adding Nussbaum's list of capabilities to Rawls' social primary goods, which have to be shared pursuant to the two established fundamental principles of justice (the Liberty Principle as well as the Equal Opportunities Principle and the Difference Principle).[58] These primary goals may not be the best for everyone, as they reflect only 'particular conceptions of the good' based on some pre-established set of values.[59] They are not necessarily the most important ones for disabled people, who require not just income but also other kinds of goods, such as healthcare and personal assistance.[60] Nussbaum's list of capabilities appears to covers largely Rawls' own list of social primary goods, and therefore it might even replace it altogether. Another way of combining both theories of justice would be to make use of capabilities theory to enhance participation in the social contract. Wong argues that the two moral powers might just be potential ones, and therefore that society should allow for enabling conditions so that disabled people can acquire such moral powers.[61] In this way, capabilities theory would be incorporated into the social contract theory. Mixing social contract and capabilities theories nonetheless presents one major hurdle. Social contract theory refers only to people's sources of income and wealth for purpose of determining how to share the burdens and benefits of social cooperation. It does not take into account the possession of natural endowments, which can be a key concern regarding disability.

The issue is also how far capabilities theory is congruent with the social model of disability (and, through this model, the philosophy underlying the CRPD). In order to underpin the view that disability is a product of societal organisation, capability theory must provide for means by which to remove barriers preventing disabled people from participating in society. A pivotal issue at stake is whether the capabilities theory provides normative ground for including disabled people through calling for modifying the environment towards this end. While it takes this environment into consideration, it does not seek to modify it for the inclusion

[56] J. Wolff and A. De-Shalit, *Disadvantage* (Oxford: Oxford University Press, 2007) 121–2.

[57] Ibid, 140–1.

[58] Richardson, 'Rawlsian Social-Contract Theory', 454 and 461.

[59] M. Sandel, *Liberalism and the Limits of Justice* (Cambridge: Cambridge University Press, 2nd edn, 1998) 27.

[60] T. Burchardt, 'Capabilities and Disability: the Capabilities Framework and the Social Model of Disability' (2004) 19 *Disability & Society* 735, 739.

[61] S. Wong, *'Duties of Justice* to Citizens with Cognitive Disabilities' (2009) 40 *Metaphilosophy* 282, 386 and 389.

of disabled people; it may even be invoked to argue in favour of their segregation.[62] If capabilities theory favours such inclusion, this is only as a way to strengthen their capabilities.

Capabilities theory itself distinguishes between three types of factors that bear upon the ability to convert resources into essential human functionings: personal, social and environmental factors.[63] Personal factors concern people's own capacity to use the resources available to them, which may be affected by the existence of impairment. Social and environmental factors relate to the social structures surrounding disabled people that have an impact on the development of their capabilities. Capabilities theory therefore acknowledges that the enhancement of capabilities may depend upon different kinds of obstacles. This is confirmed by Nussbaum's concept of 'combined capabilities', which she understands as capabilities that are to be developed through the creation of appropriate political, social and economic conditions.[64] Anderson also points out that the strengthening of capabilities involves making environments more accessible to disabled people in order to confer on them equal citizenship.[65] Capabilities theory thus highlights the importance of societal organisation to attain its objectives, which contrasts with Rawls's Theory of Justice.[66]

Despite taking into account different types of conversion factors, what the capabilities theory means for the environment per se remains to be clarified. The environment is just one of the elements that must be considered when defining the amount of resources for strengthening the capabilities. The strengthening of such capabilities, by itself, does not entail bringing changes to that environment. This contrasts with the social model, which is much more radical in its view of disability. As stated by Robeyns, social structures are only 'the means and not the ends of well-being' in relation to capabilities theory.[67] The latter remains flexible as to how to increase the level of capabilities and is not intended to provide any direction in this regard. One reason for this is that the theory takes the individual as the moral unit of analysis. It does not command how to improve existing structures; rather, it considers a number of conversion factors that affect the strengthening of capabilities.

Silver and Stein further charge that Nussbaum's approach imposes on disabled people to make personal efforts to acquire capabilities even though they might

[62] A. Silvers and M. Stein, 'Disability and the Social Contract' (2007) 74 *University of Chicago Law Review* 1615, 1627–8.

[63] I. Robeyns, 'The Capabilities Approach: A Theoretical Survey' (2005) 6 *Journal of Human Development* 93, 99; I. Robeyns, 'Justice as Fairness and the Capability Approach' in B. Kaushik and K. Ravi (eds), *Arguments for a Better World: Essays in Honor of Amartya Sen. Volume 1: Ethics, Welfare, and Measurement* (Oxford: Oxford University Press, 2009) 397, 404.

[64] Nussbaum, *Creating Capabilities*, 84; M. Nussbaum, *Women and Human Development*, 20.

[65] E. Anderson, 'What Is the Point of Equality?' (1999) 109 *Ethics* 287, 319–21.

[66] L. Terzi, 'What Metric of Justice for Disabled People? Capability and Disability' in Brighouse and Robeyns, *Measuring Justice: Primary Goods and Capabilities*, 150, 166.

[67] Robeyns, 'The Capabilities Approach: A Theoretical Survey', 110.

have good reasons for not doing so.[68] They criticise capability theory for being too paternalistic.[69] It is correct that the strengthening of the capabilities will somehow depend on people's performances. Nonetheless, it must be remembered that the capabilities theory is about entitlements. Capabilities, which are *opportunities* to perform a number of human functionings, offer disabled people the choice to use the resources on offer, inasmuch as they correlate to potential rather than achieved human functionings. As especially stressed by Sen, the individuals retain the decision whether to develop any capabilities in such a way. On the other hand, such a choice might not always be the predominant factor of wellbeing. It is arguable that, for certain disabled people, the creation of social relationships by which they can flourish may be a more important factor for their development than the protection of their freedom.[70] It has been remarked that such people may sometimes attach more importance to affection than choice.[71] Sen's approach likewise reflects the view that rationality ought to be amongst human beings' fundamental attributes.

Having said this, capabilities theory has much common ground with the CRPD.[72] While this theory does not fully accord with the social model of disability, it comes close to the Convention's understanding of disability. In a similar way to the capabilities approach, the CRPD promotes the 'acceptance of persons with disabilities as part of human diversity'.[73] The different types of conversion factors (personal, social and environmental) come into play with regard to the implementation of the Convention.[74] There are also resemblances between the list of capabilities proposed by Nussbaum and the rights protected by the CRPD. More broadly, the capabilities theory overlaps, to a large extent, with the notion of human rights, as – in Nussbaum's own words – it can be seen as 'one species of a human rights approach'.[75] Both of them give entitlements to individuals and rely on the ideals of human dignity.

Despite this convergence, capabilities theory still does not entirely uphold the Convention's objectives. It does contemplate the interaction of impairments with different kinds of barriers and entails the reconsideration of social arrangements through the distribution of resources.[76] To that degree, it converges with

[68] Silvers and Stein, 'Disability and the Social Contract', 1626.
[69] Ibid, 1626–7.
[70] J. Vorhaus, 'Capability, Freedom and Profound Disability' (2013) 28 *Disability & Society* 1047, 1057.
[71] J. Vanier, *Homme et Femme Dieu les Fit* (Paris: Presses de la Renaissance, 2009) 226.
[72] C. Harnacke, 'Disability and Capability: Exploring the Usefulness of Martha Nussbaum's Capabilities Approach for the UN Disability Rights Convention' (2013) 41 *Journal of Law, Medicine and Ethics* 769, 774–5.
[73] Article 3(d), CRPD.
[74] S. Venkatapuram, 'Mental Disability, Human Rights and the Capabilities Approach: Searching for the Foundations' (2014) 26 *International Review of Psychiatry* 408, 412–13.
[75] Nussbaum, *Frontiers of Justice*, 141.
[76] L. Terzi, *Justice and Equality in Education: A Capability Perspective on Disability and Special Educational Needs* (London/New York: Continuum, 2008) 99–101.

the approach taken by the Convention. However, the theory does not go as far as the Convention does in other respects. Besides the fact that it fails to postulate participation in society, it does not endeavour to enhance capabilities to the highest possible level for all those who are disabled. In the words of Silvers and Stein, capabilities theory does not seek to 'level the playing field'.[77] While the CRPD permits States Parties to gradually achieve its objectives,[78] its fundamental aim is to provide disabled people with the possibility of enjoying all their rights 'on an equal basis with others' regardless of the situation in which they are. Capabilities theory is moreover quite weak on the improvement of social attitudes,[79] contrary to the Convention which requires that States Parties 'promote awareness of the capabilities ... of persons with disabilities'.[80] The theory additionally displays an overall intrinsic negative view of these capabilities, as it aims more to remedy the lack thereof than to affirm their recognition. On the whole, thus, it is more or less in agreement with how the CRPD itself understands disability, but it demonstrates significant constraints in reaching the Convention's actual objectives.

3.2.2 Recognition Theory

Allocation of resources is not the only pertinent consideration in fulfilling the entitlements of disabled people under the CRPD. The notion of 'recognition' provides another conceptual lens through which to give effect to the Convention. Without such recognition, there is a distortion in the formation of our identity, which takes place through the development of social relationships.[81] According to Fraser, recognition should be at the heart of society, and she proposes a 'status model' to make participation in equal terms possible.[82] In order to achieve 'participatory parity', she argues that the recognition of social status and the distribution of resources should be treated as part of a unique normative framework.[83] As both of them are necessary for this purpose, they cannot be taken separately; rather, they need to reinforce each other. With regard to gender, for instance, policies aimed at redistribution must not lead to further devaluation and policies aimed at recognition should not entail further economic hardship for women.[84] In view of this, Fraser's

[77] Silvers and Stein, 'Disability and the Social Contract', 1634.
[78] Harnacke, 'Disability and Capability', 775–6.
[79] N. Hedge and A. Mackenzie, 'Putting Nussbaum's Capability Approach to Work: Revisiting Inclusion' (2012) 42 *Cambridge Journal of Education* 327, 335.
[80] Article 8(1)(c), CRPD.
[81] C. Taylor, 'The Politics of Recognition' in A. Gutman (ed), *Multiculturalism: Examining the Politics of Recognition* (Princeton: Princeton University Press, 1994) 25, 34–6.
[82] N. Fraser and A. Honneth, *Redistribution or Recognition? A Political-Philosophical Exchange* (London/New York: Verso, 2003) 29–31.
[83] Ibid, 34–7.
[84] N. Fraser, *Fortunes of Feminism: From State Managed Capitalism to Neoliberal Crisis* (New York: Verso, 2013) 171–3.

'participatory parity' could assist in indicating what should be undertaken in order to ensure the inclusion of disabled people.

Although Fraser herself did not focus on disability, her insight into recognition is very much in keeping with the social model of disability.[85] She spells out the necessity of recognition not by placing emphasis on the individual but by drawing attention to social institutions.[86] Whatever is done to respond to disabled people's needs should allow for the removal of obstacles created by society. The call for recognition arises as a reaction to the denial of equal social status, which depends not only on allocating resources but also on improving those mindsets that have shaped social institutions. In the words of Fraser, what is required in dealing with misrecognition is changing the 'institutionalised value patterns that impede parity of participation'.[87] These 'institutionalised [value] patterns' must cease to accord disabled people a lower social status that impedes their participation in society.[88] While the capabilities theory has attracted significant attention in debates around disability, it is surprising that this has not yet been matched by references to recognition theory given its relevance for disabled people.

An advantage of recognition theory is that it does not preclude subsequent recourse to social contract theory. The practice of mutual recognition is actually a condition for participation in the social contract.[89] It is precisely the failure to recognise some disabled people as parties to this social contract that has proven to be the most contentious issue in relation to disability.[90] Recognition theory resolves this problem by making provision for social arrangements to ensure that all of them are placed on an equal footing. It dictates that society can only be just if it is governed by rules that are based on the full appreciation of everyone.

The question that follows, once again, is whether and how recognition theory can provide direction towards including disabled people. Although this theory sets out the aim of 'participatory parity', it does not give further guidance as to what to do in order to achieve it. Human differences, however, should not just be acknowledged but should also give rise to responses that accommodate them.[91] These responses must offer disabled people genuine opportunities for participation in society. Efforts to secure equal social status, therefore, entail mechanisms

[85] G. Calder, 'Disability and Misrecognition' in S. Thompson and M. Yar (eds), *The Politics of Misrecognition* (Aldershot: Ashgate, 2011) 105, 109–10; B. Danermark and L. Gellerstedt, 'Social Justice: Redistribution and Recognition – A Non-reductionist Perspective on Disability (2004) 19 *Disability & Society* 339, 346.

[86] A. Knight, 'Democratizing Disability: Achieving Inclusion (without Assimilation) through "Participatory Partiy"' (2015) 30 *Hypatia* 97, 103.

[87] N. Fraser, 'Rethinking Recognition' (2000) 3 *New Left Review* 107, 115.

[88] Danermark and Gellerstedt, 'Social Justice: Redistribution and Recognition', 345.

[89] A. Honneth, *The Struggle for Recognition. The Moral Grammar of Social Conflicts* (Cambridge: Polity Press, 1995) 42–3.

[90] Although this problem would potentially be resolved were it to be otherwise, the fact remains that social contract theory is not concerned with obstacles to participation in society.

[91] Danermark and Gellerstedt, 'Social Justice: Redistribution and Recognition', 346–7.

of redistribution.[92] In this regard, the capabilities theory offers disabled people entitlements by proceeding to such redistribution. Even though this theory lacks clarity as to whether inclusion is the preferred option towards this end, it advances pragmatic solutions in order to overcome the multiple disadvantages encountered by such people.

As can be seen from the above analysis, a combination of both capabilities theory and recognition theory can prove useful for the inclusion of disabled people. Recognition theory, as developed by Fraser, highlights the necessity of providing an equal social status to all members of society. It postulates that such a social status is a pre-requisite for achieving 'participatory parity'. Since recognition theory views recognition and distribution as mutually intertwined, it leaves enough room for drawing on capabilities theory with a view to defining what kind of measures are necessary to remove the obstacles that prevent disabled people from participating in society. Capabilities theory entails the allocation of resources so that disabled people have opportunities to perform certain human functionings. The theory nonetheless leaves open a range of options in order to do so. While it considers various conversion factors that affect the enhancement of capabilities, it does not give priority to social and environmental factors and associates disability more often than not with personal factors. The aim of 'participatory parity' could elevate the capabilities theory to make inclusion the way forward in order to achieve the human functionings. This 'participatory parity' would become in this way the preferred channel through which disabled people acquire the capabilities in question.

Recognition theory thus allows for a shift in focus by using the equalisation of the social status of disabled people as a means strengthening of capabilities . It would re-direct capability theory towards this end through the requirement of ensuring participation in society in whatever steps are taken in order to develop such capabilities. Capabilities theory, in turn, can help translate recognition theory into practice by determining the resources to be allocated in order to remove the actual obstacles faced by disabled people. It can be used as a tool for achieving 'participatory parity', thereby facilitating inclusion in its own right.

This being said, the question can be asked as to whether recognition must be a pre-requisite to enhance capabilities. Robeyns argues that this is not the case, because recognition is already contained in the capabilities approach. Referring to Sen's approach, she argues that this theory by itself provides enough leeway to meet demands for both distribution and recognition.[93] Capabilities theory would be more appropriate for dealing with disabled people than recognition theory

[92] S. Fredman, 'Redistribution and Recognition: Reconciling Inequalities' (2007) 23 *South African Journal on Human Rights* 214, 218–19.

[93] I. Robeyns, 'Is Nancy Fraser's Critique of Theories of Distributive Justice Justified?' in K. Olson (ed), *Adding Insult to Injury: Nancy Fraser Debates Her Critics* (London: Verso, 2008) 176, 186.

(which has not made disability a focal point so far), especially since 'participatory parity' would not always be feasible for them.[94] It is true that Fraser's recognition theory remains quite vague as to how to fulfil its premises and perhaps requires more elaboration to justify its normative dimension. In any event, it would need more fine-tuning so as to direct its full potential towards disabled people, starting with consideration for their needs.

Nonetheless, arguing that recognition theory simply duplicates capabilities theory may be a step too far. Recognition theory encourages reflection upon the situation of disabled people through the objective of granting an equal social status to all individuals. By contrast, the capabilities theory does not target social institutions. More clarity on this aspect is needed in relation to disability. This can be seen in Robeyns' way of approaching disability, which would relate to decision-making, activity choices and being 'well-sheltered, well fed and well cared for'.[95] Ensuring the participation of disabled people in society is more than the sum of all of those things, however essential they are, as is well illustrated by the social model of disability.[96]

Equality theory can also be drawn upon to support the argument for taking both distribution and recognition measures for the purpose of including disabled people in society. The principle of equality has moved from one of formal equality to one of substantive equality, which involves the necessity of ensuring the attainment of *de facto* equality. As mentioned in the first chapter, the principle of substantive equality is a cornerstone of the Convention. According to Fredman, it contains four dimensions: a distribution dimension; a recognition dimension; a participation dimension and; an accommodating dimension.[97] It thus includes (and starts with) distribution and recognition, which she explicitly correlates with the capabilities and recognition theories, respectively.[98] Turning (more recently) to the question of disability, Fredman stresses that these two dimensions (distribution and recognition) must be set in motion conjointly, especially in view of the social model of disability.[99] Interestingly, the CRPD Committee expressly endorsed her way of approaching the principle of substantive equality, considering that the four dimensions together form what it calls 'inclusive equality'.[100]

Fredman's dimensions of participation and accommodating further reinforce the proposal outlined above to combine both capabilities theory and recognition

[94] Ibid, 192–3.

[95] Robeyns, 'Is Nancy Fraser's Critique of Theories of Distributive Justice Justified?', 192.

[96] Furthermore, if Sen's approach is chosen as reference for the capabilities theory, it may be pointed out that it misses a normative dimension.

[97] S. Fredman, *Discrimination Law* (Oxford: Oxford University Press, 2nd ed., 2011) 176–80.

[98] S. Fredman, 'Substantive Equality Revisited' (2016) 14 *International Journal of Constitutional Law* 712, 729–31.

[99] S. Fredman, 'Emerging from the Shadows: Substantive Equality and Article 14 of the European Convention on Human Rights' (2016) 16 *Human Rights Law Review* 273, 297–8.

[100] CRPD Committee, *General Comment on Equality and Non-discrimination*, 9 March 2018, CRPD/C/GC/6, para 11.

theory. They help define what recognition and discrimination should aim when it comes to disability. On the one hand, ensuring participation constitutes the very objective of according an equal social status for all individuals. On the other hand, accommodation is what should drive the allocation of resources between them.

The final question is what all of this means with a view to making disability an integral part of international human rights law. Capabilities theory demonstrates the importance of remedying the actual disadvantage experienced by disabled people. The CRPD turns this idea into law, although it does more than that: the Convention guarantees that they can participate in society by calling not only for the removal of those barriers that hinder such participation but also by mandating the adoption of measures so that they can live in their communities with others. This requires that they enjoy a social status that does no longer keep them at the margins of society. While this idea is not entirely new, its proclamation in a human rights treaty adds value to the entire field of international human rights law. As will be explained in the next chapter, it provides a more realistic view of what the notion of human rights should encompass for all groups of people, whoever they are.

4
Normative Background: The Dis-abled Subject in International Human Rights Law

This chapter considers how the legal subject has been construed in the field of international human rights law (4.1. The Legal Subject in International Human Rights Law). It argues that the notion of human rights has come to give priority to the able-bodied individual, with the result that disabled people have been invisible in the international human rights framework. It then suggests that the CRPD has given this notion a more real dimension through its consideration for distinct forms of embodiment. It goes on to argue that disability can help broaden the range of human variety considered in the concept of human rights (4.2. Human Diversity in International Human Rights Law). The chapter subsequently analyses Fineman's vulnerability theory and how it actually fits with the concept of disability, as well as its usefulness in providing a broader approach to dealing with disability. It finally introduces the idea of the dis-abled subject, which allows both the universality of human rights to be strengthened and the Convention's significance for the whole field of international human rights law to be revealed.

4.1 The Legal Subject in International Human Rights Law

4.1.1 The Disembodied Legal Subject

In order to fully understand the challenge posed by disability to international human rights law, it is first necessary to investigate the way in which human beings are regarded in that field. As the latter has centred upon the individual, it is individual rights that human rights aim to protect.[1] Accordingly, international human rights law has evolved so as to provide a number of entitlements to individuals. The problem in this evolution is that the concept of human rights has revolved around an abstract, interchangeable holder of rights. This becomes particularly perceptible in moral accounts of human rights. The question of which rights should qualify is a question which in turn leads to that of charting the attributes of the legal subject.

[1] A. Arstein-Kerslake, *Restoring Voice to People with Cognitive Disabilities: Realizing the Right to Equal Recognition before the Law* (Cambridge: Cambridge University Press, 2017) 2.

Disability in International Human Rights Law. Gauthier de Beco, Oxford University Press. © Gauthier de Beco 2021.
DOI: 10.1093/oso/9780198824503.003.0005

Griffin relies on the notion of personhood, by which he means capacity for normative agency.[2] Human rights, then, are those rights that safeguard this normative agency. The development of cognitive skills is central to our understanding of humanity, and therefore the lack of rationality can be a motive for restrictions. The emphasis is placed on the autonomy of individuals. If this autonomy can be facilitated by practical accommodation, people will have personhood, as is the case for those who are physically disabled.[3] Children, in principle, will also acquire such autonomy as they grow up. Others are not considered to be rights-holders. These include persons with diminished cognitive skills due to impairments as well as those whose willpower may be controlled by others for a number of different reasons.[4]

Reliance on the notion of personhood thusin the end denies moral status to people with intellectual impairments. Defining human beings by the possession of rationality leads to the view that some of these people are not worthy of moral consideration. The resolution not to grant them such moral consideration is still dominant in some theories of justice. As seen in the previous chapter, Rawls limits the parties to the social contract to those who have 'the capacity for a sense of justice and the capacity for a conception of the good' (the two moral powers that they should possess).[5] What is implicit for Rawls is explicit for Gauthier, who reckons that certain people are 'beyond the pale of morality tied to mutuality'.[6] This view indeed demonstrates 'the sliding scale of personhood',[7] which is beyond the reach of the 'severely mentally retarded'.[8] Their lives are not truly human; their existence lacks sufficient humanity.

The concept of human rights has evolved in some discordance with the extensive and numerous possibilities of human variety. It has been taken for granted that the individual is able-bodied while keeping out those who fall below the threshold. Some personal features are cast aside even though they concern all human beings. Society has given priority to a type of body, a standpoint which has affected more than just disabled people.[9] By defining what are human beings, theories of justice have made not merely abstractions but idealisations by assuming what human beings actually ought to be.[10] Such idealisations have disqualified a great part of

[2] J. Griffin, *On Human Rights* (Oxford: Oxford University Press, 2008) 33–7.

[3] Ibid, 67–8.

[4] S. Fredman, *Comparative Human Rights Law* (Oxford: Oxford University Press, 2018) 31; J. Raz, 'Human Rights Without Foundations' in S. Besson and J. Tasioulas (eds), *The Philosophy of International Law* (Oxford: Oxford University Press, 2010) 321, 325.

[5] J. Rawls, *Political Liberalism* (New York: Columbia University Press, 1993) 19.

[6] D. Gauthier, *Morals by Agreement* (Oxford: Oxford University Press, 1986) 268.

[7] P. Byrne, *Philosophical and Ethical Problems in Mental Handicap* (Basingstoke: Macmillan Press, 2000) 10.

[8] Griffin, *On Human Rights*, 34.

[9] N. Hirschmann, 'Disabling Barriers, Enabling Freedom' in B. Arneil and J. Hirschmann (eds), *Disability and Political Theory* (Cambridge: Cambridge University Press, 2017) 99, 111.

[10] O. O'Neill, *Towards Justice and Virtue: A Constructive Account of Practical Reasoning* (Cambridge: Cambridge University Press, 1996) 41–2.

humanity. It is again rationality that has been used to set the supposed boundaries between those who are abled and those who are disabled.

The crux of the issue, perhaps, is that by circumscribing the requirements of personhood there will always be individuals who do not fulfil the conditions that are laid down. Any move that purports to list people's attributes in order to define the holders of rights will run counter to those who have personal features that are not seen as reflecting the normativity of the average human being. Whatever the criteria used for defining these holders of rights, there will be some who cannot meet them. More often than not these will be disabled people and mostly those who are intellectually disabled, as special emphasis is given to the role of cognitive skills.

The notion of personhood offers a moral account of human rights that places the able-bodied individual on a pedestal. This notion raises difficult questions that are beyond the scope of the present book, including that of whether belonging to the human species should be enough of a condition to have equal moral consideration and that of whether non-human animals should be granted lower moral consideration than any human being whatever their capabilities.[11] A positive answer, at least, has the advantage of going along with any particular form of embodiment, however extraordinary and distinguishable, and of accepting the infinite range of human differences. One way of achieving this is to advance the idea that all individuals have sufficient cognitive skills to be ascribed personhood.[12] However, such a claim is open to empirical questioning especially regarding those who appear to lack any of those skills. A justification is still needed to recognise such people as rights-holders. The conclusion for the time being is that it is futile to embark on a definition of what are human beings in order to delineate the concept of human rights.

The same problem can be seen in the international framework of human rights. Feminist scholars have been criticising human rights for disguising a masculine perspective, as attested by the content of the rights proclaimed by human rights treaties. These rights more often than not do not take into consideration the specific concerns of women and place much emphasis on the public sphere which is principally occupied by men.[13] Despite its aim to achieve gender equality, it has been argued that the Convention on the Elimination of All Forms of Discrimination against Women (CEDAW) essentially compares women to men and tends to

[11] See, inter alia, P. Singer, 'Speciesism and Moral Status' (2009) 40 *Metaphilosophy* 567, 572–3; A. Jaworska and J. Tannenbaum, 'Person-Rearing Relationships as a Key to Higher Moral Status' (2014) 125 *Ethics* 242; J. McMahan, 'Challenges to Human Equality' (2008) 12 *The Journal of Ethics* 81. For a different perspective, see Byrne, *Philosophical and Ethical Problems in Mental Handicap*, 53–5.

[12] Arstein-Kerslake, *Restoring Voice to People with Cognitive Disabilities*, 44–7.

[13] H. Charlesworth and C. Chinkin, *The Boundaries of International Law* (Manchester: Manchester University Press, 2000) 231–7; H. Charlesworth, C. Chinkin and S. Wright, 'Feminist Approaches to International Law' (1991) 85 *American Journal of International Law* 613, 625–31.

concentrate on male-centred issues.[14] While feminist critiques have been arguing this for some time, the fact that the concept of human rights similarly adopts an able-bodied perspective is rarely stressed, if at all. What has been done at the expense of women has likewise been done at the expense of disabled people.

This limited understanding of the human condition is reflected in the attributes of the legal subject. There is a false impression that this legal subject is neutral in appearance, thereby surpassing different forms of embodiment. In the words of Grear, there has been 'a tendency in abstractionism towards (incomplete) disembodiment', which started onwards from the UDHR.[15] The model shaped by the normativity of the average human being that lies beneath such abstractionism has taken the form of a fixed and distant figure who is disconnected from others and capable of living only by itself. This abstractionism led to Marx's famous allegation that human rights do not 'go beyond egoistic man . . . an individual withdrawn into himself, into the confines of his private interests and private caprice, and separated from the community'.[16] Such an individual holds on to the ideal of maleness, whiteness, heterosexuality and, so it is argued, 'able-bodiedness'. It is because of the disembodiment of the legal subject that human rights have appeared to benefit such a limited number of individuals. Detached from any pre-conceived interest, the legal subject finds itself 'beyond the reach of experience'.[17] Human rights are defined with limited regard for the many possibilities of human variety notwithstanding their pretension to universality. As well described by Taylor, 'the very idea of such ['blind' liberalisms] . . . may be a kind of pragmatic contradiction, a particularism masquerading as the universal'.[18]

As a result, the able-bodied individual is taken to represent the 'norm' which serves as a benchmark for the legal subject. Disabled people are then regarded as others, because they deviate from this 'norm' and because they are supposedly different. They fall short of the average human being fashioned by the concept of human rights, as they clash with the ideal of 'able-bodiedness'. This clash, however, makes disability an important question to be resolved in the field of international human rights law.

[14] D. Otto, 'Women's Rights' in D. Moeckli et al (eds), *International Human Rights Law* (Oxford: Oxford University Press, 3rd edn, 2018) 309, 317–9; Charlesworth, Chinkin and Wright, 'Feminist Approaches to International Law', 631–2.

[15] A. Grear, '"Framing the Project" of International Human Rights Law: Reflections on the Dysfunctional "Family" of the Universal Declaration' in Gearty and Douzinas, *The Cambridge Companion to Human Rights Law* 17, 32.

[16] K. Marx, *On the Jewish Question* in K. Marx and F. Engels (eds), *Collected Works* (Lawrence & Wishart: London, 1975) 146, 164.

[17] M. Sandel, *Liberalism and the Limits of Justice* (Cambridge: Cambridge University Press, 2nd edn, 1998) 62.

[18] C. Taylor, 'The Politics of Recognition' in A. Gutman (ed), *Multiculturalism: Examining the Politics of Recognition* (Princeton: Princeton University Press, 1994) 25, 40.

The categorisation of 'otherness' has denied personhood in particular to those who are intellectually disabled.[19] It has come to mean that such people cannot have human rights, sincethere is too great a divergence between them and the individuals that human rights aim to protect. The standing prevalence given to the principle of autonomy in this context is a legacy of philosophical thought since the Enlightenment. It is reflected in Article 1 of the UDHR which stipulates that human beings are 'endowed with reason and conscience'. The ensuing prejudice has also targeted other marginalised groups of people, including women and ethnic minorities as well as people from a poorer background, all of whom have sometimes been considered disabled.[20] While such misapprehension has been dispelled to a large degree,[21] the reality of impairment means that this prejudice is still enduring with those who are disabled. The ideal of 'able-bodiedness' makes of disability the 'last frontier of unquestioned inferiority'.[22]

The result has been the trivialisation of the particular needs of disabled people. In the absence of the CRPD, there was no direction as to how human rights could have real meaning for them. While a number of human rights treaties were adopted for other marginalised groups of people, disabled people remained invisible in international framework of human rights. Their specific situation was of no concern to the legal subject. The issue of disability belonged to the realm of charity, and therefore it fell outside of the domain of human rights.

Disabled people were subjects of welfare and, in a limited manner, objects of rights if they needed some form of particular protection. Early international instruments on disability were mainly confined to welfare policies.[23] This is the reason why most of the attention with regard to disability went to the International Covenant on Economic, Social and Cultural Rights (ICESCR) and why the International Covenant on Civil and Political Rights (ICCPR) was little used in this regard,[24] a situation which somewhatcontinues to hold true even today. In a similar vein, it has been remarked that the CRC's separate article on disabled children does not truly follow a rights-based approach,[25] in contrast to the CRPD's own separate article on disabled children. What the CRPD has done is to definitively revoke the

[19] G. Quinn and A. Arstein-Kerslake, 'Restoring the "Human" in "Human Rights" – Personhood and Doctrinal Innovation in the UN Disability Convention' in C. Gearty and C. Douzinas (eds), *The Cambridge Companion to Human Rights Law* (Cambridge: Cambridge University Press, 2013) 36, 39–40.

[20] M. Jones and L. Basser Mark, 'Law and the Social Construction of Disability' in M. Jones and L. Basser Mark (eds), *Disability, Divers-Ability and Legal Change* (The Hague: Martinus Nijhoff Publishers 1999) 3, 5.

[21] Arstein-Kerslake, *Restoring Voice to People with Cognitive Disabilities*, 11.

[22] T. Siebers, *Disability Theory* (Ann Arbor: University of Michigan Press, 2008) 6.

[23] GA, *Declaration on the Rights of Mentally Retarded Persons*, 20 December 1971, A/RES/26/2856; GA, *Declaration on the Rights of Disabled Persons*, 9 December 1975, A/RES/3447 (XXX).

[24] G. Quinn and T. Degener, *The Current Use and Future Potential of United Nations Human Rights Instruments in the Context of Disability* (New York/Geneva: UN, 2002) 54.

[25] Ibid, 192–3.

prevailing welfarist approach in dealing with disability with its latent medicalised dimension. This is not to deny that welfare policies remain necessary in order to improve the life of disabled people. As indicated in the previous chapter, disabled people rely upon both recognition and redistribution in order to participate in society. The Convention acknowledges that the removal of barriers for disabled people involves the allocation of resources, but such allocation is not its central purpose.[26] The central purpose is to give them 'the full and equal enjoyment of all human rights',[27] which of course requires but entails more than the adoption of welfare policies.

Conversely, it has been noted that anti-discrimination law has lost sight of the need for welfare.[28] As seen in the first chapter, the prohibition of discrimination itself does not suffice for the purpose of combating the marginalisation of disabled people, while adopting welfare policies remains essential for the purpose. The CRPD has therefore consolidated, surpassed and even converted the need for welfare into a question of human rights. It has retrieved disability from the realm of charity towards the provision of equal opportunities for participation in society. Both the welfarist approach and the rights-based approach may conflict with one another, since disability can be used as a motive for imposing restrictions,[29] although it has been suggested that it is possible to combine them in order to expand the reach of anti-discrimination law.[30] The Convention has overcome this conflict by considering how welfare policies can contribute to the enjoyment of human rights. Admittedly, there has been some disagreement as to whether welfare can take the form of human rights. No-one will have responsibilities for entitlements if there are no institutions tasked with fulfilling them.[31] The question remains though why there would be no entitlements as a consequence of there not being any such institutions.[32] By incorporating the welfare approach into a rights-based approach, the Convention had created a legal basis for such entitlements.

The question of disability has thus raised doubts about the assumed universality of human rights. The CRPD requires a departure from the model shaped by the normativity of the average human being that has been used to demarcate the concept of human rights up till now. The 'human' component of the concept has taken the shape of an individual who is independent, autonomous and self-conscious.[33]

[26] F. Mégret, 'The Disabilities Convention: Towards a Holistic Concept of Rights' (2008) 12 *International Journal of Human Rights* 261, 265–6.

[27] Article 1, CRPD.

[28] S. Bagenstos, 'The Future of Disability Law' (2004) 114 *Yale Law Journal* 1, 4;

[29] H. Hagtvedt et al, 'Histories of Human Rights in the Nordic Countries' (2018) 3 *Nordic Journal of Human Rights* 189, 198.

[30] A. Satz, 'Disability, Vulnerability, and the Limits of Antidiscrimination' (2008) 83 *Washington Law Review* 513, 556–7.

[31] O'Neill, *Towards Justice and Virtue*, 131–2.

[32] J. Tasioulias, The Moral Reality of Human Rights' in T. Pogge (ed), *Freedom from Poverty as a Human Right: Who Owes What to the Very Poor?* (Oxford: Oxford University Press, 2007) 75, 91–3.

[33] Quinn and Arstein-Kerslake, 'Restoring the "Human" in "Human Rights"', 37.

This is the same individual whose personhood human rights would preserve. This individual represents what is considered to be the 'norm', whereas others supposedly deviate from that 'norm'. The CRPD challenges such a view both by proclaiming all the rights of disabled people and by imposing obligations to make these rights more of a reality. Nowhere is this shift clearer than with the right to equal recognition before the law, which not only guarantees legal capacity but also prescribes support for its exercise.[34] The CRPD is itself evidence that theories of justice have been lagging behind developments at the international level.[35] International human rights law has moved forward without robust philosophical foundations in the background.

What must be done now is to build upon the criticism made by feminism to confront the legal subject ever more with the reality of disability and to break open its covert neutrality.[36] This legal subject must be re-embodied and liberated, at last, from its disembodied conception in international human rights law. It should thereby allow for a greater recognition of the full variety of human possibilities, including the occurrence of impairment, consistent with the CRPD. Making space for disability will help free the concept of human rights from its lack of acknowledgement of the whole range of human differences.

International human rights law has neglected disabled people, and the CRPD reveals this in the full light of day. The notion of human rights disregarded some of the essential personal features of human beings. While the Convention represents a significant step in removing this drawback, the imperative to ground disability more deeply in the canon of human rights still stands. Otherwise, as argued by Byrne, 'there is a risk that [the CRPD] further naturalises the existing human rights framework, itself based initially, through the [UDHR], on a conception of an able-bodied rights holder'.[37] The way to avoid this naturalisation is more than just a re-thinking of such conception in light of the Convention. As indicated by Quinn and Degener (prior to the CRPD), it is also important to ensure that all human rights treaties benefit disabled people even apart from that (future) Convention.[38] This includes the ICESCR and the ICCPR, with the latter specifically being able to underscore the need for a rights-based approach. In order to do so, it is necessary to investigate how the CRPD's consideration for distinct forms of embodiment can spill over into the entire field of international human rights law.

[34] Article 12 (2) and (3), CRPD.

[35] B. Arneil, 'Disability in Political Theory versus International Practice: Redefining Equality and Freedom' in Arneil and Hirschmann, *Disability and Political Theory*, 20, 28.

[36] F. Campbell, 'Legislating Disability: Negative Ontologies and the Government of Legal Identities' in S. Tremain (ed), *Foucault and the Government of Disability* (Ann Arbor: University of Michigan Press, 2005) 108, 112.

[37] B. Byrne, 'Dis-Equality: Exploring the Juxtaposition of Disability and Equality' (2018) 6 *Social Inclusion* 9, 16.

[38] Quinn and Degener, *The Current Use and Future Potential of United Nations Human Rights Instruments in the Context of Disability*, 294.

4.1.2 The Embodied Legal Subject

The human rights treaties devoted to particular marginalised groups of people have taken different approaches in defining those whose rights they aim to protect. The International Convention on the Elimination of All Forms of Racial Discrimination (ICERD), the oldest one, does not define race. Nor – unconsciously – does CEDAW define gender. By contrast, the CRC provides that 'a child means every human being below the age of eighteen'.[39] This is however a rather static definition of a child. The CRC does not refer to any of the personal features of its recipients other than that of being younger than the said age even if it requires, in some of its provisions, that States Parties take into consideration the exact age of the child.[40] The Convention therefore takes a purely biological approach to defining who is 'a child' without seeking any further understanding of childhood. While it was stressed earlier that it has much in common with the CRPD, this is probably the main difference between both human rights treaties. The CRPD understands disability much more flexibly and, in fact, does not attempt any definition at all. It provides that disabled people 'include those who have long-term physical, mental, intellectual or sensory impairments which in interaction with various barriers may hinder their full and effective participation in society'.[41] The Convention thus draws attention to the effects of such barriers on those who have different kinds of impairments.

Article 1 of the CRPD is no more than a way of establishing the scope of the Convention (which interestingly it does alongside establishing its aims – in a section entitled 'Purpose'). The reason there is no definition of disability is not just to avoid the risk of ruling out certain categories of disability. It is inherent in the concept of disability itself. As shown in Chapter 2, the meaning of disability has significantly evolved over time, and there is still no consensus on the matter. The CRPD was adopted at a time when the social model had reached its highest level of acceptance, although the model itself had already attracted criticism from different sides in view of its radical standpoint. Given the disagreement on the concept in question, disabled people's organisations (DPO's) simply preferred not to embark on any definition of disability.[42]

Having said that, there was also a general willingness to recognise the fact that disability is a product of societal organisation. Be that as it may, the CRPD's drafters were inspired by the social model of disability. This, however, created a situation like the serpent biting his own tail, as it raises the question as to how such a model can be turned into reality through a legally binding international

39 Article 1, CRC.

40 This includes the right of the child to be heard (Articles 12(1)) and the right to rest and leisure (Article 31(1)).

41 Article 1, CRPD.

42 Arneil, 'Disability in Political Theory versus International Practice', 26.

instrument. Should the Convention be solely for people with impairments who are encountering barriers, it would be of no use to those who are really able to participate fully in society. Disability emerges only when they are unable to participate due to how their impairment interacts with these barriers. Hence, the more society is inclusive, the fewer disabled people there would be according to the Convention. Unless the term 'people with disabilities' used throughout this Convention (except in Article 1 and the Preamble) is replaced with 'people with impairments', it would not apply to anybody in an ideal and perfect world, which of course does not and never will exist.

Despite this mix-up, the CRPD is very much in keeping with the current view of disability. While acknowledging that it is society that in fact disables those with all kinds of impairments, the Convention considers that embodiments can take very different forms and have multiple practical implications. What matters is not so much who exactly is 'disabled', but how the different kinds of impairments impact upon their lives in the social context they inhabit. Although the Convention in some way does identify what disability is, it focuses above all on what an impairment *does* to those who have the disability. Such a focus makes the legal subject less neutralthan it was before in international human rights law. The CRPD furthers the vision of the embodied legal subject both by restoring human variety in the concept of human rights and by putting into perspective different forms of embodiment. This vision reflects the objective of no longer trying to 'fix' disabled people but of modifying the environment in a way that considers 'the widest possible range of human form and function'.[43] The Convention, therefore, is probably the human rights treaty that moves the furthest from the individualism that has dominated the field of international human rights law to date.

It is worth emphasising further that disability, which establishes the scope of the CRPD, is dissimilar to other characteristics. While these characteristics can similarly be seen as a social construct, there are notable differences. Gender, for instance, refers to a single characteristic even though it has multifarious elements (and is not to be confused with sex). On the other hand, disability refers to a characteristic that is extremely diverse given its association with many different kinds of impairments. The number of intra-group variations between disabled people is both significant and extensive. Another fundamental difference is that intrinsic to disability are some negative consequences that need to be taken into consideration, as pointed out by the critics of the social model.[44] While sex is also a particular

[43] R. Garland-Thomson, 'Misfits: A Feminist Materialist Disability Concept' (2011) 26 *Hypatia* 591, 603.

[44] T. Shakespeare, *Disability Rights and Wrongs Revisited* (London/New York: Routledge, 2nd edn, 2014) 21–3 and 77; L. Terzi, 'The Social Model of Disability: A Philosophical Critique' (2004) 21 *Journal of Applied Philosophy* 141, 152; J. Morris, 'Impairment and Disability: Constructing an Ethics of Care that Promotes Human Rights' (2001) 16 *Hypatia* 1, 14; L. Barclay, 'Natural Deficiency or Social Oppression? The Capabilities Approach to Justice for People with Disabilities' (2012) 9 *Journal of Moral Philosophy* 500, 520.

physical but again single characteristic, it has no such negative consequences.[45] This prevents a straightforward and simple comparison of disabled people with other historically marginalised groups of people.

Disabled people also possess characteristics other than that of disability. As seen in Chapter 1, intersectionality may lead to specific disadvantages that cannot be reduced to a summing-up of those that result from prejudices based on distinct grounds. While the issue has not received much attention with regard to disability in international human rights law,[46] extra-group differences can make a significant difference in the way in which any person has to cope with whatever kind of impairment. Disability thus may be exacerbated by disadvantages that are associated with gender, age, race, sexual orientation and so on. Women, children, people belonging to racial or ethnic minorities and lesbian, gay, bisexual, transgender and intersex (LGBTI) people who are disabled are often subject to extreme forms of discrimination.

In contrast to intra-group differences, extra-group differences of course are not peculiar to those who are disabled but cut across all marginalised groups of people. The CRPD is nonetheless the human rights treaty more than any other that considers these extra-group differences. The Convention deals with intersectionality in many of its provisions, especially with regard to disabled children and women (on whom it has separate articles).[47] By considering both the intra-group differences and the extra-group differences amongst disabled people, it makes the legal subject even more embodied than it has been in the field up until now.

This confirms that disability is not a fixed characteristic. Despite its plurality, it is attributed to an entire group whose members are supposed to share a number of common personal features.[48] There is however considerable heterogeneity in this group and even within some well-established categories of disability.[49] This heterogeneity, again, can be put further into perspective, as disabled people may simultaneously belong to other marginalised groups of people (that is, women, children, people from racial or ethnic minorities and LGBTI people and so on). Whatever categories are made in order to distinguish disabled people, it remains practically impossible to capture the entire phenomenon.

[45] D. Wasserman, 'Is Disability Discrimination Different?' in D. Hellman and S. Moreau (eds), *Philosophical Foundations of Discrimination Law* (Oxford: Oxford University Press, 2014) 269, 273; A. Silver, 'An Essay on Modeling: The Social Model of Disability' in C. Ralston and J. Ho (eds), *Philosophical Reflections on Disability* (New York: Springer, 2012) 1, 32.

[46] See, however, G. de Beco, 'Intersectionality and Disability in International Human Rights Law' (2020) 24 *International Journal of Human Rights* 593; R. de Silva de Alwis, 'Mining the Intersections: Advancing the Rights of Women and Children with Disabilities within an Interrelated Web of Human Rights' (2009) 18 *Pacific Rim Law & Policy Journal* 293.

[47] Articles 6 and 7, CRPD.

[48] This is symbolized by the image of the wheelchair that is misleadingly supposed to represent all of them in public places.

[49] R. Garland Thomson, 'Disability, Identity, and Representation' in T. Titchkosky and R. Michalko (eds), *Rethinking Normalcy* (Toronto: Canadian Scholar's Press, 2009) 63, 69.

Disabled people therefore form too varied a group to make wide generalisations. Whatever the measures taken to facilitate their participation in society, these same measures will have to handle an extensive amount of varied needs. This diminishes the benefit of a collective approach that would generate undifferentiated solutions in order to meet these needs. The experience of disability is indeed universal but always particular and even unique. As argued by Stein, a 'disability-based framework [moves] from group-based protection to individualized assessment'.[50] The CRPD does not see disabled people as a well circumscribed group of people; rather, it considers disability as a human rights issue that calls for a large set of differentiated responses.

To make matters even more complex, there are many borderline cases. Such cases can be triggered by one-off events that create disabilities or have a risk of repetition, and they also include so-called 'invisible disabilities'. Sometimes, it may simply not possible to establish whether a person is disabled, even when resorting to the notion of impairments. This impossibility leads to the problem of defining the boundaries of the group in question and disqualifies any strict dichotomy between able and disabled. With more knowledge on the experience of disability in the future, the group is likely to expand even more and include more individuals. Disabled people, in fact, potentially include anyone and everyone, especially since impairments are mostly acquired after birth.[51] The chances of acquiring such impairments are increasing as time goes on, an important factor given the growing proportion of the ageing population. The constant addition of new people further reduces the stability of the group which will have further members in its midst, with the result that it will make the category very difficult to circumscribe. Disability is and will always remain a concept in search of its own definition.

In light of this, it is no wonder that the various sub-groups of disabled people have had limited relations with each other. Deaf persons and autistic people, to take just two examples, have very divergent needs and claims to make upon society. It is only lately that disabled people have started to gather forces to form alliances. The ambition of obtaining a human rights treaty for themselves has played a pivotal role in the process of formation. What disabled people have in common, is that they experience a 'misfit' with the world around them.[52] They face similar practices of exclusion, because social institutions are designed in a way that ignores particular forms of embodiment. According to Barnes, disability refers to a solidarity that arose as a result of this shared experience, which, in turn, gave birth to the disability rights movement.[53] Nevertheless, the question remains how is it possible for

50 M. Stein, 'Disability Human Rights' (2007) 95 *California Law Review* 75, 116.

51 Siebers, *Disability Theory*, 71.

52 Garland-Thomson, 'Misfits: A Feminist Materialist Disability Concept', 597.

53 E. Barnes, *The Minority Body. A Theory of Disability* (Oxford: Oxford University Press, 2016) 43–8.

such a movement to represent all the various categories of disability, some of which raise deeply-seated questions.

It is therefore remarkable that the CRPD places such a heterogeneous group of people under a single umbrella. The CRPD's drafters were somewhat aware of the problem. Its Preamble declares that States Parties recognise 'the diversity of persons with disabilities'.[54] Article 1 of the Convention explicitly mentions 'physical, mental, intellectual or sensory impairments' and uses the term 'include' when listing these, thereby making disabled people part of an open-ended group of people.[55] The CRPD has more provisions concerning particular kinds of impairments and focuses on disabled women and children. This again is something that is only done in this Convention, so that no comparisons can be made in this regard with other human rights treaties. The Preamble goes even further by providing that disability is 'an evolving concept',[56] which takes stock of on-going discussions on this concept. Such a terminology re-enforces the suggestion that the CRPD does not attempt to define that concept, but rather gives direction on how the issue should be addressed by States Parties. Hence, there is a need for 'relativising the concept of disability' within the meaning of the Convention.[57]

Returning to the heterogeneity of the group, the CRPD had to address intra-group differences. Not much thought is required to grasp that human rights raise different issues regarding those who are physically disabled, those who have diminished cognitive skills and those who are experiencing mental health issues not to mention those who have sensory disabilities, such as deafness or blindness. It would be senseless to apply human rights in a similar manner to all of them. Although the Convention offers disabled people guarantees in general terms, it acknowledges this heterogeneity throughout its provisions.

In this way, the CRPD has brought humanity back into the notion of human rights. By avoiding a 'one size-fits all approach', it puts into question the normativity of the average human being that has been relied upon in order to define the holders of rights. While the concept of human rights has had a rather generic view of the individual, the Convention has opened up debate on what 'human' really stands for in the notion of human rights. Its adoption is a response to the need for greater sensitivity to human differences.

This being said, the CRPD has not completely catered for the absence of homogeneity amongst those whom it concerns. The Convention provides for a general catalogue of rights for individuals finding themselves in wholly different situations. Some of its provisions may seem less relevant to some categories of disability. A legitimate question, however, is to ask whether the task of drafting an international

[54] Preamble(i), CPRD.
[55] Article 1, CRPD.
[56] Preamble(e), CRPD.
[57] Mégret, 'The Disabilities Convention: Towards a Holistic Concept of Rights', 274.

instrument for all of those categories was a feasible one and, going further, whether it was not preferable to adopt distinct human rights treaties even though this begs the question of how many such human rights treaties would ultimately be needed. Indeed, the elaboration of an all-encompassing legally binding international instrument for disabled people has been the battleground of the Convention's negotiation process. With the exception of those who are 'blind, deaf or deafblind',[58] it is noticeable that the CRPD does not explicitly refer to any particular kind of impairment.

The question thus remains whether the CRPD provides adequate and comprehensive protection to all sub-groups of disabled people. The deaf community expressed its opinion emphatically when it came to that question during the negotiation process, which explains the high level of attention paid to deaf people. Especially with regard to education, it stressed their negative experiences and the fear that inclusive education would aim to assimilate them into mainstream settings.[59] While references to the 'deaf community' and 'deaf culture' were inserted in the Convention as a compromise,[60] participation in society actually means something very different for those who are deaf. As deaf people consider themselves primarily to be a linguistic community, they regard sign language as something more than a tool of communication.[61] Deaf people see the maintenance of ties with their peers as an essential aspect of their lives, which does not sit very well with the ideals of inclusion. DPOs are still sceptical about whether this can ever be achieved for deaf people even if the CRPD proclaims the right to inclusive education.[62]

Even more debatable is '[r]espect for autonomy', which is one of the general principles of the CRPD and which contains 'the freedom to make one's own choices'.[63] While autonomy is essential to be able to exercise human rights, it may collide with obstacles for some of those who are disabled. The Convention guarantees the provision of 'support they may require in exercising their legal capacity', but this provision cannot be isolated from other important factors. It might be said that the Convention expects too much from people with cognitive impairments.[64] It can be hard, if not impossible, to remove any obstacles which these people face in such a way that they can actually enjoy their human rights. Freedom may perhaps

[58] Article 24(3)(c), CRPD.

[59] WBU, WFD and DbI, 'Article 17 Statement on Inclusive Education for Persons who are Deaf, Blind and Deafblind: The Rationale for Choice in Education', https://static.un.org/esa/socdev/enable/rights/ahcstata24sevscomments.htm#multi.

[60] Articles 24(3)(b)) and 30(4), CRPD.

[61] S. Batterbury, 'Language justice for Sign Language Peoples: the UN Convention on the Rights of Persons with Disabilities' (2012) 11 *Language Policy* 253, 256–8.

[62] J. Murray, M. De Meulder and D. le Maire, 'An Education in Sign Language as a Human Right?: The Sensory Exception in the Legislative History and Ongoing Interpretation of Article 24 of the UN Convention on the Rights of Persons with Disabilities' (2018) 40 *Human Rights Quarterly* 37, 59–60.

[63] Article 3(a), CRPD.

[64] K. Johnson, 'The UN Convention on the Rights of Persons with Disabilities: A Framework for Ethical and Inclusive Practice?' (2013) 7 *Ethics & Social Welfare* 218, 226–7.

not even be what at particular times is most needed for them.[65] The focus on the principle of autonomy is certainly the Achilles heel of the whole CRPD. It exposes the difficulties involved in eliminating reliance on the notion of personhood in determining the content of human rights.

As a result, the CRPD might be accused of conformism, in that it envisions what disabled people ought to be even if it applies regardless of any forms of impairments. While the accusation may be exaggerated, the Convention has been drafted in such a way that it might give more appropriate consideration and be more appealing for certain disabled people. From the perspective of capabilities theory, it could be argued that it assumes or presupposes the human functionings disabled people should be allowed to nurture in order to live in dignity, even when there are circumstances where those human functionings cannot be made available or are not what really matters the most to them. The CRPD represents unfinished business, as the debate remains open as to whether its normative underpinnings are valid for all categories of disability. Although the CRPD expanded 'pre-existing conceptualizations of freedom', it has itself inherent limitations especially regarding those with very severe forms of impairments.[66] It is however worth recalling that the Convention has had to both compensate for the silence around disability in preceding human rights treaties and face up to a persisting vacuum in political theory. This Convention has had to find its place within the international human rights system as it stood right until its adoption.

4.2 Human Diversity in International Human Rights Law

4.2.1 The Vulnerable Subject

There have been attempts to take the legal subject out of its straitjacket. Involving a high degree of self-sufficiency, the liberal subject does not offer an accurate picture of the human condition. According to Fineman, the vulnerable subject has the potential to recognise that suffering harm is possible at any point in the lifetime of every single individual.[67] Vulnerability is not related to any particular group of people, although it can take multiple forms and be experienced in many ways, which makes it both universal and particular at the same time.[68] It is therefore a constant and universal experience of all human beings. Vulnerability theory invites

[65] J. Vorhaus, 'Capability, Freedom and Profound Disability' (2013) 28 *Disability & Society* 1047, 1057.

[66] I. Bostad and H. Hanisch, 'Freedom and Disability Rights: Dependence, Independence, and Interdependence' (2016) 47 *Metaphilosophy* 371, 381.

[67] M. Fineman, 'The Vulnerable Subject: Anchoring Equality in the Human Condition' (2008) 20 *Yale Journal of Law & Feminism* 1, 10–12.

[68] M. Fineman, 'The Vulnerable Subject and the Responsive State' (2010) 60 *Emory Law Journal* 251, 266–7.

us to reconsider the legal subject in order to better capture the complex nature of human beings.[69]

What the vulnerable subject does by putting the liberal subject in question is to produce a shift in focus to social institutions. By requiring the State to address all forms of injustice, it places vulnerability at the core of social responsibility.[70] The vulnerability theory reflects the need to help individuals with dependency not just in the private sphere but also in the public sphere. It postulates that States must be responsive to any occurring harm by allowing these individuals to build up reserves of resilience.[71] The result would not be a status of invulnerability, which cannot be achieved and which only exists in fiction. It would be the provision of different types of resources by social institutions so as to enable people to cope with their vulnerabilities. This responsive State finds parallel in the role of the State in the international framework of human rights through the fulfilment of the obligations enshrined in different human rights treaties.[72]

Fineman does not deal with disability even though she lists it alongside other aspects of the human experience that may produce vulnerability.[73] A closer look reveals though that both the concept of vulnerability and the concept of disability have much in common and that her way of approaching vulnerability allows for a deeper understanding of disability. Vulnerability not only includes but also closely correlates with disability. Precisely because the vulnerability theory allows for particular forms of embodiment, it can be useful in addressing the specific situation of disabled people. The theory similarly calls for responses by the State, and these responses require the re-arrangement of social institutions.

The vulnerability theory does not isolatedisability as a human experience, but it is also concerned with other affiliated issues, such as gender and age. Instead, it sees disability as a particular manifestation of vulnerability. The vulnerable subject thus draws first and foremost attention to what is common to humanity, including the multiple forms of embodiment. The emphasis lies not on any differences between disabled and non-disabled people but on those commonalities amongst all human beings who will suffer frommany sorts of harm throughout their lifetime. It is indeed the strong emphasis on these differences and the denial of shared humanity that has perpetuated the social oppression of disabled people.[74] The advantage of looking at the commonalities among all human beings is that doing so has the

69 M. Fineman, 'Vulnerability and Inevitable Inequality' (2017) 4 *Oslo Law Review* 133, 142.

70 Fineman, 'The Vulnerable Subject: Anchoring Equality in the Human Condition', 20–2; Fineman, 'The Vulnerable Subject and the Responsive State', 273–5.

71 M. Fineman, 'Equality, Autonomy, and the Vulnerable Subject in Law and Politics' in M. Fineman and A. Grear (eds), *Vulnerability: Reflections on a New Ethical Foundation for Law and Politics* (Farnham: Ashgate, 2013) 13, 22.

72 M. Heikkilä, H. Katsui and M. Mustaniemi-Laakso, 'Disability and Vulnerability: A Human Rights Reading of the Responsive State' (2020) 24 *International Journal of Human Rights* 1180, 1186.

73 M. Fineman, 'Equality and Difference – The Restrained State' (2015) 66 *Alabama Law Review* 609, 619–20; Fineman, 'Vulnerability and Inevitable Inequality', 144–5.

74 Morris, 'Impairment and Disability', 6.

potential to contribute to the 'normalization' of disability. As argued by Clough, the vulnerability theory highlights 'the particular experience' that emanates from the 'individual's interaction with society' akin and maybe more than the social model of disability itself.[75] Disability is seen here as an expression of human variety that affects participation in society, rather than as a characteristic associated with a particular group of people.

With the vulnerability theory, States are asked to consider any form of dependency as part of a series of concerns. If a certain manifestation of vulnerability is associated exclusively with a particular group of people and not seen as an issue that may be subject to species-wide variation, these same people are more likely to be categorised as different in comparison to others and seen as a burden to society.[76] The theory therefore resists a group-based approach to addressing vulnerability. Fineman reckons that focusing on group identities overlooks the more general problems of disadvantage and, thereby, disregards the effects of social institutions.[77] Such a view advises against the use of disability to situate people on one side (disabled) or on the other (able).[78]

The concept of vulnerability has further parallels with that of disability, two of which deserve to be highlighted.

The first parallel is that disability just like vulnerability is a universal experience. As argued by Zola, we need to accept 'the near universality of disability and that all its dimensions (including the biomedical) are part of the social process by which the meanings of disability are negotiated'.[79] Disability refers to a broad range of impairments that may occur to anyone on many occasions during one's lifetime, and therefore it encompasses the entire population. These impairments vary not only in kind but also in their level of severity, with the result that establishing the threshold for having any particular impairment can sometimes be very difficult. Disability will furthermore have an impact on the families of disabled children, since they will have to bear additional costs arising from the disability. Parents may therefore face difficulties in coping with their lives and have often diminished employment opportunities.[80]

All individuals have needs that are similar to those associated with disability, regardless of whether they themselves are considered disabled or not. According to Bickenbach, disability is therefore a 'universal feature of the human condition'

[75] B. Clough, 'Disability and Vulnerability: Challenging the Capacity/Incapacity Binary' (2017) 16 *Social Policy & Society* 469, 479.

[76] J. Scully, 'Disability and Vulnerability: On Bodies, Dependence, and Power' in C. Mackenzie, W. Rogers and S. Dodds (eds), *Vulnerability New Essays in Ethics and Feminist Philosophy* (Oxford: Oxford University Press, 2014) 204, 218–19.

[77] Fineman, 'The Vulnerable Subject: Anchoring Equality in the Human Condition', 21–2.

[78] J. Herring, 'The Disability Critique of Care' (2014) 8 *Elder Law Review* 1, 14.

[79] I. Zola, 'Toward the Necessary Universalizing of a Disability Policy' (1989) 67 *The Milbank Quarterly* 401, 420.

[80] A. Rimmerman, *Family Policy and Disability* (Cambridge: Cambridge University Press, 2015) 38.

and not one that 'demarcates one portion of humanity'.[81] While society has viewed disability as a marginal issue, it is actually a central aspect of the human experience. In the words of Garland-Thomson, it can even be declared that '[w]hat we call disability is perhaps the essential characteristic of being human'.[82] This understanding of disability calls for the adoption of measures for the benefit of all those who may face different challenges that are related to disability.[83] It triggers social responsibility in terms of State responses indeed in a way analogous to vulnerability.

The second parallel is that disability has a bearing on a large set of experiences. These experiences will vary according to the circumstances and cannot be captured through the use of binaries. The differences between disabled and non-disabled people once more are not as rigid as it may seem and not as easy to establish as is often commonly assumed. Rather, we need to see ability and disability as the two ends of a long spectrum. Both are parts of a 'continuum', upon some point of which any individual will find herself.[84] Anyone possesses or lacks a certain ability and be more or less able or disabled depending on the circumstances. As with the vulnerability theory, the social model of disability also sees vulnerability as detached from a particular identity.[85] More than a question of binaries, therefore, disability is about the 'the sheer diversity of embodied experience'.[86]

Consequently, disability has no opposite notwithstanding what the term by itself suggests. As with vulnerability, a status of ability is neither used in such terms, nor does it exist in reality. The status of ability, in effect, is an ideal. Those who are considered to be able are only 'temporally abled', because they might become disabled sooner or later.[87] No-one will ever be fully able. Conversely, those who are seen as disabled are only 'temporally disabled', and they still have capacities in many respects, a fact which too often has been forgotten. They just have a number of limitations for some aspects of life. This makes again disability a matter of degree rather than a question of binaries.[88] Of course, it will become more significant for some severe kinds of impairments, which can impact on how disability is actually experienced.

[81] J. Bickenbach, 'Minority Rights or Universal Participation: The Politics of Disablement' in Jones and Basser Mark, *Disability, Divers-Ability and Legal Change*, 101, 112.

[82] R. Garland-Thomson, 'The Case for Conserving Disability' (2012) 9 *Bioethical Inquiry* 339, 342.

[83] J. Bickenbach, S. Rubinelli and G. Stucki, 'Being a Person with Disabilities or Experiencing Disability: Two Perspectives on the Social Response to Disability' (2017) 49 *Journal of Rehabilitation Medicine* 543, 546–7.

[84] Zola, 'Toward the Necessary Universalizing of a Disability Policy', 406; Bickenbach, 'Minority Rights or Universal Participation', 112.

[85] Heikkilä, Katsui, Mustaniemi-Laakso, 'Disability and Vulnerability', 1184.

[86] E. Hall and R. Wilton, 'Towards a Relational Geography of Disability' (2017) 41 *Progress in Human Geography* 727, 740.

[87] Siebers, *Disability Theory*, 71.

[88] K. Malleson, 'Equality Law and the Protected Characteristics' (2018) 81 *Modern Law Review* 598, 607–8. B. Clough, 'New Legal Landscapes: (Re)Constructing The Boundaries of Mental Capacity Law' (2018) 2 *Medical Law Review* 246, 270.

A similar point has been made with regard to gender, which comprises elements that transcend the dichotomy between male and female.[89] Gender, too, is not a fixed characteristic that can be attributed to one particular group of people, although this characteristic is less to be situated on a linear scale than disability and emphasises more – but not always – a sense of identity. The 'sex dualism' that international human rights law has hinged on to define gender has similarly missed the 'bodily diversity' that lies across such binaries.[90]

In reverse, the question of disability could be used as a means to advance vulnerability theory. It could make this theory more practical and bring its premises ever closer to the human condition, since it allows the fine-tuning of vulnerability in a way that better accounts for the different forms of embodiment. Disability is admittedly only one of the various manifestations of vulnerability. However, as its experience is universal, it touches upon the whole of the vulnerable subject. The very nature of disability requires attention to be drawn to a series of demands upon society that specifically result from the existence of impairment. Recognising such form of vulnerability may lead to a deeper appreciation of the full range of human differences. For this to happen, it is important no longer to despise disability but to treat it as an intrinsic aspect of the human experience. The point again holds true with regard to vulnerability itself.[91]

Still, this way of regarding disability carries its own dangers. Highlighting particular forms of embodiment may result in losing sight of vulnerability as a universal experience, but not doing so could lead to real needs being ignored. The fundamental question is how to respond to these needs if it is not recognised that some manifestations of vulnerability provide a basis for the construction of identities. Such recognition, in turn, requires establishing the distinctiveness of any categories, thereby inevitably proceeding to some degree of essentialism.[92] Identities indeed are needed in remedying vulnerabilities, since it would be impractical to register all the characteristics of each and every single individual. States need to proceed to generalisation if they are to be able to take effective action, as it will enable them to define not only the type of response but also how to allocate resources towards this end. It can indicate that a certain group of people generally requires a specific kind of support in order to deal with a particular vulnerability.[93] The law would therefore face challenges if it were to define characteristics

[89] D. Otto, 'Queering Gender 'Identity' in International Law' (2015) 33 *Nordic Journal of Human Rights* 299, 312–13.

[90] W. O'Brien, 'Can International Human Rights Law Accommodate Bodily Diversity?' (2015) 15 *Human Rights Law Review* 1, 5.

[91] M. Fineman, '"Elderly" as Vulnerable: Rethinking the Nature of Individual and Societal Responsibility' (2012) 20 *The Elder Law Journal* 71, 126.

[92] I. Young, *Justice and the Politics of Difference* (Princeton: Princeton University Press, 1990) 172.

[93] J. Herring, *Vulnerable Adults and The Law* (Oxford: Oxford University Press, 2016) 30.

without any reference to identities.[94] These identities can also be a powerful tool for leveraging different forms of collective mobilisation. The point is not to reject essentialism altogether but to increase awareness of the pitfalls of relying exclusively on identities in addressing vulnerability.

In the words of Sully, 'there is a fine balance to be struck' in order to avoid a unique focus on the different manifestations of vulnerability, thereby ending up keeping particular groups of people in a perpetual state of 'social and political marginalization'.[95] This tension is inherent to the vulnerable subject, which disability more than any other characteristic throws into relief. Focusing too much attention on identities in order to define particular groups of people might culminate in stigmatisation. This might have the contrary effect of sabotaging inclusion, by considering these groups as different and burdensome.

The result would be another form of vulnerability stemming from the conjuncture of the State's responses themselves. According to Mackenzie, vulnerability can be not only ontological but also situational and even pathogenic.[96] 'Pathogenic vulnerability' arises from dysfunctional social relationships that affect one's self-image through the very adoption of the policies that are supposed to remedy vulnerabilities.[97] By creating further vulnerabilities, such policies, in fact, place those for whom they are adopted in a worse position than that in which they were initially. If any measures humiliate individuals despite their objective of redressing disadvantages, their reach will be limited and antagonism will be more likely.[98] This is the case when these measures underestimate the real needs of disabled people, by pushing them towards ever higher levels of autonomy,[99] or when they overestimate those real needs, by dismissing their capacities altogether.

In short, States must incorporate the question of disability into their overall strategies for combating marginalisation. This not only acknowledges the universal experience of disability but also avoids the consideration of some groups of people as inherently dependent. Policies directed to disabled people should be applicable to all individuals. Instead of singling them out, they must take the form of shared responses subject to variation across the whole population. The effect of the action taken, in that case, would extend to other marginalised groups for such responses actually would serve the inclusion of all.

[94] Malleson, 'Equality Law and the Protected Characteristics', 617.

[95] Scully, 'Disability and Vulnerability', 219.

[96] C. Mackenzie, 'The Importance of Relational Autonomy and Capabilities for an Ethics of Vulnerability' in Mackenzie, Rogers and Dodds, *Vulnerability New Essays in Ethics and Feminist Philosophy*, 30, 9.

[97] Ibid, 9 and 44–5; S. Dodds, 'Dependence, Care, and Vulnerability' in Mackenzie, Rogers and Dodds, *Vulnerability New Essays in Ethics and Feminist Philosophy*, 181, 197.

[98] J. Wolff and A. De-Shalit, *Disadvantage* (Oxford: Oxford University Press, 2007) 171–2.

[99] Dodds, 'Dependence, Care, and Vulnerability', 198.

4.2.2 The Dis-abled Subject

The vulnerability theory paves the way for the adoption of a universal approach that regards disability as a constant and universal experience of all human beings. This approach can be realised, it is suggested, through introducing the idea of the dis-abled subject. The dis-abled subject epitomises the fact that disability is encountered by everyone on many occasions during one's lifetime. This universal approach does not consider disability as a characteristic attributed to a particular group of people only and allows for the more explicit integration of disability into the whole field of international human rights law.

As argued earlier, there is a need for abandoning the dichotomy between able and disabled. The hyphen in 'dis-ability' highlights that ability and disability themselves do not exist, but rather that both ability and disability are at the end of a long spectrum, and therefore that any individual is to a certain extent simultaneously abled and disabled. The prefix ('dis') is arguably a problem given its etymological construction,[100] although there is no other alternative for the time being.[101] There is in fact no term that refers to ability and disability in a non-binary manner, and this fosters resistance to abandoning the dichotomy between able and disabled. At the same time, the prefix ('dis') concedes that the experience of impairment can have intrinsic consequences for the lives of those concerned. Disability is indeed not a neutral phenomenon that would relate only to societal organisation, but, in the absence of a more accurate term, it can be considered the most appropriate one to describe the idea of the dis-abled subject.

Disability provides a useful entry point for reconsidering the universality of human rights. This universality has come to refer to the common values that underpin these rights. It correlates with the very notion of human rights, although it has come under attack by cultural relativism. It has however been demonstrated that universalism and particularism are not mutually exclusive,[102] and that both are essential to fully understand the notion of human rights.[103] The antagonism might perhaps be due to the alleged expansive reach of universality, which in fact

[100] Barness, *The Minority Body. A Theory of Disability*, 176.

[101] Arneil, 'Disability in Political Theory Versus International Practice', 34–5. Originating from Latin, 'dis' is a prefix used to indicate 'apart'.

[102] C. Tomuschat, *Human Rights: Between Idealism and Realism* (Oxford: Oxford University Press, 2003) 68–70; M. Freeman, 'Universalism of Human Rights and Cultural Relatisivism' in S. Sheeran and N. Rodley (eds), *Routledge Handbook of International Human Rights Law* (Abingdon: Routledge, 2014) 49, 54–7; F. de Varennes, 'The Fallacies in the "Universalism Versus Cultural Relativism" Debate in Human Rights Law' (2006) 7 *Asia-Pacific Journal on Human Rights and the Law* 67, 76–82.

[103] S. Fredman, *Comparative Human Rights Law* (Oxford: Oxford University Press, 2018) 55–6; J. Donnelly, *Universal Human Rights in Theory and Practice* (Ithaca: Cornell University Press, 3rd edn, 2013) 104–5.

does not reject the possibility of divergent political visions as well as national or local sensitivities.[104]

The same line of thought applies to those for *whom* human rights have been proclaimed. The notion of universality appertains not just to the definition of legal standards but also to that of rights-holders.[105] While it has been taken for granted that the rights-holders can be any one, the alleged neutrality of the legal subject has come to mean that disabled people are largely unaccounted for. The idea of the dis-abled subject thus shifts the focus from the side of 'rights' to the side of the 'human' in the notion of human rights. Universality then is about those who are the beneficiaries of human rights protection. Although this question has not been discussed as much, it is of the utmost importance to those who are disabled, which is why having the CRPD was a necessity. The adoption of a human rights treaty for disabled people by itself can be seen as proof of the limited reach of the traditional legal subject.[106] If the concept of universality fails to consider the question of disability, it becomes a pure contradiction in terms. There would actually not be much left of the 'human' if disabled people were left out of the concept of human rights. This concept has to be elevated if it is to retain its intended meaning. Otherwise the spotlight will continue to be on a restricted number of people, excluding those who are in just as much or even greater need of human rights protection, such as disabled people. The dis-abled subject is a device to bring them back to the centre of attention in the field of international human rights law.

In order to be truly universal, human rights must embrace ever more the reality of each and every single individual and override any masculine, white, heterosexual or able-bodied perspective. The legal subject should do away with the normativity of the average human being that has made it such a poor representation of humanity. Persisting with this normativity would continue casting doubts on the assumed universality of human rights. In order to include those who fail to meet the 'norm', difference itself should be given a much broader basis than has been afforded it up until now.[107] Recognising that particular needs cannot be met through the adoption of a 'one size-fits all approach', the dis-abled subject personifies the fact that all individuals have different demands to make upon society. Such needs require a degree of particularism in the adoption of measures so as to guarantee that these individuals are able to enjoy their human rights. The dis-abled subject

[104] N. Walker, 'Universalism and Particularism in Human Rights: Trade-off or Productive Tension? Old Problems, New Possibilities' in D. Kinley, W. Sadurski and K. Walton (eds), *Human Rights Old Problems, New Possibilities* (Cheltenham: Edward Elgar, 2013) 89, 102–3.

[105] J. Petman, 'The Special Reaching for the Universal: Why a Special Convention for Persons with Disabilities?' in J. Kumpuvuori and M. Scheinin (eds), *United Nations Convention on the Rights of Persons with Disabilities – Multidisciplinary Perspectives* (Helsinki: The Center for Human Rights of Persons with Disabilities in Finland, 2012) 2, 30.

[106] Grear, '"Framing the Project" of International Human Rights Law', 29.

[107] M. Minow, *Making All the Difference. Inclusion, Exclusion, and American Law* (Ithaca: Cornell University Press, 1990) 95–6.

thus perfects the notion of universality by expanding the concept of human rights to the very boundaries of the human experience. Siebers concludes by stating that 'disability rights hold the key to universal human rights'.[108]

Following this line of reasoning, a number of scholars have argued that the CRPD is relevant to all individuals.[109] In order to make such an argument, it is necessary though to disconnect the concept of disability from whatever group is in question. While the Convention already treats this group as open-ended, the concept should not be confined even to that group. Arneil makes such a disconnection by suggesting that disability is, at any one time, a universal experience 'over the entire lifespan' and, at any other time, an experience that will only be lived by 'a minority of people'.[110] As she considers that disability is – partially – an experience concerning all human beings, she infuses both the universal approach and the group-based approach. What is left unclear is how both of them work individually and how they are mutually imbricated. Bickenbach, Rubinelli and Stuki similarly distinguish between 'persons with disabilities' and 'experiencing disability' while attempting to reconcile both perspectives.[111] Even though they concede that the power of the group-based approach is actually also its weakness, they propose to maximise the respective advantages of the two perspectives through this reconciliation.[112] More investigation would be required in order to establish how such a group-based approach could still yield results alongside its universal counterpart.

By contrast, the dis-abled subject warns against the group-based approach, a view it likewise borrows from the vulnerable subject. The motivation behind this argument is not just that all individuals could gain from getting to grips with disability. It is also that the use of identities in order to define some groups of people is testament to the existence of a 'norm' against which these groups are measured.[113] Although a total relinquishment of these identities would be problematic in terms of effective action, it is indispensable to constrain this kind of essentialism. By overriding any group-based approach, the dis-abled subject brings a new dimension to the notion of universality. The Convention includes in its general principles the 'acceptance of persons with disabilities as part of human diversity'.[114] While this provision does refer to disabled people, it conveys the message of their sameness with other human beings. Distinguishing between those who are disabled

[108] Siebers, *Disability Theory*, 185.

[109] Mégret, 'The Disabilities Convention: Towards a Holistic Concept of Rights', 274; Quinn and Arstein-Kerslake, 'Restoring the "Human" in 'Human Rights', 37–8; A. Dhanda, 'Constructing a new Human Rights Lexicon: Convention on the Rights of Persons with Disabilities' (2008) 5 *International Journal on Human Rights* 43, 55.

[110] Arneil, 'Disability in Political Theory versus International Practice', 41.

[111] Bickenbach, Rubinelli and Stucki, 'Being a Person with Disabilities or Experiencing Disability', 543.

[112] Ibid, 548–9.

[113] Young, *Justice and the Politics of Difference*, 169.

[114] Article 3(d), CRPD.

and those who are non-disabled will by itself lead to the castigation of disability.[115] Doing so maintains the relegation of disabled people into the position of outsiders.

The CRPD exacerbates this tension between universalism and particularism by incorporating the different forms of embodiment into the legal subject. The Convention, at last, displays the latent schism that has sprung up between the legal standards and rights-holders.[116] It 'sends out the message that disabled people are equal subjects of rights with non-disabled people' – a message which was apparently needed – and contends that particular manifestations of vulnerability call for different ways of human rights protection.[117] As argued in relation to the legal standards, 'common particularization' points to a number of concerns that are raised with regard to parts of the population.[118] While disability admittedly is just one of these concerns, the concept itself is extremely vast and still represents a missing piece of the human rights puzzle notwithstanding the CRPD.

It is against this backdrop that the universality of human rights unlocks the Convention. As stated by Mégret:

> While the Convention speaks of 'disabled persons' – and there sometimes seems to be a sense that disability is an inherent characteristic of individuals – disability can be a very fluid concept and a very transient state, so that the frontier that separates disability from non-disability is in fact quite porous ... In understanding that 'we are all disabled', at least potentially, lies one way in which the Disabilities Convention can be seen as being about more than its title.[119]

What Mégret implicitly seeks to do here is to expand the scope of the CRPD by making all of us disabled. Such expansion resolves the dichotomy between able and disabled implicit in the concept of disability by granting membership to any individuals. Going a step further, the dis-abled subject separates both the concept and the group from each other, for this allows for viewing disability as something that affects each and every single individual. The point is not to extend disabled people to the whole of humanity but rather to detach the concept from the group. This avoids categorising certain people even if it is just to put all of them in the group in question.

It is worth highlighting that the CRPD undertakes to explicate disability in its Preamble while setting out who are 'persons with disabilities' in Article 1. Itss

[115] R. Mallett and K. Runswick-Cole, *Approaching Disability: Critical Issues and Perspectives* (Abington: Taylor Francis, 2014) 102–4.

[116] Quinn and Arstein-Kerslake, 'Restoring the "Human" in "Human Rights"', 37–8.

[117] J. Scully, 'The Convention on the Rights of Persons with. Disabilities and Cultural Understandings of Disability' in J. Anderson and J Philips (eds), *Disability and Universal Human Rights: Legal, Ethical, and Conceptual. Implications of the Convention on the Rights of Persons with Disabilities* (Utrecht: Netherlands Institute of Human Rights, 2012) 71, 81.

[118] Walker, 'Universalism and Particularism in Human Rights', 108–10.

[119] Mégret, 'The Disabilities Convention: Towards a Holistic Concept of Rights', 274.

drafters, in an unconscious manner, thus too blended the concept and the group, both of which are described in an almost identical manner in the Convention. Unfortunately, this amalgamation gives pre-eminence to the group-based approach from which the dis-abled subject precisely attempts to take a distance. To its credit, the CRPD remains a group-specific human rights treaty, as evidenced by its title. By contemplating the concept of disability (and not the group of disabled people), the Preamble nonetheless attests that the Convention is centred upon a specific issue of concern. Such a view is pushed further by its recognition that 'disability is an evolving concept'.[120] This Preamble thus confirms that the CRPD not only understands disability dynamically but also that the concept can be detached from the group with regard to this Convention. This further strengthens the argument that the CRPD does not deal only with those who are disabled.

As disability stands above and beyond the identity used to define disabled people, it is a question that concerns the entire population. From a legal point of view, the question may be asked whether group-specific rights can protect those who do not belong to the target group. The answer must be positive, since it is not because a right has special relevance for a group that this right cannot also benefit those outside of that group who might potentially gain from it.[121] As far as the CRPD is concerned, the group-specificity of its rights, is, in fact, quite limited. Although Mégret argues that the Convention 'comes very close to either creating new rights or formulating rights in the context of disability that have never been framed as such',[122] Arajävi considers the 'rights that apply only to [disabled people] ... amount to a relatively small number'.[123] Not much therefore stands in the way of opening out these rights, or at least the great majority of them, to the benefit of all individuals. There is even no reason why those rights that are most specific to disabled people cannot be used in the furtherance of this end. As stated by Zola, 'what is done in the name of disability today will have meaning for all of society's tomorrows'.[124]

This view is well in keeping with the universality of human rights. It resolves the boundary problems related to disability by not falling into the trap of a narrow usage of the concept of disability. While it has been argued that groups-specific rights are non-universal,[125] this is thwarted by impracticable implementation. The Convention applies to all individuals, wherever questions are raised by how

[120] Preamble(e), CRPD.

[121] A. Goldiner, 'Membership Rights: The Individual Rights of Group Members' (2019) 32 *Canadian Journal of Law & Jurisprudence* 343, 362–3; J. Nickel, *Making Sense of Human Rights* (Oxford: Blackwell Publishing, 2nd edn, 2007) 161–2.

[122] F. Mégret, 'The Disabilities Convention: Human Rights of Persons with Disabilities or Disability Rights' (2008) 30 *Human Rights Quarterly* 494, 497.

[123] P. Arajävi, 'UN CRPD and the Human Rights of Persons with Disabilities' in Kumpuvuori and Scheinin, *United Nations Convention on the Rights of Persons with Disabilities*, 34, 47.

[124] Zola, 'Toward the Necessary Universalizing of a Disability Policy', 422.

[125] Jones, 'Collective and Group-Specific', 54–6.

disability affects participation in society. Rather than concerning a particular group of people, the CPRD therefore offers 'a unique opportunity to rethink how we conceive the human rights of *all* [people]'.[126]

As will be illustrated in Part II, the Convention rights draw attention to challenges that every single individual can face at one time or another, challenges which must be resolved by some alleviation of the barriers embedded in society. Be it with regard to legal capacity, education, employment or political participation, individuals may be excluded from any or all of them due to the system's lack of consideration for the full range of human differences. The universality of disability calls for the real accommodation of human differences by actually modifying the environment itself.

The CRPD has taken a vital step forward in international human rights law insofar as it enunciates the rights of disabled people in a way which at the same time upgrades human rights in general. This Convention comprises elements that human rights treaties found not worth clarifying and that continue to disadvantage a large part of the population. It creates an obligation to take the necessary measures so as to facilitate participation in society, ranging from the provision of support and the guarantee of accessibility to improving social arrangements and the undertaking of awareness raising. By offering responses to a large variety of needs, these measures will provide States with the capacity to handle disability-related issues which unaddressed have long affectedthe real enjoyment of human rights.

By arguing that this Convention 'is of much more general interest beyond disability', Quinn and Arstein-Kerslake take another route to arrive at the same conclusion.[127] Instead of considering disability as universal experience, they broaden the CRPD's application by demonstrating its bearing upon all human beings. Although it remains unclear what that view entails for the concept of disability itself and although it may push the influence of this Convention too far, the idea again is that the CRPD goes much deeper than its object by uncovering a number of fallacies attached to the very notion of human rights. It confirms that the Convention rights can be used to elevate this notion more generally.

The conclusion is that the adoption of the CRPD is about much more than protecting the rights of disabled people. By recognising the universal experience of disability, the dis-abled subject makes the most possible out of that Convention for the sake of humanity. Rather than considering how to blend disability with the existing paradigm of the able-bodied individual, it re-shapes the substratum of international human rights law itself. The dis-abled subject offers all individuals further human rights protection through its embrace of the multifarious possibilities of human variety.

[126] Mégret, 'The Disabilities Convention: Towards a Holistic Concept of Rights', 274 (emphasis in the original).

[127] Quinn and Arstein-Kerslake, 'Restoring the "Human" in "Human Rights"', 38.

II

STANDARDS: HUMAN RIGHTS FOR DISABLED PEOPLE AND BEYOND

5

Legal Capacity: A Challenging Priority

This chapter analyses the right to legal capacity. It examines how the right was guaranteed prior to the CRPD and how it is protected for disabled people by the Convention (5.1. The Right to Legal Capacity). It not only discusses the issues raised by the notion of legal capacity and but also explains the way in which the Convention addresses deficits in mental capacity through its requirement to provide support for the exercise of legal capacity. It goes on to examine the concept of legal capacity within the meaning of the CRPD (5.2. Implications for International Human Rights Law). It explores what disability brings to the fore in respect of support by focusing on the role of social relations in achieving decision-making. It also considers the consequences of the right to legal capacity for the whole of international human rights law as well as outstanding issues in the understanding of this right.

5.1 The Right to Legal Capacity

5.1.1 Prior to the CRPD

The right to equal recognition before the law is one of the oldest and most long-established rights in the field of international human rights law. It is rooted in the principle that human beings have a legal personality which provides them with corresponding rights and duties. While non-human entities can also be regarded as legal persons, it has not always been so for any individuals. The issue has created contention in political theory with regard to those who lack cognitive skills. It therefore concerns especially intellectual disabilities, as well as mental health conditions which can affect decision-making.

The right to legal capacity is related to equal recognition before the law. However, this right does more than guarantee that individuals have the ability to hold rights and duties by granting them legal personality. It also gives them the ability to exercise those rights and duties. International human rights law did however not provide explicitly for such a right to legal capacity.

The International Covenant on Civil and Political Rights (ICCPR), just as the Universal Declaration of Human Rights (UDHR), states that '[e]veryone shall have the right to recognition everywhere as a person before the law'.[1] This right has

[1] Article 16, ICCPR; Article 6, UDHR.

Disability in International Human Rights Law. Gauthier de Beco, Oxford University Press. © Gauthier de Beco 2021.
DOI: 10.1093/oso/9780198824503.003.0006

received scant attention and unfortunately suffers from vagueness in its wording. While the Covenant recognises individuals' legal personality, it appears to leave open the possibility of imposing certain restrictions on legal capacity.[2] Such understanding corresponds to the exception that was made for 'persons of unsound mind' (amongst several other groups) in the second paragraph of the initial version.[3] Although this paragraph was subsequently deleted, it signalled that the international community was not ready to provide the same right to equal recognition before the law to all human beings.

Women have been denied legal capacity throughout human history. While they sometimes did have legal capacity, it was limited with respect to property rights, especially the property rights of married women. They were usually represented by their husbands, or other male relatives, and could not participate in the legal system. They are still under guardianship in countries like, instance, Saudi Arabia. The Convention on the Elimination of all Forms of Discrimination against Women (CEDAW) sought to put an end to this 'civil death'. In contrast to Article 16 of the ICCPR, Article 15 of CEDAW stipulates that 'States Parties shall accord to women, in civil matters, a legal capacity identical to that of men and the same opportunities to exercise that capacity'.[4] CEDAW thereby acknowledges that they must be able to *exercise* such legal capacity, as confirmed by requirement to 'give women equal rights to conclude contracts and to administer property and … treat them equally in all stages of procedure in courts and tribunals'.[5] Its drafters however pointed out that this provision was not meant to proscribe exceptions for others.[6] While women have for a long time been treated as disabled people or as children with whom they were often categorised, CEDAW requires that States Parties grant them – but only as women – legal capacity, that is, 'a legal capacity identical to that of men'.[7]

Other groups, especially racial minorities, have also been denied legal capacity.[8] By attributing a lower level of mental capacity to them, disability has been used to justify denials of legal capacity. Children are still treated in this way by law, but this is for other reasons. Unlike disabled people, children are supposed to acquire the

[2] S. Joseph, J. Schultz and M. Castan, *The International Covenant on Civil and Political Rights: Cases, Materials and Commentary* (Oxford University Press: Oxford, 3rd ed., 2013) 336.

[3] M. Bossuyt, *Guide to the Travaux Préparatoires the International Covenant on Civil and Political Rights* (Dordrecht: Martinus Nijhoff, 1987) 336.

[4] Article 15(2), CEDAW.

[5] Ibid.

[6] S. Goonesekere, 'Article 15' in M. Freeman, C. Chinkin and B. Rudolf (eds), *The UN Convention on the Elimination of All Forms of Discrimination against Women: A Commentary* (Oxford: Oxford University Press, 2012) 387, 390–1.

[7] Article 15(2), CEDAW.

[8] A. Arstein-Kerslake and E. Flynn, 'The Right to Legal Agency: Domination, Disability and the Protections of Article 12 of the Convention on the Rights of Persons with Disabilities' (2014) 10 *International Journal of Law in Context* 22, 25; T. Siebers, 'Disability and the Right to Have Rights' (2007) 27 *Disability Studies Quarterly*; http://dsq-sds.org/article/view/13/13.

skills to make decisions in adulthood. This means they have no legal capacity for the time being until they reach a certain age. The CRPD has nonetheless created tensions with regard to the CRC, which will be discussed later.

Disabled people therefore have had no right to legal capacity under international human rights law, at least, until the CRPD. As the denial of legal capacity is generally correlated to disability in domestic laws, these people have often been subject to guardianship systems and mental health legislation. The removal of their legal capacity may also lead to involuntary treatment and compulsory confinement.[9] Having themselves no decision-making powers, they are unable to challenge the decisions made on their behalf.

The existing international instruments before the CRPD's adoption, explicitly or implicitly, conceded that disabled people may be deprived of their legal capacity.[10] Both the Declaration on the Rights of Mentally Retarded Persons and the Principles for Protection of Persons with Mental Illness and the Improvement of Mental Health Care allowed for restrictions on their legal capacity.[11] The Standard Rules for the Equalisation of Opportunities for Persons with Disabilities do not mention this issue. Nor did the Committee on Economic, Social and Cultural Rights (CESCR Committee) in its general comment on the situation of disabled people.[12] No general comment has been adopted by the Human Rights Committee on the right to equal recognition before the law. In light of this, the discussions on legal capacity during the negotiation process touched upon questions that had never been addressed before.

5.1.2 Article 12 of the CRPD

The importance of the right to legal capacity for disabled people is invaluable. It is instrumental to the enjoyment of all the rights of disabled people, including the right to liberty, the right to integrity, the right to independent living, the right to family life and the right to access to justice, not to mention equality and non-discrimination.[13] Beyond guardianship systems and mental health legislation, legal capacity has ramifications in family law, contract law, consumer law and criminal

[9] World Health Organisation (WHO) and World Bank, *World Report on Disability* (Geneva: WHO, 2011) 77–8.

[10] A. Kanter, *The Development of Disability Rights under International Law. From Charity to Human Rights* (Abingdon: Routledge, 2015) 244–5.

[11] GA, *Declaration on the Rights of Mentally Retarded Persons*, 20 December 1971, A/RES/26/2856, Article 7; GA, *Principles for Protection of Persons with Mental Illness and the Improvement of Mental Health Care*, 17 December 1991, A/RES/46/119, Principle 1.6.

[12] CESCR Committee, *General Comment No 5: Persons with Disabilities*, 9 December 1994, E/1995/22.

[13] P. Gooding, 'Supported Decision-Making: A Rights-Based Disability Concept and its Implications for Mental Health Law' (2013) 20 *Psychiatry, Psychology and Law* 431, 437.

law.[14] As will be seen in chapter 9, the right to legal capacity is also linked to political rights including the right to vote. Its denial, however, is deeply entrenched in legal systems. In view of this, the Committee on the Rights of Persons with Disabilities (CRPD Committee) decided to elaborate its first general comment on the right to equal recognition before the law.[15] It drafted this general comment with the collaboration of disabled people's organisations as well as experts and academics.

Article 12 of the CRPD is entitled 'Equal recognition before the law'. According to article 12(1), States Parties 'reaffirm that persons with disabilities have the right to recognition everywhere as persons before the law'. Article 12(2) of the Convention adds that States Parties 'recognize that persons with disabilities enjoy legal capacity on an equal basis with others in all aspects of life'. While the first paragraph is a reminder of the general right to equal recognition before the law, the second paragraph is about the right to legal capacity itself. The Convention thus goes further than merely conferring legal personality upon disabled people. It moreover stresses the right to legal capacity's all-encompassing scope by using the phrase 'all aspects of life'.

Before moving on with the remaining provisions, it is necessary to inquire into the relevant concepts in greater detail. Cognitive impairment is supposed to reduce someone's level of mental capacity. More often than not this is translated into the removal of her legal capacity. However, mental capacity and legal capacity are two separate and distinguishable concepts.[16] On the one hand, mental capacity concerns decision-making skills, 'which naturally vary from one person to another' according to the CRPD Committee.[17] On the other hand, legal capacity is a construct which gives the powers to make decisions. While mental capacity is a flexible notion that depends on the circumstances, legal capacity allows individuals to form legally binding relations and protects them against coercive action.

Nevertheless, a link is made between the two concepts (mental capacity and legal capacity), which is usually done through the use of three different tests: status, functional or outcome.[18] These tests – the most common of which is the functional one – may result in the denial of legal capacity. The CRPD, in fact, breaks the link made between both concepts. In the view of the CRPD Committee, Article 12

[14] Y. Maker et al, 'Ensuring Equality for Persons with Cognitive Disabilities in Consumer Contracting: An International Human Rights Law Perspective' (2018) 19 *Melbourne Journal of International Law* 178; E. Verney, 'Redefining contractual capacity? The UN Convention on the Rights of Persons with Disabilities and the incapacity defence in English contract law' (2017) 37 *Legal Studies* 493; T. Minkowitz, 'Rethinking Criminal Responsibility from a Critical Disability Perspective: The Abolition of Insanity/Incapacity Acquittals and Unfitness to Plead, and Beyond' (2014) 23 *Griffith Law Review* 434.

[15] CRPD Committee, *General Comment No 1. Article 12: Equal Recognition Before the Law*, 19 May 2014, CRPD/C/GC/1, para 13.

[16] E. Flynn and A. Arstein-Kerslake, 'Legislating Personhood: Realising the Right to Support in Exercising Legal Capacity' (2014) 10 *International Journal of Law in Context* 81, 83.

[17] CRPD Committee, *General Comment No 1. Article 12*, para 13.

[18] Flynn and Arstein-Kerslake, 'Legislating Personhood', 85–7.

warns that 'perceived or actual deficits in mental capacity must not be used as justification for denying legal capacity'.[19]

Yet, such an understanding of the right to legal capacity can be fraught with difficulties as regards domestic legislation. The drafters of the CRPD indeed struggled to achieve sufficient consensus on Article 12. Two problems in particular spurred debate and need clarification. One underlies while the other overlies the right to legal capacity.

The first problem is that in the great majority of civil law countries a distinction is made between a capacity for rights and a capacity to act. One possibility is to grant all individuals legal personality, as done by the ICCPR. As mentioned earlier, people are then given the ability to hold rights and duties. There was no objection to disabled people having legal capacity in this sense. Another possibility is to recognise them also as persons capable of performing acts with legal effect. Legal capacity in that sense requires that the legal system does not take away decision-making powers. The former concerns 'legal standing' and grants individuals legal personality; the latter is about 'legal agency which allows them to make decisions by themselves. Offering disabled people both 'legal agency' and 'legal standing' somehow turned out to be an insurmountable obstacle for those making the distinction between a capacity for rights and a capacity to act.

The problem was the object of a footnote to Article 12(2) of the CRPD (a never seen feature in international human rights law up until then). It was introduced to indicate that in Arabic, Chinese and Russian, legal capacity was limited to capacity for rights.[20] Although it was pushed forward by Arab States, it confirmed that granting 'legal agency' to all disabled people was unacceptable to many governments. Despite this opposition, the footnote was eventually dropped by the Ad Hoc Committee, which declared that legal capacity carried the same meaning in the different languages.[21] In other words, the term invariably stands for both a capacity for rights and a capacity to act (or, at least, a capacity to act which implies a capacity for rights).[22]

The Convention attests this interpretation of the right to legal capacity by providing that disabled people have the right to manage their property and to sign financial contracts such as 'bank loans, mortgages and other forms of financial credit'.[23] It is therefore in continuity with CEDAW's provision that women shall

[19] CRPD Committee, *General Comment No 1. Article 12*, para 13.

[20] A. Dhanda, 'Legal Capacity in the Disability Rights Convention: Stranglehold of the Past or Lodestar for the Future?' (2007) 34 *Syracuse Journal of International Law and Commerce* 429, 453–4; T. Minkowitz, 'The United Nations Convention on the Rights of Persons with Disabilities and the Right to be Free from Nonconsensual Psychiatric Interventions' (2007) 34 *Syracuse Journal of International and Comparative Law* 405, 411.

[21] Dhanda, 'Legal Capacity in the Disability Rights Convention', 454–5.

[22] A. Arstein-Kerslake, *Restoring Voice to People with Cognitive Disabilities. Realizing the Right to Equal Recognition Before the Law* (Cambridge: Cambridge University Press, 2017) 235.

[23] Article 12(5), CRPD.

be able 'to exercise that capacity',[24] meaning the capacity to act in the view of the CEDAW Committee.[25] Were the negotiating parties not to recognise such a capacity to act, they might have introduced an exception for disabled people that was not to be found in CEDAW itself,[26] exception which would have been endorsed, paradoxically, by the CRPD.

Although the negotiating parties thus refrained from limiting the right to legal capacity to a capacity for rights, this debate not only demonstrates the difficulties of refusing to restrict disabled people in their legal capacity but also brings out the ensuing need for transforming the legal system for this very purpose. The resistance to leaving decision-making powers in the hands of any disabled person reflects the view that States did not see legal capacity as a human rights issue.

The second problem is that 'substituted decision-making' is a common feature of most legal systems. 'Substitute decision-making' is when a third party (a guardian) is appointed to make decisions for the person whose legal capacity has been restricted. According to the CRPD Committee, it involves that 'any decision ... is based on what is believed to be in the objective "best interests" of the person concerned, as opposed to being based on the person's own will and preferences'.[27] The CRPD purposely does not mention 'substituted decision-making'. It requires that the disabled person retains the powers to make decisions by having respect for her 'will and preferences'. Rather than defining what is in the individual's 'best interests', 'the [S]tate must protect choice' if the right to legal capacity is to be fulfilled.[28]

Having said this, the right to legal capacity so interpreted raises practical challenges. Cognitive impairment by itself can sometimes prevent people from making decisions. Aware of the difficulties involved in guaranteeing legal capacity to all disabled people, the drafters needed to find a solution in order to enable them to do so. Article 12(3) of the Convention provides that 'States Parties shall take appropriate measures to provide access by persons with disabilities to the support they may require in exercising their legal capacity'. Such provision of support can be indispensable for the actual preservation of 'legal agency'. The CRPD Committee considers that 'substitute decision-making [must] be replaced by 'supported decision-making', which 'requires both the abolition of substitute decision-making regimes and the development of supported decision-making alternatives'.[29] While the Convention itself does not prescribe such abolition, this is the way towards realising the right to legal capacity. The requirement of providing support for the exercise of legal

[24] Article 15(2), CEDAW (emphasis added).

[25] CEDAW Committee, *General Recommendation No 21: Equality in Marriage and Family Relations*, thirteenth session 1994, A/49/38, para 7.

[26] Dhanda, 'Legal Capacity in the Disability Rights Convention', 443–4.

[27] CRPD Committee, *General Comment No 1. Article 12*, para 27.

[28] A. Arstein-Kerslake, 'An Empowering Dependency: Exploring Support for the Exercise of Legal Capacity' (2016) 18 *Scandinavian Journal of Disability Research* 77, 87.

[29] CRPD Committee, *General Comment No 1. Article 12*, para 28.

capacity signals a major change of perspective in the field of international human rights law. As argued by Quinn and Arstein-Kerslake, Article 12 of the Convention creates a shift in focus 'from a deficits-orientated guardianship paradigm … to a support paradigm that uses the fact of a deficit to explore ways in which support can be put in place to enable capacity to grow and to be exercised'.[30]

This shift in focus ought to be lauded. Article 12 of the CRPD is more than a mere statement of principle as it provides for access to support in the exercise of legal capacity. The Convention thereby displays sensitivity to some of the inherent effects of cognitive impairment. Without such sensitivity, the right to legal capacity – in the sense of 'legal agency' – is only of theoretical value. 'Both the question of 'legal standing' vs 'legal agency' and the question of 'substituted decision-making' vs 'supported decision-making', therefore, are intrinsically related. The transition to 'supported decision-making' is key to the actual preservation of 'legal agency'.

5.1.3 The CRPD's New Emphasis

In the majority of legal systems, mental capacity serves as a benchmark to determine whether or not to remove someone's legal capacity and instead install guardianship, in full or in part. Disabled people are tested for determining whether they have this mental capacity, because they are assumed not to have the necessary decision-making skills. This approach overlooks how such skills can take varied forms and how cognition is not the only relevant element in the evaluation.[31] Diminished cognition conversely is not necessarily attached to disability and, even if it were, the way it may be so connected is often difficult to gauge.[32]

By guaranteeing legal capacity to all disabled people, international human rights has taken a revolutionary turn. The CPRD requires that States Parties recognise the ability of such people to exercise their rights and duties as much as any other people. In the words of Dhanda, Article 12 is 'a foundational assertion of the right to be human'.[33] What may have been implicit in the past and still unclear for many is now explicit in the Convention. The CPRD therefore represents a significant evolution in the field of international human rights law. It mandates that any restrictions on legal capacity differentiate no longer between disabled and non-disabled, which can be difficult to absorb by today's international human rights framework.

[30] G. Quinn and A. Arstein-Kerslake, 'Restoring the 'Human' in 'Human Rights'. Personhood and Doctrinal Innovation in the UN Disability Convention' in C. Gearty and C. Douzinas (eds), *The Cambridge Companion to Human Rights Law* (Cambridge: Cambridge University Press, 2013) 36, 47.

[31] A. Dhanda, 'Universal Legal Capacity as a Universal Human Right' in M. Dudley, D. Silove and F. Gale (eds), *Mental Health and Human Rights: Vision, Praxis and Courage* (Oxford: Oxford University Press, 2012) 177, 183.

[32] Arstein-Kerslake, *Restoring Voice to People with Cognitive Disabilities*, 11–12.

[33] Dhanda, 'Legal Capacity in the Disability Rights Convention', 457.

Article 12 of the CRPD has been a source of considerable tension in most countries. While States Parties are reviewing their national legislation to implement this Convention, legal systems are still wedded to the provision that disability can be a motive for imposing restrictions on legal capacity. As explained in chapter 3, political theory has been calling upon the notion of personhood in order to deny moral status to disabled people. The recognition of legal capacity puts into question the liberal subject regarded as a rational human being. Article 12 is thus much concerned with the 'human' in the concept of human rights, which it attempts to depict 'in some realistic way'.[34]

This leads to the question of whether the CRPD's vision is no more than wishful thinking. Such seems to be the position of the European Court of Human Rights. While the Court is prepared to deal with procedural matters and the consequences of denying legal capacity, it is not yet ready to condemn such denial itself and examine its legality in light of the CRPD.[35] For instance, in the *M.S. vs Croatia (No 2)* case, it considered that the compulsory confinement of a disabled person without appropriate procedural safeguards violated the European Convention on Human Rights, but it did not rule on the fact that the disabled person had been deprived of legal capacity.[36] More recently, in the *Rooman vs Belgium* case, the Court decided that a person of 'unsound mind' may be detained for the purpose of treatment provided that person also receives appropriate care to facilitate a return to society.[37]

The social model of disability can serve as a lens to explain what is at stake here: society erects barriers that target those with cognitive impairments. Guided by the criterion of rationality as part of the fundamental attributes of human beings, its response to deficits in mental capacity is the categorisation of certain people and stripping of their autonomy. As a result, it is quite possible that no legal system will altogether abolish any regimes of 'substituted decision-making' in the immediate future.

The way forward again lies in 'supported decision-making'. The guarantee that disabled people must obtain 'the support they may require in exercising their legal capacity' gives real content to the right to equal recognition before the law.[38] It is absent in CEDAW, where skills to make decisions indeed are taken for granted. Its provision that women must have 'the *same opportunities* to exercise that capacity'[39] still points to the necessity of creating 'a supportive context' for such exercise.[40]

[34] E. Celik, 'The Role of the CRPD in Rethinking the Subject of Human Rights' (2017) 2 *International Journal of Human Rights* 933, 948.

[35] Arstein-Kerslake, *Restoring Voice to People with Cognitive Disabilities*, 118–34.

[36] European Court of Human Rights, *M.S. vs Crotia (No 2)*, 19 February 2015, Appl No 75450/12, para 160.

[37] European Court of Human Rights, *Rooman vs Belgium*, 31 January 2019, Appl No 18052/11, para 210.

[38] Article 12(3), CRPD.

[39] Article 16(2), CEDAW (emphasis added).

[40] Goonesekere, 'Article 15', 396.

It takes into account women's continued marginalisation and the need to support them, for instance, in terms of education. The CRPD goes a step further by prescribing the provision of support for the purpose of achieving decision-making itself. This support ought not only to improve knowledge but also to enhance autonomy for this purpose. The requirement to do this is what makes Article 12 of the Convention a great innovation in international human rights law.

Legal capacity therefore is no longer seen in a negative way but as an impetus towards receiving support for its exercise.[41] This approach fits in with Wong's suggestion that society should establish enabling conditions to acquire Rawls's two moral powers for participation in the social contract.[42] As seen in Chapter 3, it is not a question of yes or no but of what ought to be done in order to develop those moral powers.

According to Kanter, the CRPD has created a 'right to support' which challenges traditional approaches to the notion of autonomy.[43] Whether the Convention introduces such a new right or provides a more accurate understanding of an existing one is open to debate. What is sure is that the CRPD has brought a new emphasis on the right to equal recognition before the law by imposing upon States Parties the obligation to offer disabled people support so that they can make decisions by themselves.

The right to legal capacity thereby challenges the usual dichotomies of international human rights law. This right is considered to belong to civil and political rights, as it emanates from a right proclaimed by the ICCPR (that is, the right to equal recognition before the law).[44] However, this understanding ignores the CRPD's new emphasis, which extends this right into the socio-economic sphere. While legal capacity perhaps has a civil rights dimension already within it, the support for its exercise is essentially related to economic and social rights.[45] In the absence of support, the right to legal capacity loses its real significance. The very nature of the right to legal capacity is opposed to its being assigned to either one or the other set of rights for it extends to both. Pursuing too far the division into civil and political and economic and social rights renders hollow the content of human rights, since it ignores the deeper connection between the two sets of rights.[46]

This is not the prevailing opinion. According to the CRPD Committee, 'the *rights* provided for in article 12 apply at the moment of ratification and are subject

[41] Celik, 'The Role of the CRPD in Rethinking the Subject of Human Rights', 948.

[42] S. Wong, '*Duties of Justice* to Citizens with Cognitive Disabilities' (2009) 40 *Metaphilosophy* 382, 393–4. The two moral powers are 'the capacity for a sense of justice and the capacity for a conception of the good' (J. Rawls, *Political Liberalism* (New York: Columbia University Press, 1993) 19).

[43] Kanter, *The Development of Disability Rights under International Law*, 266–7.

[44] Arstein-Kerslake, *Restoring Voice to People with Cognitive Disabilities*, 35–7.

[45] While she explicitly rejects the idea, Arstein-Kerslake still considers that the right to legal capacity is 'a unique marriage between the right to liberty and the right to social support for the exercise of liberty' (Arstein-Kerslake, *Restoring Voice to People with Cognitive Disabilities*, 57).

[46] G. de Beco, 'The Indivisibility of Human Rights and the Convention on the Rights of Persons with Disabilities' (2019) 68 *International & Comparative Law Quarterly* 141, 153–4.

to immediate realization' and 'the obligation ... to provide access to support in the exercise of legal capacity is an obligation for the fulfilment of [civil and political rights]'.[47] Although any delay in meeting this obligation will breach its international commitments, this view does not help towards the realisation of the right to legal capacity. Not only is it impossible to provide adequate support to all those needing it in the short term, but also a State Party must develop a strategy for attaining this goal.[48] Assigning the right to legal capacity only to civil and political rights misses the target if the State Party has not adopted measures for enhancing decision-making skills.

5.2 Implications for International Human Rights Law

5.2.1 The Universality of Legal Capacity

Diminished or, at least, imperfect, decision-making skills, is a proper feature of all human beings. A lack thereof, however, has mainly been attributed to disabled people, but it has sometimes been ascribed to other groups. Mental capacity is moreover correlated to social context. As stated by the CRPD Committee, it 'may be different for a given person depending on many factors, including environmental and social factors'.[49] This view is confirmed by prejudice against disabled people that is exacerbated by characteristics other than disability. Disabled women, for instance, face acute forms of discrimination and often suffer from violence and sexual abuse.[50] There is also much stereotyping against disabled LGBT people.[51] Intersectionality thus increases the likelihood of the denial of legal capacity.

The CRPD enjoins States Parties to dissociate states of mind from any particular groups of people. In view of this, Dhanda reckons that the Convention advances 'universal legal capacity'.[52] The CRPD Committee has taken up the idea, considering that 'universal legal capacity' involves the recognition that 'all persons, regardless of disability or decision-making skills, inherently possess legal capacity.[53] The right to legal capacity therefore pertains to all individuals.

[47] CRPD Committee, *General Comment No 1. Article 12*, para 30 (emphasis added).

[48] In any event, it seems that the CRPD Committee confuses itself by adding that 'States Parties must immediately begin taking steps towards the realization of the rights provided for in article 12'. The immediacy refers here to the 'steps' and no longer to the 'realization' itself (Ibid, para 30).

[49] Ibid, para 13.

[50] C. Frohmader and S. Ortoleva, *The Sexual and Reproductive Rights of Women and Girls with Disabilities* (Issues Paper commissioned by the ICPD International Conference on Human Rights), July 2014, 4–5; http://www.womenenabled.org/pdfs/issues_paper_srr_women_and_girls_with_disabilities_final.pdf.

[51] S. Dudek, 'Institutionalized Queers: Homosexuality in Residential Facilities for People with Cognitive Disabilities' (2006) 26 *Disability Studies Quarterly*; http://dsq-sds.org/article/view/698/875.

[52] Dhanda, 'Universal Legal Capacity as a Universal Human Right', 181.

[53] CRPD Committee, *General Comment No 1. Article 12*, para 25.

Everyone relies on others for proper decision-making so that legal capacity can only be exercised if support is available for its exercise. As argued by Mackenzie, interdependency acknowledges that autonomy is relational and contingent on social relations.[54] For instance, Series defines 'supported decision-making' as 'helping [people] to obtain and understand information relevant to the decision, talking through the pros and cons of different available options, or helping a person to communicate with others'.[55] This way of defining the term appreciates that the achievement of independence depends on the opportunity to rely on others.

In fact, 'supported decision-making' has its origins in existing social relations and entered only later on into legal practice.[56] The support required, therefore, does not necessarily refer to external intervention; rather, it draws upon 'both informal and formal support arrangements'.[57] In the words of Gooding, it is 'a broad spectrum, some of which may engage legal mechanisms, some of which may not'.[58] This includes support that spontaneously emerges in any social context.

Unfortunately, this spontaneous support has diminished with the growing levels of marginalisation. Its ready availability has become more and more reduced especially in modern democracies, such as the US.[59] As a result, many people find themselves isolated with no help at hand and sometimes end up in even ever more dramatic situations.[60] The CRPD Committee consciously recommends to 'facilitate the creation of support, particularly for people who are isolated and may not have access to naturally occurring support in the community'.[61] It furthermore considers this 'naturally occurring community support (including friends, family and schools) … as key to supported decision-making'.[62] What is therefore needed is to expand the 'naturally occurring community support', which is currently in decline. While human rights aim to protect individuals, they can be used towards this end by means of strengthening social relations.[63] In order to realise the right to legal capacity, the most effective strategy would arguably be to broaden any

[54] C. Mackenzie, 'The Importance of Relational Autonomy and Capabilities for an Ethics of Vulnerability' in C. Mackenzie, W. Rogers and S. Dodds (eds), *Vulnerability New Essays in Ethics and Feminist Philosophy* (Oxford: Oxford University Press, 2014) 30, 42–3.

[55] L. Series, 'Relationships, Autonomy and Legal Capacity: Mental Capacity and Support Paradigms' (2015) 40 *International Journal of Psychiatry* 80, 85.

[56] P. Gooding, A *New Era for Mental Health Law and Policy: Supported Decision-Making and the UN Convention on the Rights of Persons with Disabilities* (Cambridge: Cambridge University Press, 2017) 241–2.

[57] CRPD Committee, *General Comment No 1. Article 12*, para 15.

[58] Gooding, *A New Era for Mental Health Law and Policy*, 123.

[59] Kanter, *The Development of Disability Rights under International Law*, 267.

[60] J. Craigie et al, 'legal Capacity Mental Capacity and Supported Decision-Making: Report from a Panel Event' (2019) 62 *International Journal of Law and Psychiatry* 160, 162.

[61] CRPD Committee, *General Comment No 1. Article 12*, para 29(d).

[62] Ibid, para 45.

[63] J. Herring, 'Forging a Relational Approach: Best Interest or Human Rights?' (2013) 13 *Medical Law International* 32, 49.

support available through family and friendship rather than create further legal mechanisms.

This discussion shows how limited remains the consideration of the kind of the support that is necessary for the exercise of legal capacity. Attention is generally focused on the 'will and preferences' of the person in a number of complex situations. The identification this 'will and preferences' is then detached from the social context and limited to only some decisions that are heavy with consequence. This is all done with the aid of experts who are specifically designated persons. It is true that support within the meaning of the CRPD must be provided only for exercising legal capacity,[64] but its impact will be upon a wide range of issues.

Indeed, there is little guidance on the support to be provided in keeping with the CRPD. The CRPD Committee only mentions 'peer support, advocacy … or assistance with communication'.[65] It has been yet noted that the CRPD directs attention to any social relations that could provide support for the exercise of legal capacity.[66] Even if the Convention tends to accentuate the need for expertise, it allows for leaning on those social relations in order to get this support. At the end of its general comment, the Committee itself cites the 'opportunities to build social networks' as a means to 'support the exercise of legal capacity'.[67] It thus points to the necessity of providing support not only within but also through communities. The latter can both help expand the availability of support and act as a check on how it is actually being used.

According to Arstein-Kerslake, 'the organic formation of supported decision-making that naturally occurs in families and communities', which has been obstructed by the long-time segregation of disabled people, can awaken support for the exercise of legal capacity.[68] It is in these 'families and communities' that first-hand knowledge is available on how to give disabled people control of their lives.[69] This also concerns the so-called 'hard cases', as it is precisely in such cases that this first-hand knowledge will allow the judgement upon what the person would have really liked at times when she still was able to communicate this or in case she were able to do so.

It is therefore the social relations wherein support mostly originates that ought to be strengthened. Such strengthening can sustain or even expand those social networks which all individuals draw upon so as to enjoy their right to legal capacity. The purpose would be to stimulate non-legal mechanisms by allowing communities to enhance everyone's decision-making skills. Such non-legal mechanisms could provide to all people, including those who are disabled, information, advice and

[64] Arstein-Kerslake, *Restoring Voice to People with Cognitive Disabilities*, 178; C. de Bhailís and E. Flynn, 'Recognising Legal Capacity: Commentary and Analysis of Article 12 CRPD' (2017) 13 *International Journal of Law in Context* 6, 13.

[65] CRPD Committee, *General Comment No 1. Article 12*, para 17.

[66] Series, 'Relationships, Autonomy and Legal Capacity', 83.

[67] CRPD Committee, *General Comment No 1. Article 12*, para 52.

[68] Arstein-Kerslake, *Restoring Voice to People with Cognitive Disabilities*, 198.

[69] Gooding, *A New Era for Mental Health Law and Policy*, 193.

guidance in order to enable them to make decisions by themselves. In so doing, the CRPD nevertheless insists that States Parties must 'provide for appropriate and effective safeguards to prevent abuse',[70] thus guaranteeing that the support provided does not increase dependency but is actually conducive to autonomy. In order to avoid shifting responsibilities, it remains essential to have a legal framework that not only guarantees the release of the necessary resources but also offers the option of declining the support on offer and seeking it from elsewhere if necessary. This legal framework must ensure that any support on offer is reliable and that it respects both the person's wishes and actual circumstances. In the end, disabled people should themselves be able to determine who provides them with this support, whether families or friends, professionals or, perhaps, even a mix of both.

All in all, the right to legal capacity is about the attainment of social cohesion. While this right is crucial in order to realise the right to independent living, the converse is equally true. It is constrained without the connectedness to others that allows for its realisation.[71] Facilitating the 'naturally occurring support in the community' simultaneously diminishes needs for formal support.[72] Inclusion is therefore the very means of widening decision-making skills. Ensuring the provision of support but stopping short of strengthening social relations makes the task even harder and fails to release the CRPD's full potential.

The question moreover is whether States Parties will agree to divert their resources towards 'supported decision-making' away from guardianship systems in accordance with the CRPD. The CRPD Committee's views on the right to legal capacity has already been the cause of dismay by stakeholders.[73] The reality is such that it is unlikely that all disabled people will be able to get support 'at nominal or no cost' in order to exercise their legal capacity,[74] including through 'trusted support persons to assist them'.[75] As this is unlikely to ever happen anytime soon coupled with the fact that isolation is becoming more common than ever, there is a good argument to direct resources to real-world communities so as to yield support for the exercise of such legal capacity.

In sum, the right to legal capacity has received a lot of attention. There are indeed good reasons for putting it high on the international agenda. Our legal capacity allows to decide where, how and with whom we live. The right to legal capacity has therefore raised a lot of controversy and poses both practical and conceptual challenges. While recognising the importance of this right, it can be asked though not

[70] Article 12(4), CRPD.

[71] G. Quinn, *Rethinking Personhood: New Directions in Legal Capacity Law and Policy. An Ideas Paper, April 2011, University of British Columbia, Vancouver*, 17–8; https://www.inclusionireland.ie/sites/default/files/attach/basic-page/846/rethinkingpersonhood-newdirectionsinlegalcapacitylawandpolicy-gerardquinn-april2011.docx.

[72] CRPD Committee, *General Comment No 1. Article 12*, para 29(d).

[73] Craigie et al, 'legal Capacity Mental Capacity and Supported Decision-Making', 65.

[74] CRPD Committee, *General Comment No 1. Article 12*, para 29(e).

[75] Ibid, para 17.

only whether the attention given to that right has helped to break the stalemate but also whether it has not been somewhat at expense of attention to the other Convention rights, which, in turn, have an impact on the right in question.

5.2.2 Closing the Gap

The right to legal capacity is one of the most important rights of the CRPD. Legal capacity is an essential aspect of the right to equal recognition before the law, which the Convention has finally affirmed with regard to all disabled people. This was a welcome move after it being sidelined by the ICCPR which made exceptions specifically with these people in mind.[76] The right to legal capacity entails that all human beings are allowed to make choices about their lives, including choices not deemed by others to be in their own best interests.

From this it follows that legal capacity implies a certain level of risk taking. However, the threshold in this regard is not set at the same level for those who are disabled. The latter are believed to have a greater propensity to make 'bad' decisions, whereas others are free to make any decisions they like, good or bad. The question is: Why tolerate risk for all individuals except for disabled people?[77] A frequent answer is that the 'bad' decisions will have consequences not only for the individual but also for others who will have 'to pick up the inevitable pieces' even if this holds true for just about anyone.[78] If things go badly, society's response should not vary between disabled and non-disabled people. In the UK, for instance, those with a mental health condition that causes particular tendencies (whether or not they manifest themselves) are left unprotected by the Equality Act 2010.[79] As stated by the CRPD Committee, any protection against abuse must respect the 'will and preferences', including 'the right to take risks and make mistakes'.[80] States must be able to set limits on people's choices, but these limits should be the same for every individual and not be placed just on certain groups.

Still, there can be doubts as to whether this is really feasible. While it is fundamental to provide legal capacity on a universal level, there can be difficulties in its actual implementation. One of them is the requirement to follow disabled people's 'will and preferences',[81] which must inform '[a]ll forms of support in the exercise of legal capacity' according to the CRPD Committee.[82] Social relations, as a rule,

[76] Joseph, Schultz and Castan, *The International Covenant on Civil and Political Rights*, 336.
[77] Series, 'Relationships, Autonomy and Legal Capacity', 88.
[78] Quinn, *Rethinking Personhood*, 5 and 15.
[79] P. Harpur, *Ableism at Work: Disablement and Hierarchies of Impairment* (Cambridge: Cambridge University Press, 2019) 106–7 and 119. See Regulation 4(2) of The Equality Act 2010 (Disability) Regulations 2010.
[80] CRPD Committee, *General Comment No 1. Article 12*, para 22.
[81] Article 12(4), CRPD.
[82] CRPD Committee, *General Comment No 1. Article 12*, para 29(b).

involve exposure to influence by others, for better or for worse. They constrain us, but, at the same time, we rely on them and they give sense to who we are. Basing the exercise of legal capacity exclusively on the 'will and preferences' rests on the assumption that human beings are always capable of defining what is of value to them. This championing of such 'will and preferences' further perpetuates the notion of personhood grounded in the capacity for normative agency which human rights are supposed to safeguard.

If society accepts a certain level of risk taking, it should also similarly accept a certain level of influence. There is once again no reason to set a lower threshold for those who are disabled here.[83] The problem is how to set such a threshold, as it might be impossible to know whether a particular choice truly reflects one's 'will and preferences'.[84] The CRPD provides that 'measures relating to the exercise of legal capacity … [must be] free of … undue influence'.[85] However, it can sometimes be difficult to establish when influence is 'undue' although there are cases where this is evident, which makes it important to establish 'effective safeguards'. Some degree of 'undue influence' might be present in any support offered to enable people to make decisions. Its presence is inherent to any social relations, which relations entail responsibilities that are not always appreciated by the law.[86] Several scholars still maintain that finding out what are indeed 'will and preferences' remains the objective whatever the circumstances.[87] The CRPD Committee similarly recommends that if 'it is not practicable to determine the will and preferences of an individual, the "best interpretation of will and preferences" must replace the "best interests" determinations'.[88] It might in fact turn out that this 'best interpretation of will and preferences' will dominate in most cases and likewise will become a sort of substitution.

The question also is what 'will and preferences' truly mean in the CRPD.[89] The two terms (will and preferences) might produce contradictory results in practice: the first one emanates from one's overall life goals, while the second one is more time-bound.[90] Support may not always help resolve such contradiction or elicit what are the person's real 'will and preferences'.

[83] P. Gooding, 'Navigating the Flashing Amber Lights of the Right to Legal Capacity in the United Nations Convention on the Rights of Persons with Disabilities: Responding to Major Concerns' (2015) 15 *Human Rights Law Review* 45, 56.

[84] P. Bartlett, 'The United Nations Convention on the Rights of Persons with Disabilities and Mental Health Law' (2012) 75 *Modern Law Review* 752, 766.

[85] Article 12(4), CRPD.

[86] J. Herring, *Vulnerable Adults and the Law* (Oxford: Oxford University Press, 2016) 258–9.

[87] Flynn and Arstein-Kerslake, 'Legislating Personhood', 99; de Bhailís and Flynn, 'Recognising Legal Capacity', 16–17.

[88] CRPD Committee, *General Comment No 1. Article 12*, para 21.

[89] Gooding, *A New Era for Mental Health Law and Policy*, 237.

[90] G. Szmukler, '"Capacity", "Best Interests", "Will and Preferences" and the UN Convention on the Rights of Persons with Disabilities' (2019) 18 *World Psychiatry* 34, 39–40.

Consequently, there might never be a pure form of 'supported decision-making'. Some element of substitution – which, too, is a grey area – will always be present in the provision of support. While the CRPD lacks clarity on the issue,[91] it acknowledges that legal capacity does not take place in a void. It highlights that what matters is the quality of the social context wherein skills to make decisions can be maximised. In the words of Kanter, Article 12 of the CRPD 'may provide a new model of social relations that offers support for people with and without disabilities alike'.[92] This confirms that the right to legal capacity is ultimately about social cohesion.

The CRPD thus questions the common understanding of the right to equal recognition before the law, as initially protected by the ICCPR and subsequently expanded by CEDAW. What matters is a lower level of mental capacity is addressed by the provision of support rather than by the removal of legal capacity. In order to bring about 'universal legal capacity',[93] it is this provision of support that must be the point of attention. The deeper question is how to shape the social context in a way that enables all individuals to make choices about their life. The right to legal capacity involves not only accepting that autonomy is always relational but also putting aside the exclusive focus on its civil rights dimension.

The key message is that restrictions on legal capacity should not be used as a response to deficits in mental capacity instead of ensuring that mechanisms, which can be legal or not, are in place for the purpose of achieving decision-making. If restrictions on legal capacity are required, they must be applied impartially and find their justification in international human rights law as a whole.[94] The difficulty in so doing though is that such restrictions have been established precisely for those with particular kinds of impairments. While the CRPD provides for safeguards against abuse 'in accordance with international human rights law',[95] human rights treaties allow for exceptions to be made by the very fact of impairment. As a result, the UN treaty bodies persevere with those regimes that tolerate coercive action against disabled people.[96] There is a long road ahead before these treaty bodies integrate the Convention's vision into their work while reconciling their recommendations with those of the CRPD Committee. Further dialogue of them is essential towards this end, although the normative gap makes such reconciliation difficult.[97] The CRPD Committee has moreover no mandate to work across the range of human rights treaties.

91 Gooding, 'Supported Decision-Making', 437–8.
92 Kanter, *The Development of Disability Rights under International Law*, 268.
93 A. Dhanda, 'Universal Legal Capacity as a Universal Human Right', 183.
94 Arstein-Kerslake, *Restoring Voice to People with Cognitive Disabilities*, 90; Gooding, *A New Era for Mental Health Law and Policy*, 236.
95 Article 12(4), CRPD.
96 Szmukler, '"Capacity", "Best Interests", "Will and Preferences"', 35–6.
97 P. Bartlett, 'Will and Preferences in the Overall CRPD Project' (2019) 18 *World Psychiatry* 48, 49.

A final point is that children have no right to legal capacity under international human rights law. Instead, they are prepared so that they can make decisions by themselves once they reach adulthood. Others thus make decisions on their behalf, but they must apply the 'best interests' principle. As provided by the CRC, '[i]n all actions concerning children … the best interests of the child shall be a primary consideration'.[98] This provision has been replicated in the CRPD.[99] The same Convention, however, would denounce the 'best interests' principle in its drive to develop 'supported decision-making' regimes. In the words of the CRPD Committee, this principle 'is not a safeguard which complies with article 12 *in relation to adults*',[100] thereby admitting it can be so regarding children.

Like the 'will and preferences', the 'best interests' principle is subject to uncertainties, which include how 'best interests' are to be defined and how to handle conflicting claims.[101] The principle should also be read in conjunction with children's 'right to express [their] views freely in all matters affecting [them]' protected by the CRC.[102] The right of the child to be heard is cardinal for determining what are the 'best interests' of the child, because it guarantees that her wishes are taken into account in any decision-making process.[103] It is likewise provided for – in the same wording – in the CRPD, which adds that disabled children should 'be provided with disability and age-appropriate assistance to realize that right'.[104]

There is therefore a double standard in international human rights law. The CPRD has inherited the general rule that a lower level of mental capacity by virtue of age naturally implies a denial of legal capacity.[105] While it rejects the 'best interests' principle for adults, it maintains it as far as children are concerned. This principle is reminiscent of the welfarist approach to dealing with disability, which adheres to a medical perspective on disabled people.[106] Disabled children do need the enhancement of their decision-making skills, as do all the children, if they are to be able to exercise their legal capacity as adults. It is more likely they will have this legal capacity removed at a later stage if they themselves are not provided earlier with any opportunity to make choices about their lives.

[98] Article 3, CRC.

[99] Article 7(2), CRPD.

[100] CRPD Committee, *General Comment No 1. Article 12*, para 21 (emphasis added).

[101] M. Freeman, *A Commentary on the United Nations Convention on the Rights of the Child: Article 3. The Best Interests of the Child* (Leiden/Boston Martinus Nijhoff, 2007) 36–8.

[102] Article 12(1), CRC.

[103] J. Zermatten, 'The Best Interests of the Child Principle: Literal Analysis and Function' (2010) 18 *International Journal of Children's Rights* 483, 496–7.

[104] Article 7(3), CRPD.

[105] R. Sandland, 'Lessons for Children's Rights from Disability Rights' in E. Brems, E. Desmet and W. Vandenhole (eds), *Children's Rights Law in the Global Human Rights Landscape: Isolation, Inspiration, Integration?* (Abingdon: Routledge, 2017) 109, 124–5.

[106] B. Byrne, 'Minding the Gap? Children with Disabilities and the United Nations Convention on the Rights of Persons with Disabilities' in M. Freeman (ed), *Law and Childhood Studies* (Oxford: Oxford University Press, 2012) 419, 428.

The resulting uneasiness is visible in the CRPD Committee's recommendations. With a single stroke, it recalls the principle of the 'best interests' – as enunciated in both the CRC and the CRPD – and recommends States Parties 'to ensure that the will and preferences of children with disabilities are respected'.[107] One can wonder how it is possible to do both at the same time.

This begs the question why deficits in mental capacity should lead to either substitution (because of age) or support (because of disability) with no middle way in-between. While the CRPD's drafters could not offer disabled children more rights than children in general, the Convention encourages a move towards 'supported decision-making' for all children alike.[108] Such a move requires taking a distance from focusing onthe 'best interests' of the child and creating opportunities to increase decision-making skills during childhood. So doing would recognise not only that mental capacity evolves over time but also that support is always needed towards this end. The support would help both disabled and non-disabled children to gradually achieve decision-making, but it may have to be pursued later on depending on the circumstances. It would give effect to the right of the child to be heard, as it underpins the need to recognise and enhance their emerging autonomy. The move towards 'supported decision-making' for any children is paved further by the obligation to provide 'disability and *age*-appropriate assistance' for the realisation of this right set out in the CRPD.[109]

As explained in Chapter 1, the two human rights treaties share similarities, but they go in opposite directions as far as legal capacity is concerned. On the one hand, the CRC endorses the standpoint that society should make decisions on children's behalf. On the other hand, the CRPD rejects substitution altogether for those who are adult. This antagonism calls for some relaxation (and a pardoning of the CRPD Committee's confusion). It shows perhaps that the future lies in balancing a child's 'will and preferences' with her 'best interests' regardless of disability *and* age. This does not mean that children should simply have 'legal agency', but that further alignment must be sought between both human rights treaties in order to allow all individuals to make decisions in adulthood.

[107] CRPD Committee, *General Comment No 1. Article 12*, para 36.
[108] Sandland, 'Lessons for Children's Rights from Disability Rights', 125.
[109] Article 7(3), CRPD (emphasis added).

6
Inclusive Education: A Hidden Priority

This chapter examines the right to inclusive education. It explains how the CRPD has incorporated the goal of inclusive education into international human rights law and what it expects from States Parties for the realisation of the right to inclusive education (6.1. The Right to Inclusive Education). It subsequently explores the Convention's new emphasis on the right to education while looking at the measures to be adopted in order to achieve inclusive education. It continues by examining the renewed commitment to inclusiveness with regard to education in the field of international human rights law (6.2. Implications for International Human Rights Law). The chapter upholds that inclusive education is universal and that the right to inclusive education applies to all children alike even if it has disability-specific aspects. It finally investigates what this right actually means for education systems as well as the remaining challenges in its implementation.

6.1 The Right to Education

6.1.1 Prior to the CRPD

The right to education is well-recognised in the field of international human rights law. The Universal Declaration of Human Rights (UDHR) declares that '[e]veryone has the right to education'.[1] This right to education is generally protected by the International Covenant on Economic, Social and Cultural Rights (ICESCR) and the Convention on the Rights of the Child (CRC),[2] both of which outline different obligations relating to primary, secondary and tertiary education.[3] Although the right to education primarily belongs to economic and social rights, it also pertains to civil and political rights. It covers both the content of education (called the 'social aspect' of the right) and the right of parents to choose the education of their children according to their religious and moral convictions (called the 'freedom

[1] Article 26(1), UDHR.
[2] Articles 13 and 14, ICESCR; Articles 28 and 29, CRC.
[3] Article 13(2), ICESCR; Article 28(1), CRC. While the CRC repeats most of the standards enunciated in the ICESCR, it contains a number of new elements which include measures relating to vocational guidance, school attendance and school discipline (Articles 28(1)(d) and (e) and 28(2), CRC).

Disability in International Human Rights Law. Gauthier de Beco, Oxford University Press. © Gauthier de Beco 2021.
DOI: 10.1093/oso/9780198824503.003.0007

aspect' of the right).[4] The right to education, therefore, is a good example attesting to the indivisibility of human rights.

There is ample guidance available on how to put into effect the right to education according to international human rights law. Such guidance is provided by the CESCR Committee in two general comments on this right, one on the right in general and the other on action plans for primary education.[5] The CRC Committee adopted its first ever general comment on the aims of education.[6]

This being said, no human rights treaty had addressed disabled people's education prior to the CRPD. Adopted by UNESCO in 1960, the Convention against Discrimination in Education prohibits discrimination on the basis of a number of different grounds but omits disability.[7] By contrast, the CRC explicitly refers to 'disability' in its general anti-discrimination clause, unlike previous human rights treaties, and even contains a separate article on disabled children.[8] There is, however, no provision on how to protect their right to education in this Convention. It took the CRPD's enactment to articulate that right as a distinctive right under international human rights law.

Along a parallel path, a number of international instruments have considered the matter in a way that would subsequently influence international human rights law. Following the World Conference on Education in Jomtien in 1990, the World Declaration on Education for All: Meeting Basic Learning Needs (Jomtien Declaration) declared that '[s]teps need to be taken to provide equal access to education to every category of disabled persons as an integral part of the education system'.[9] The Standard Rules on the Equalization of Opportunities for Persons with Disabilities (Standard Rules), adopted in 1993, similarly recommended that '[e]ducation for persons with disabilities should form an integral part of national educational planning, curriculum development and school organisation'.[10]

The major next step was the UNESCO World Conference on Special Needs Education: Access and Equality held in 1994, where for the first time specific attention was paid to the goal of inclusive education.[11] The ensuing Salamanca Statement and Framework for Action on Special Needs Education (Salamanca

[4] The latter aspect is provided for both by Article 13(3) of the ICESCR and by Article 18(4) of the International Covenant on Civil and Political Rights.

[5] CESCR Committee, *General Comment No 13: The Right to Education (Art. 13)*, 8 December 1999, E/C.12/1999/10; CESCR Committee, *General Comment No 11: Plans of Action for Primary Education (Art. 14)*, 10 May 1999, E/C.12/1999/4.

[6] CRC Committee, *General Comment No 1: The Aims of Education (Art. 29(1))*, 17 April 2001, CRC/GC/2001/1.

[7] Convention against Discrimination in Education (1962) 429 UNTS 93.

[8] Articles 2(1) and 23, CRC.

[9] Article 3(5), Jomtien Declaration.

[10] Rule 6(1), Standard Rules.

[11] World Conference on Special Needs Education: Access and Equality, *Salamanca Statement and Framework for Action on Special Needs Education*, 7–10 June 1994; available at: https://unesdoc.unesco.org/ark:/48223/pf0000098427.

Statement) stated that 'those with special educational needs must have access to regular schools which should accommodate them within a child-centred pedagogy capable of meeting these needs'.[12] It also provided for a series of steps to be taken in order to achieve inclusive education even though they were not legally binding. By acknowledging the need for accommodating all types of pupils in the general education system, these international instruments paved the way for the right of disabled children to education.

There were nonetheless still doubts about whether inclusion was to be the preferred option in every circumstance. The Salamanca Statement urged States 'to adopt as a matter of law or policy the principle of inclusive education, ... unless there are compelling reasons for doing otherwise'.[13] The Standard Rules went further by providing that '[i]n situations where the general school system does not yet adequately meet the needs of all persons with disabilities, special education may be considered'.[14] This wording not just legitimised exceptions to the rule, but it also diluted the meaning of inclusive education itself.

Shortly before the CRPD's adoption (during the very course of the Ad Hoc Committee's discussions on the content ofthen Article 17), the CRC Committee issued its general comment on the situation of disabled children. In this general comment, it expressed the view that inclusive education 'should be the goal of educating children with disabilities'.[15] This was the clearest assertion of this goal so far by any treaty body. Yet, the general comment also reflected differences with regard to the education of disabled people. The CRC Committee indeed considered that 'the measure in which the inclusion occurs, may vary' and that '[a] continuum of services and programme options must be maintained in circumstances where fully inclusive education is not feasible to achieve in the immediate future'.[16] It was thus still unclear what the standards concerning education would be in the future convention.

6.1.2 Article 24 of the CRPD

The right to education is of utmost importance for all human beings. This right works as a multiplier for it enhances both economic and social rights, such as the right to work and right to food, and civil and political rights, such as the right to vote and freedom of expression. This is particularly true for disabled people who will remain on the margins of society unless they receive adequate education. The

[12] Para 2, Salamanca Statement.
[13] Para 3, Salamanca Statement.
[14] Rule 6(3), Standard Rules.
[15] CRC Committee, *General Comment No 9: The Rights of Children with Disabilities*, 27 February 2007, CRC/C/GC/9, para 66.
[16] Ibid.

right to education empowers them to take control of their lives and facilitates their full participation in society. The issue was the subject of a resolution by the UN Human Rights Council (HRC) in 2014.[17] It received even greater attention following the adoption of a general comment by the CRPD Committee entitled 'The Right to Inclusive Education' in 2016.[18]

Article 24(1) of the CRPD proclaims that 'States Parties recognize the right of persons with disabilities to education'. It goes on to provide that '[w]ith a view to realizing this right ... States Parties shall ensure an inclusive education system at all levels and life long learning'. This is the ideal towards which they must strive by committing a sufficient level of resources based on an appropriate educational strategy. By incorporating the goal of inclusive education into international human rights law, the CRPD has endorsed the right to inclusive education. Article 24(2) of the Convention not only prohibits the exclusion of disabled people from education but also sets outs what must be done in order to realise the right to inclusive education.

The road to Article 24 has not been easy though. The education of disabled people sparked heated debate during the negotiation process, and the right to education was discussed at length by the Ad Hoc Committee. It was only towards the end of the Convention's negotiation process that its drafters agreed upon the goal of inclusive education.

A core point of contention was whether special education had still to be made available by the States Parties. Discussions concentrated on parents' right to choose the form of education for their children. While some considered that special education should continue to exist, others considered that inclusive education should always constitute the norm.[19]

Consensus started to emerge that inclusive education should be rule for disabled people even though special education could still be provided for them if their needs so required.[20] Following a final version circulated by the facilitator,[21] the negotiating parties eventually agreed to drop this exception to the rule. It was decided that inclusive education had to feature as an explicit guarantee for all disabled people. By stipulating that 'States Parties shall ensure an inclusive education system at all levels and lifelong learning',[22] the Convention put aside the reservations expressed in earlier international instruments.[23] More than two decades after

[17] HRC, *The Right to Education of Persons with Disabilities*, 24 March 2014, A/HRC/25/L.30.

[18] CRPD Committee, *General Comment No 4. Article 24: Right to Inclusive Education*, 2 September 2016, CRPD/C/GC/4.

[19] B. Byrne, 'Hidden Contradictions and Conditionality: Conceptualisations of Inclusive Education in International Human Rights Law' (2013) 28 *Disability & Society* 332, 239.

[20] G. de Beco, 'Comprehensive Legal Analysis of Article 24 of the Convention on the Rights of Persons with Disabilities' in G. de Beco, J. Lord and S. Quinlivan (eds), *The Right to Inclusive Education in International Human Rights Law* (Cambridge: Cambridge University Press, 2019) 58, 65.

[21] Report of the Working Group to the Ad Hoc Committee, 17 August 2005, A/60/266.

[22] Article 24(1), CRPD.

[23] The Centre for Studies on Inclusive Education's proposal to explicitly prohibit segregation was nonetheless rejected by the Convention's drafters (B. Shaw, 'Inclusion or Choice? Securing the Right to

the Salamanca Statement, the goal of inclusive education was given a legal basis in international human rights law.

Article 24 of the CRPD is therefore silent on special schools. It neither compels States Parties to maintain such schools, nor does it demand that all disabled children attend regular schools. The Convention simply does not use such terms as 'special schools' or 'regular schools'. It expresses a strong preference for inclusiveness, but it apparently leaves open the possibility of alternative ways to educate disabled people. This lack of indication as to whether special schools are contravening international human rights law even now continues to raise controversy about the potential benefits of inclusive education. It not only shows the difficult position in which the Convention's drafters found themselves but also the challenges that still lie ahead in reducing the availability of special schools.

The question, then, is what States Parties must do in order to realise the right to inclusive education. The CRPD stipulates that they must ensure that '[p]ersons with disabilities are not excluded from the general education system on the basis of disability'.[24] Refusal to enrol a child on such a basis results in direct discrimination, which can be precluded through a so-called 'non-rejection clause'.[25] Courts in different jurisdictions have condemned the denial of education to disabled children who are considered to be 'uneducable', including in the US (which led to the enactment of the Individuals with Disabilities Education Act of 1990 (IDEA)) and Ireland.[26] The Convention further requires that States Parties ensure that 'children with disabilities are not excluded from free and compulsory primary education, or from secondary education'. It thereby echoes both the ICESCR and the CRC,[27] although it makes less differentiation between the different levels of education.[28] The CRPD also provides that '[p]ersons with disabilities can access an inclusive, quality and free primary education and secondary education ... in the communities in which they live'.[29] Infrastructure, including classrooms and toilets, as well as transport to school must therefore be made fully accessible to them.[30] The right to

Inclusive Education for All' in M. Sabatello and M. Schulze (eds), *Human Rights & Disability Advocacy* (Philadelphia: University of Pennsylvania Press, 2013) 58, 63).

[24] Articles 24(2)(a), CRPD.

[25] OHCHR, *Thematic Study on the Right of Persons with Disabilities to Education*, 18 December 2013, A/HRC/25/29, para 26.

[26] US District Court E.D. Pennsylvania, *Pennsylvania Association for Retarded Children (PARC) v Pennsylvania* 343 F Supp 279 (E.D. Pa 1972); US District Court Columbia, *Mills v Board of Education* 348 F Supp 866 (D.D.C. 1972); Irish High Court, *O'Donoghue v Minister for Health* [1996] 2 IR 20.

[27] Article 13(2)(a) (b), ICESCR; Article 28(1)(a) and (b), CRC.

[28] de Beco, 'Comprehensive Legal Analysis of Article 24 of the Convention on the Rights of Persons with Disabilities', 71.

[29] Article 24(2)(b), CRPD.

[30] UNICEF Innocenti Research Centre, *Promoting the Rights of Children with Disabilities* (Florence: UNICEF, 2007) 16–17; Inclusion International, *Better Education for all When We are Included Too. A Global Report. People with an Intellectual Disability and their Families Speak out on Education for All, Disability and Inclusive Education*, October 2009, 82; available at: http://ii.gmalik.com/pdfs/Better_Education_for_All_Global_Report_October_2009.pdf.

inclusive education calls for removing all the obstacles, of whatever kind, that disabled children face in accessing education.

States Parties must furthermore guarantee that '[r]easonable accommodation of the individual's requirements is provided'.[31] The duty to provide reasonable accommodation is thus not only enunciated with regard to all the rights protected by the CRPD,[32] but is also repeated in relation to education.[33] The CRPD Committee has affirmed that the provision of such accommodation should not only be cost-free, but also that it should be made straight away upon request by any disabled person,[34] and this applies to both public and private actors. States Parties must ensure that reasonable accommodation is in fact provided to disabled children and set out the obligation to do that in their national legislation. The CRPD considers that refusal to do this is a form of discrimination,[35] as confirmed by the European Court of Human Rights in the context of education.[36]

One category of disabled people which expressed serious concerns about the goal of inclusive education was deaf, blind or deaf-blind people. The World Blind Union (WBU), World Federation of the Deaf (WFD) and Deafblind International (DbI) insisted that different forms of education should continue to be made available during the negotiation process given that there is 'no one educational solution that is suitable for all deaf, blind and deafblind children'.[37] The Convention therefore stipulates that States Parties must ensure that 'the education of persons, and in particular children, who are blind, deaf or deaf-blind, is delivered ... in environments which maximize academic and social development'.[38] Although the phrase 'in environments which maximize academic and social development' can be understood as code for special education – called the 'sensory exception' –,[39] the CRPD Committee has interpreted it as meaning education in mainstream settings.[40] It is probably one of the most delicate provisions of the entire CRPD.

[31] Article 24(2)(c), CRPD.

[32] Article 5(3), CRPD.

[33] It is even repeated twice, as Article 24(5), which is related to higher education, also requires 'that reasonable accommodation is provided to persons with disabilities'.

[34] CRPD Committee, *General Comment No 4. Article 24*, paras 23 and 27.

[35] Article 2, CRPD.

[36] European Court of Human Rights, *Çam v Turkey*, 23 May 2016, Appl No 51500/08, para 68. See also European Court of Human Rights, *Enver Şahin v Turkey*, 30 January 2018, Appl No 23065/12, para 60.

[37] WBU, WFD and DbI, 'Article 17 Statement on Inclusive Education for Persons who are Deaf, Blind and Deafblind: The Rationale for Choice in Education'; available at: https://static.un.org/esa/socdev/enable/rights/ahcstata24sevscomments.htm#multi.

[38] Article 24(3)(c), CRPD.

[39] J. Murray, M. De Meulder and D. le Maire, 'An Education in Sign Language as a Human Right?: The Sensory Exception in the Legislative History and Ongoing Interpretation of Article 24 of the UN Convention on the Rights of Persons with Disabilities' (2018) 40 *Human Rights Quarterly* 37, 45–6.

[40] B. Byrne, 'Dis-Equality: Exploring the Juxtaposition of Disability and Equality' (2018) 6 *Social Inclusion* 9, 12.

Blind, deaf or deaf-blind people are the only category explicitly mentioned in this Convention with the exception of the reference to 'physical, mental, intellectual or sensory impairments'.[41]

Those who are deaf often self-identify as members of a cultural and linguistic community and view sign language as more than a tool of communication.[42] As such, they lay claim to a distinct identity associated with 'Deaf culture', and this was also taken up in the CRPD.[43] Pointing to the failure of education systems to meet their needs, they argued in favour of special schools offering deaf children the opportunity to sustain relations with their peers.[44] More recently, it has been shown how different models of 'bilingual education' can achieve participation in the general education system in accordance with the Convention.[45] While further study is needed in order to establish what the right to inclusive education actually means for deaf, blind or deaf-blind people, their position on the issue reveals that it should not impose assimilation on them but favour communication in their preferred language as widely as possible.

6.1.3 The CRPD's New Emphasis

Disabled children are particularly excluded from education. In many parts of the world, these children cannot go to school because of their disability.[46] In high-income countries, most of them are educated in special schools.[47] Besides leading to the segregation of disabled children, the special schools offer them a lower standard of education and decrease their prospects of employment.

Through its requirement to enable disabled children to participate in the general education system, the CRPD has placed a new emphasis on the right to education. The Convention not only proclaims the right to inclusive education but also lays down what is required for its fulfilment. While Article 24 does not define the concept of inclusive education itself, it spells out what should be the aims of

[41] Article 1, CRPD.

[42] S. Battersbury, 'Language justice for Sign Language Peoples: the UN Convention on the Rights of Persons with Disabilities' (2012) 11 *Language Policy* 253, 256–8.

[43] Article 30(4) of the CRPD stipulates that disabled people should be 'entitled ... to recognition and support of their specific cultural and linguistic identity, including sign languages and deaf culture'. Note that 'deaf' is without capital letter here.

[44] R. Kayess and J. Green, 'Today's Lesson is on Diversity: A Reflection on Inclusive Education' in P. Blanck and E. Flynn (eds), *Routledge Handbook of Disability Law and Human Rights* (London: Routledge, 2016) 53, 66.

[45] J. Murray et al, 'Intersectional Inclusion for Deaf Learners: Moving beyond General Comment no. 4 on Article 24 of the United Nations Convention on the Rights of Persons with Disabilities' (2018) 24 *International Journal of Inclusive Education* 691, 699–701.

[46] UNICEF, *The State of the World's Children 2013*. Children with disabilities (New York: UNICEF, 2013) 27–8.

[47] UNICEF Innocenti Research Centre, *Promoting the Rights of Children with Disabilities*, 17.

the 'inclusive education system' to be developed towards this end. In doing so, the Convention has expanded upon similar provisions from both the ICESCR and the CRC. It is therefore possible to draw inspiration from those provisions, not only to understand the right to inclusive education itself but also to determine how the CRPD through recognising this right has fine-tuned the right to education for disabled people.

According to the Convention, the aims of establishing an 'inclusive education system' ought to be threefold.

First, the 'inclusive education system' should 'be directed' to '[t]he full development of human potential and sense of dignity and self-worth, and the strengthening of respect for human rights, fundamental freedoms and human diversity'.[48] This provision is a replication of the ICESCR,[49] to which have been added the terms 'self-worth' and 'human diversity'. While 'self-worth' is important to counter the image of disabled children as inferior, 'human diversity' reflects the Convention's general principle of fostering the 'acceptance of persons with disabilities as part of human diversity and humanity'.[50]

Second, the CRPD stipulates that the 'inclusive education system' should strive for '[t]he development by persons with disabilities of their personality, talents and creativity, as well as their mental and physical abilities, to their fullest potential'.[51] This is largely copied from the CRC.[52] The CRPD Committee has recommended that States parties 'support the creation of opportunities to build on the unique strengths and talents of each individual with a disability.[53] The CRC Committee also stated that education concerns 'the broad range of life experiences and learning processes which enable children ... to develop their personalities, talents and abilities.'[54] The right to inclusive education therefore entails having those 'personalities, talents and abilities' enhanced rather than using these as justification for segregating those who are disabled.

Third, the 'inclusive education system' should aim at '[e]nabling persons with disabilities to participate effectively in a free society'.[55] The ICESCR provides for the same aim,[56] but the CRPD has expanded its meaning insofar as '[f]ull and effective participation and inclusion in society' is one of its general principles.[57] 'Full and effective participation and inclusion' embodies the deeper purpose of inclusive education, which is to equip disabled children to face adult life challenges

48 Article 24(1)(a), CRPD.
49 Article 13(1), ICESCR.
50 Article 3(d), CRPD.
51 Article 24(1)(b), CRPD.
52 Article 29(1)(a), CRC.
53 CRPD Committee, *General Comment No 4. Article 24*, para 16.
54 CRPD Committee, *General Comment No 1*, para 2.
55 Article 24(1)(c), CRPD.
56 Article 13(1), ICESCR.
57 Article 3(c), CRPD.

and to foster relations with those who are non-disabled. Inversely, inclusive education may itself be a vehicle to the improvement of social attitudes towards disabled people.

In light of this, the CRPD requires working through the entire process of transforming the education system so that disabled children can effectively be educated alongside any other children. Rather than enrolling these children in regular schools without making further adjustments,[58] inclusive education involves 'a process of systemic reform embodying changes and modifications in content, teaching methods, approaches, structures and strategies in education'.[59] Thus, the Convention is concerned with the development of an 'inclusive education system' that is not only responsive to the varied needs of disabled children but also embraces human difference in all its various aspects.

Amongst the measures to be adopted in order to achieve inclusive education, two are particularly important. These are the support of disabled children and the training of staff members, which are covered by Article 24. Each contributes to realising the right to inclusive education in its own way.

First, the CRPD stipulates that disabled people must 'receive the support required within the general education system, to facilitate their effective education'.[60] This support can take the form of specific equipment, such as Braille and sign-language, or of 'a qualified learning support assistant, either shared or on a one-to-one basis.[61] As emphasised by the phrase 'within the general education system', it must be provided by regular schools, for instance, by means of an individual education plan.[62] The fact that most resources for disabled children are allocated to special schools indeed complicates this objective. In order to realise the right to inclusive education, governments must transfer these resources from the special schools to the regular schools.[63]

The Convention furthermore requires that States Parties ensure that '[e]ffective individualised support measures are provided in environments that maximize academic and social development, consistent with the goal of full inclusion'.[64] At first sight, this seems to repeat the provision mentioned above. While both provisions were originally part of a single paragraph,[65] their wording

[58] G. Thomas, 'Inclusive Schools for an Inclusive Society' (1997) 24 *British Journal of Special Education* 103, 103; A. Liasidou, *Inclusive Education, Politics and Policymaking* (London: Continuum, 2012) 8–9.

[59] CRPD Committee, *General Comment No 4. Article 24*, para 11.

[60] Article 24(2)(d), CRPD.

[61] CRPD Committee, *General Comment No 4. Article 24*, para 32.

[62] OHCHR, *Thematic Study on the Right of Persons with Disabilities to Education*, 46–7.

[63] G. de Beco, 'The Right to Inclusive Education According to Article 24 of the UN Convention on the Rights of Persons with Disabilities: Background, Requirements and (Remaining) Questions' (2014) 32 *Netherlands Quarterly of Human Rights* 263, 277.

[64] Article 24(2)(e), CRPD.

[65] de Beco, 'Comprehensive Legal Analysis of Article 24 of the Convention on the Rights of Persons with Disabilities', 81–2.

varies in a number of ways. One simply mentions 'support', whereas the other refers to 'individualised support'. Another difference is the phrase 'in environments which maximize academic and social development'. While this phrase replaced the 'effective alternative support ... where the general education system can not adequately meet the support needs of persons with disabilities' in the initial version,[66] it also comes up in the provision relating to 'blind, deaf or deaf-blind people' discussed earlier.[67] The obligation to provide 'individualized support' then would allow for even more individualisation of the measures. The Convention nonetheless adds that the support must be 'consistent with the goal of full inclusion'.[68] In other words, this support should not lead to segregating disabled children despite any ambiguity.

Second, the CRPD stipulates that States Parties must 'employ teachers, including teachers with disabilities, who are qualified in sign language and/or Braille, and to train professionals and staff who work at all levels of education'.[69] Featuring again – implicitly – blind, deaf or deaf-blind people, this provision reveals that training is an essential part of inclusive education. As stated by the CRPD Committee, States Parties must 'ensure that all teachers are trained in inclusive education'.[70] The Convention specifies that '[s]uch training shall incorporate disability awareness and the use of appropriate augmentative and alternative modes, means and formats of communication, educational techniques and materials to support persons with disabilities'.[71] It is probably the starting point of developing any 'inclusive education system' by the State Party, as the implementation of new teaching methods will take some time.

The Convention emphasises another key element concerning the right to inclusive education. It underscores that the corpus of staff members should encompass people who are disabled themselves (through its reference to 'teachers with disabilities'). The employment of disabled teachers is not only a way to actually involve disabled people in the steps taken but also a stepping stone towards obtaining greater knowledge of how to achieve inclusive education. According to the CRPD Committee, such teachers can 'bring unique expertise and skills into learning envionments, contribute to breaking down barriers and serve as important role models'.[72] For this to be done though, it is necessary to include more disabled people in teacher programmes and encourage them to enter the profession in the first place.

66 Six Session of the Ad Hoc Committee, *Article 24. Consolidation of Proposals Submitted by the Facilitator*; available at https://www.un.org/esa/socdev/enable/rights/ahcstata24ssfacilitator.htm.
67 Article 24(3)(c), CRPD.
68 Article 24(2)(e), CRPD.
69 Article 24(4), CRPD.
70 CRPD Committee, *General Comment No 4. Article 24*, para 35.
71 Article 24(4), CRPD.
72 CRPD Committee, *General Comment No 4. Article 24*, para 36.

6.2 Implications for International Human Rights Law

6.2.1 The Universality of Inclusive Education

Inclusive education is not just about disabled children. Not only are all children entitled to education, but also efforts to pursue inclusiveness appertains to all of them. Leaving non-disabled children aside in those efforts in fact undermines the very idea of inclusion. In addition, research has demonstrated that inclusive education is equally good for them.[73]

The CRPD Committee seems to agree with this view. It considers that '[t]he right to inclusive education . . . involves strengthening the capacity of the education system to reach out to *all learners*'.[74] It further envisages that '[i]nclusive education is to be understood as . . . [a] fundamental human right of *all learners*'.[75] Going a step further, the Special Rapporteur on the Right to Education reckons that inclusive education is not only about children who are disabled but also about 'students with different cultural and linguistic backgrounds or, in general, any student who requires additional support to succeed in the education system'.[76]

This universality of inclusive education is in keeping with the CRPD. Article 24 of the Convention again provides that 'the right of persons with disabilities to education' is to be realised by ensuring 'an inclusive education system at all levels and life long learning'.[77] States Parties must thus realise this right *through* the establishment of such 'an inclusive education system'. This requires the whole organisation of education to be rethought, which cannot but touch upon the entire school population. Indeed, a unique focus on disabled children is hardly practicable if the goal of inclusive education is ever to be attained. It faces the obstacle that disability can be experienced in a multitude of ways bearing on every single child and rendering untenable any dichotomy between able and disabled. The development of an 'inclusive education system' concentrated exclusively around the particular needs of disabled children would depend on strict decisions as to who are its actual beneficiaries, thereby artificially treating such children as if they formed a discrete and homogenous group.

Such a view is furthermore compatible with the social model of disability. Although this model is centred on those with impairments, it shifts attention away

[73] C. Causton-Theoharis et al, 'Schools of Promise: A School District – University Partnership Centered on Inclusive School Reform' (2011) 32 *Remedial and Special Education* 192; R. Martyn and L. Florian, 'Inclusion and Achievement: Student Achievement in Secondary Schools with Higher and Lower Proportions of Pupils Designated as Having Special Educational Needs' (2006) 10 *International Journal of Inclusive Education* 481.

[74] CRPD Committee, *General Comment No 4. Article 24*, para 9 (emphasis added).

[75] Ibid, para 10 (emphasis added).

[76] B. Boly Barry, Report of the Special Rapporteur on the *Right to Education*, 29 September 2017, A/72/496, para 26.

[77] Article 24(1), CRPD.

from these impairments to the barriers embedded in society. It exposes how the education systems themselves fall short of catering for different types of pupils by categorising them as if they were inherently less capable than others. Seeing inclusive education as universal is consistent with the social model's proposition to modify the environment itself, conceding that it is the organisation of education that stands in the way of its achievement.

The right to inclusive education applies to all children alike – to disabled children first but to all other children as well. For instance, education systems often lack consideration for the linguistic and cultural particularities of children from racial minorities.[78] Being labelled as disabled, these children are likely to suffer from the same prejudices as disabled children. This happens to boys more than to girls, thereby adding a gender dimension to the issue.[79] An example is Roma children who are frequently referred to special schools in Eastern European countries, a practice condemned on several occasions by the European Court of Human Rights.[80] The education systems should provide these children with the means of enhancing their skills and abilities instead of regarding their human differences as constituting a motive for segregation. By acknowledging the complexity of human diversity, regular schools should be in a better position to meet the needs of every single child.

The expansion of inclusive education towards including all children highlights the need for avoiding labels that single out some types of pupil.[81] While labels can be necessary to assess disabled children's needs, by the same token it assigns them deficiencies.[82] Disabled children often try and resist such labelling even though they may be conscious of the barriers that confront them in education.[83] In this regard, some scholars have criticised the reference to 'individualised support' in the CRPD,[84] because it escalates 'the difficulties children themselves have with legitimised practices of teaching and learning'.[85] In order to avoid stigmatisation, it is essential to make any provision of support part of States Parties' overall educational

[78] G. de Beco, 'Intersectionality and Disability in International Human Rights Law' (2020) 24 *International Journal of Human Rights* 593, 604.

[79] S. Tomlinson, 'Special Education and Minority Ethnic Young People in England. Continuing Issues' (2015) 37 *Discourse: Studies in the Culture and Politics of Education* 513, 514 and 522; S. Strand and G. Lindsay, Ethnic Disproportionality in Special Education: Evidence from an English Population Study' (2009) 43 *Journal of Special Education* 174, 175.

[80] European Court of Human Rights, *D.H. and others v Czech Republic*, 13 November 2007, Appl No 57325/00; *Sampanis and others v Greece*, 5 June 2008, Appl No 32526/05; *Oršuš and others v Croatia*, 16 March 2010, Appl No 15766/03; *Horváth and Kiss v Hungary*, 29 January 2013, Appl No 11146/11.

[81] J. Florian and J. Spratt, 'Enacting Inclusion: a Framework for Interrogating Inclusive Practice' (2013) 28 *European Journal of Special Needs Education* 119, 122 and 133.

[82] J. Ravet, Inclusive/Exclusive? Contradictory Perspectives on Autism and Inclusion: The Case for an Integrative Position' (2011) 15 *International Journal of Inclusive Education* 667, 669–71.

[83] C. Connors and K. Stalkers, 'Children's Experiences of Disability: Pointers to a Social Model of Childhood Disability' (2007) 22 *Disability & Society* 19, 31.

[84] Article 24(2)(d), CRPD.

[85] Byrne, 'Hidden Contradictions and Conditionality', 241.

strategy. Such provision must take the form of responses that are problem- rather than person-orientated, not only in order to be practicable but also to preserve esteem. Those responses will furthermore have greater legitimacy in the eyes of others.[86]

Despite its value, it can be argued that this view may result in applying the right to inclusive education at the expense of disabled children, as it might lose sight of their real needs. The risk inherent in over-accentuating inclusive education's universality is that those real needs actually remain unmet. The argument is employed by those who are suspicious of a right to inclusive education and who see in special schools still the best solution for many disabled children.[87]

A closer look reveals that the CRPD restricts the right to inclusive education to disabled children. This is the case not only with the provision of reasonable accommodation but also with the guarantee of access to education. The Convention stipulates that States Parties must ensure that that 'persons with disabilities can access an inclusive, quality and free primary education and secondary education',[88] which reinforces the goal of inclusive education with reference to 'persons with disabilities'. The guarantee of access to education is made explicitly to them, although it requires the adoption of measures that are general in nature. As explained by the CRPD Committee, '[a]ccessibility is related to groups, whereas reasonable accommodation is related to individuals'.[89] Both may overlap though, since the provision of reasonable accommodation 'can be used as a means of ensuring accessibility for [a disabled person] in a particular situation'.[90]

Accessibility in respect of education has been understood as a matter of non-discrimination or as relating to physical and economic obstacles by the CESCR Committee.[91] In international human rights law, it calls for both compliance with the prohibition of discrimination and improving school location and affordability.[92] The CRPD has extended this understanding by prescribing the adoption of

[86] S. Lynch and A. Irvine, 'Inclusive Education and Best Practice for Children with Autism Spectrum Disorder: An Integrated Approach' (2009) 13 *International Journal of Inclusive Education* 845, 853–4.

[87] G. Hornby, 'Inclusive Special Education: Development of a New Theory for the Education of Children with Special Educational Needs and Disabilities' (2015) 42 *British Journal of Special Education* 234, 239–40; J. Kauffman and J. Badar, 'It's Instruction over Place – Not the Other Way Around!' (2017) 98 *Phi Delta Kaplan* 55, 56–7; D. Anastasiou and J. Kauffman, 'Disability as Cultural Difference: Implications for Special Education' (2012) 33 Remedial and Special Education 139, 143–4.

[88] Article 24(2)(b), CRPD.

[89] CRPD Committee, *General Comment No 2. Article 9: Accessibility*, 22 May 2014, CRPD/C/GC/2, para 25.

[90] Ibid, para 26.

[91] CESCR Committee, *General Comment No 13: The Right to Education (Art. 13)*, para 6.

[92] B. Saul, D. Kinley and J. Mowbray, *The International Covenant on Economic, Social and Cultural Rights. Commentary, Cases, and Materials* (Oxford: Oxford University Press, 2014) 1097; C. Courtis and J. Tobin, *'Article 28. The Right to Education'* in J. Tobin, *The UN Convention on the Rights of the Child. A Commentary* (Oxford: Oxford University Press, 2019) 1056, 1068–9. See also M. Verheyde, *A Commentary on the United Nations Convention on the Rights of the Child. Article 28. The Right to Education* (Leiden/Boston Martinus Nijhoff, 2006) 17–19; T. Tomasevski, *Education Denied. Cost and Remedies* (London/New York: Zed Books, 2003) 51.

'measures to ensure to people with disabilities access to the physical environment, to transportation, to information and communications, including information and communications technologies and systems'.[93] Such measures are fundamental for the realisation of all Convention rights. As highlighted by the CRPD Committee, accessibility is 'the precondition for persons with disabilities to live independently, participate fully and equally in society, and have unrestricted enjoyment of all their human rights'.[94] It is also one of the Convention's general principles,[95] which explicitly refers to 'schools' in this regard.[96]

Access to education in the CRPD, therefore, has a broader reach than the notion of accessibility – in the narrow sense – under international human rights law, but this broader reach only relates to disabled people. It is not just about issues like infrastructure and transport as well as different kinds of cost, or only a matter of non-discrimination. Rather, it touches upon the delivery of education as a whole. In the words of the CRPD Committee, '[t]he entire education system must be accessible',[97] which applies to 'not just buildings, but all information and communication' and also the '[m]odes and means of teaching'.[98] Seen in such a way, accessibility covers certain aspects of the right to inclusive education that do remain specific to disability.

While the right to inclusive education contains disability-specific aspects, in the same manner it does not cover any challenges that learners may encounter in regular schools. Both the ICESCR and the CRC provide for the standards that States have chosen for that purpose. The right to inclusive education is there to protect all children whose actual learning experience is undermined by the education system's disregard for human differences. Although education can raise many questions with respect to human rights (such as those about gender, religion, sexual identity and so on), it is exclusion from education for those kinds of reasons that the right to inclusive education seeks to eliminate.

What the CRPD nonetheless can do is to give new direction to international human rights law through the elevation of the right to education itself. Such elevation can be illustrated by the case of children belonging to linguistic minorities, which has parallels with deaf children who also qualify in some sense. A system of 'bilingual education' can actually be advantageous to all children alike even though it empowers explicitly specifically only some of them.[99] The CRPD thus stresses the need for all of the education systems to acknowledge the importance of respect for

[93] Article 9(1), CRPD.
[94] CRPD Committee, *General Comment No 2. Article 9: Accessibility*, para 14.
[95] Article 3(f), CRPD.
[96] Article 9(1)(a), CRPD.
[97] CRPD Committee, *General Comment No 4. Article 24*, para 8.
[98] CRPD Committee, *General Comment No 2. Article 9: Accessibility*, para 39.
[99] D. Réaume, 'Individuals, Groups, and Rights to Public Goods' (1998) 38 *University of Toronto Law Journal* 1, 18–19.

human diversity and to provide adequate support for all types of pupils so as to facilitate social interaction.

6.2.2 Closing the Gap

While human rights treaties protected the right to education in general, they did not provide for a right to *inclusive* education. The segregation of particular types of pupils was not a matter of rights. It did not even amount to discrimination as there was no denial of education as such and segregation could be justified on 'separate-but-equal' grounds. In 1954, in the *Brown vs Board of Education* case, the US Supreme Court, ruling that segregation on the basis of race was unconstitutional, considered that '[s]eparate educational facilities are inherently unequal'.[100] This consideration was yet to be extended to disabled children who very often were confined to separate settings, if educated at all.

The right to inclusive education, therefore, was unknown to international human rights law. The Standard Rules and Salamanca Statement – which were adopted in the early 1990s – constituted a step towards recognising such a right. However, not only were they not legally binding, but they also used rather non-committal language.

The CRC itself did not explicitly consider disability in relation to education. Its separate article on disabled children was aimed more at offering assistance than guaranteeing inclusion.[101] The Convention still contains a list of values informing the 'preparation of the child for responsible life',[102] which encourage an attitude of tolerance towards all people regardless of any characteristic.[103] Although it upheld the goal of inclusive education in its general comment on the situation of disabled children, the CRC Committee still allowed for exceptions to the rule.[104] The CRPD soon hereafter set aside those exceptions by endorsing the right to inclusive education.

Until then, disabled people's right to education had been secured through the prohibition of discrimination. This prohibition mainly served as a lens when considering the question of disability under international human rights law,[105] although it did not provide disabled people with adequate human rights protection.[106]

[100] US Supreme Court, *Brown vs Board of Education of Topeka* 347 US 483 (1954) 495.
[101] Article 23, CRC.
[102] Article 29(1)(d), CRC. This list has not been taken over in the CRPD.
[103] L. Lundy and J. Tobin, 'Article 29. The Aims of Education' in *J. Tobin (ed.), The UN Convention on the Rights of the Child. A Commentary* (Oxford: Oxford University Press, 2019) 1116, 1142–5.
[104] CRC Committee, *General Comment No 9: The Rights of Children with Disabilities*, para 66.
[105] Saul, Kinley and Mowbray, *The International Covenant on Economic, Social and Cultural Rights*, 1010–11.
[106] C. O'Cinneide, 'Extracting Protection for the Rights of Persons with Disabilities' in O. Arnardóttir and G. Quinn (eds), *The UN Convention on the Rights of Persons with Disabilities. European and Scandinavian Perspectives* (2009) 163, 172–3.

While the CRC mentioned 'disability' in its general non-discrimination clause for the first time in a human rights treaty,[107] it again offered disabled people a kind of 'separate-but-equal' status.

By proclaiming the right to inclusive education, the CRPD has done more than ensuring the equal treatment of disabled people. While the focus hitherto had been on the quality of the education in order to enhance skills and abilities, the CRPD has integrated the idea of inclusion into the existing right to education. It goes further than combating discrimination on the basis of disability as it sets out the requirements with a view to creating accessible educational environments.

The reality is that change on the ground remains low notwithstanding the Convention's high level of ratification. Barriers are hard to overcome both in low-income countries, where resources are an ongoing challenge, and in high-income countries, where disabled children continue to be segregated. While most State Parties have changed their national legislation so that disabled children can enrol in regular schools, there are no or, at most, limited resources to make it work. The support to be provided is missing or inadequate compared to those children's needs.[108] Most teachers employed in regular schools also are not equipped to deal with issues related to disability.[109]

The question is: What can be done in order to bring improvement? There is widespread resistance to inclusive education. Disabled children often feel unaccepted by regular schools and are even subject to violence, including harassment and bullying.[110] Worrying that they will be mistreated, their parents prefer special schools for them.[111] In a recent case about a child with Down syndrome who had been referred to a special school, the CRPD Committee urged the State Party to '[c]onduct an effective investigation into the allegations of abuse and discrimination', which had rendered the school a hostile place to learn.[112] From the teachers' perspective, staff members face a lot of pressure from above that makes their work difficult.[113] They fear being unable cope with disabled children, which fear is further fuelled by the fact that the tests that are used to measure educational attainment are very much inappropriate for inclusive education.[114]

[107] Articles 2(1), CRC.

[108] Inclusion International, *Better Education for All: When We're Included Too*, 65–6.

[109] UNICEF, *The State of the World's Children 2013*, 32.

[110] M. Rioux and P. Pinto, 'A Time for the Universal Right to Education: Back to the Basics' (2010) 31 *British Journal of Sociology of Education* 621, 630–1.

[111] Global Campaign for Education and Handicap International, *Equal Right, Equal Opportunity. Inclusive Education for Children with Disabilities*, 2013, 26; available at: http://www.campaignforeducation.org/docs/reports/Equal%20Right,%20Equal%20Opportunity_WEB.pdf.

[112] CRPD Committee, *Calleja Loma and Calleja Lucas v Spain*, 30 September 2020, CRPD/C/23/D/41/2017, para 9(iii).

[113] UNICEF, *The State of the World's Children 2013*, 33.

[114] A. Liasidou, 'Inclusive Education and Critical Pedagogy at the Intersections of Disability, Race, Gender and Class' (2012) 10 *Journal for Critical Education Policy Studies* 168, 175.

What is therefore needed is to transform the education system in order to enable regular schools to accommodate human differences. Instead of segregating disabled children, States Parties should remove the obstacles by bringing these children back to the centre. One particular way of following through is using Universal Design for Learning (UDL). The CRPD itself commits States Parties to support 'research and development of universally designed goods, services, equipment and facilities' which do not require further adaptations as far as possible.[115] As stated by the CRPD Committee, UDL implies providing 'a structure to create adaptable learning environments and develop instruction to meet the diverse needs of all learners'.[116] Another critical area is changing social attitudes towards disabled people, which is pivotal to pursuing inclusiveness. The CRPD itself provides for awareness-raising through '[f]ostering at all levels of the education system ... an attitude of respect for the rights of persons with disabilities'.[117] Without combating stereotypes surrounding disability, solutions for making the education system more inclusive risk to be futile.

While there is clearly little or no goodwill on the part of governments, the question is still whether a state of inclusiveness as imagined in the CRPD – and proffered by the CRPD Committee – can ever be translated into reality. A number of scholars have pointed out the flaws in thinking that regular schools should be able to educate all disabled children.[118] Impairments can vary indefinitely and, whatever progress is made, some obstacles will remain in the path of realising the right to inclusive education. The issue is particularly acute when it comes to cognitive impairments. Be that as it may, this is no reason to halt progress, as challenges encountered should not narrow or set limits to the goal of inclusive education itself.[119]

Having said this, the right to inclusive education constitutes a significant evolution in the field of international human rights law. The obligations which this right creates pose difficulties for the States Parties, especially regarding these resources that have been made available for special schools and now have to be allocated to bring about inclusion.[120] More fundamentally, inclusive education puts into questioning the emphasis on literacy and numeracy skills as well as the sciences.[121] Such emphasis requires that all children adapt themselves to live up to the same

[115] Article 4(f), CRPD.

[116] CRPD Committee, *General Comment No 4. Article 24*, para 25.

[117] Article 8(2)(b), CRPD.

[118] Hornby, 'Inclusive Special Education', 244; Kauffman and Badar, 'It's Instruction over Place – Not the Other Way Around!', 56–7; Anastasiou and Kauffman, 'Disability as Cultural Difference', 143–4.

[119] G. de Beco, 'The Right to Inclusive Education: Why is There so much Opposition to its Implementation?' (2018) 14 *International Journal of Law in Context* 396, 410.

[120] B. Byrne, 'How Inclusive is the Right to Inclusive Education? An Assessment of the UN Convention on the Rights of Persons with Disabilities' Concluding Observations' (2020) *International Journal of Inclusive Education*, 12, https://doi.org/10.1080/13603116.2019.1651411.

[121] K. Runswick-Cole, 'Time to End the Bias Towards Inclusive Education?' (2011) 38 *British Journal of Special Education* 112, 116–7.

requirements as they are set in educational targets. While this is a global trend in high-income countries,[122] it adversely affects those who are disabled.

These difficulties prompt the raising of the question of whether inclusive education as a concept really has any place in a human rights treaty. There is no consensus but rather many viewpoints on what it actually means in academic scholarship.[123] This makes it hard to give sense to the 'inclusive' component that has been included in the 'generic' right to education. It has notably been suggested that '[t]urning to the law to begin to determine a viable definition of inclusive education is not propitious'.[124] For its part, the CRPD Committee is somewhat overbroad with its own definition of inclusive education.[125] Such a definition nonetheless is imperative in order to assess whether the steps taken in order to achieve inclusive education have yielded the desired results. The complexities involved in doing so may explain why the right to inclusive education's potential has not been leveraged as yet in the field of international human rights law.

[122] This trend is promoted, for instance, by the Programme for International Student Assessment (PISA) in the Organisation for Economic Co-operation and Development (OECD).

[123] Rioux and Pinto, 'A Time for the Universal Right to Education', 638.

[124] E. Shyman, Towards a Globally Sensitive Definition of Inclusive Education Based in Social Justice' (2015) 62 *International Journal of Disability, Development and Education* 351, 352.

[125] CRPD Committee, *General Comment No 4. Article 24*, para 11.

7
Work: A Needed Priority

This chapter analyses the right to work. It examines how the CRPD has come to provide for the participation of disabled people in the 'open labour market' and examines the various barriers that limit such participation (7.1. The Right to Work). It also considers alternative forms of employment, including sheltered and supported employment, as well as how they relate to the new emphasis brought on the right to work by the CRPD. It subsequently focuses on the extent to which the Convention calls into question those working arrangements that ignore the complexity of human diversity (7.2. Implications for International Human Rights Law). It further appraises the provision of equal employment opportunities for disabled people warning against certain limits in the consideration of employment as nothing but gainful employment in international human rights law.

7.1 The Right to Work

7.1.1 Prior to the CRPD

The right to work is a fundamental right under international human rights law. Article 23(1) of the Universal Declaration of Human Rights (UDHR) provides that '[e]veryone has the right to work'. Article 6(1) of the International Covenant on Economic, Social and Cultural Rights (ICESCR) stipulates that States Parties 'recognize the right to work, which includes the right of everyone to the opportunity to gain his living by work which he freely chooses or accepts'. This right also includes the right to the enjoyment of just and favourable conditions of work, which is protected by Article 7 of the Covenant. Being composed of a series of work-related rights all of which are contingent upon each other, the right to work is more of an 'aggregate right' than a single and all-compassing one.[1]

The Committee on Economic, Social and Cultural Rights (CESCR Committee) issued two general comments on the right to work, namely one on the right to work itself and another one, more recent, on the right to the

[1] F. Coomans, 'Education and Work' in D. Moeckli et al (eds), *International Human Rights Law* (Oxford University Press, 3rd edn, 2018) 232, 245.

Disability in International Human Rights Law. Gauthier de Beco, Oxford University Press. © Gauthier de Beco 2021.
DOI: 10.1093/oso/9780198824503.003.0008

enjoyment of just and favourable conditions of work.[2] It is further worth noting that the International Labour Organisation (ILO), created in 1919, has been an important advocate for the different work-related rights, which it defined in a number of conventions.

As a social right, the right to work calls for progressive realisation within a State's available resources, but it also has some implications for freedom.[3] This encompasses freedom from forced labour, which is guaranteed by the International Covenant on Civil and Political Rights (ICCPR).[4] The right to work also extends to political rights through its collective dimension enshrined in the right to join trade unions, which is protected by both the ICESCR and the ICCPR.[5]

Disability had attracted limited attention in the world of work; in fact, it has rather been regarded as an obstacle to employment. Disability is not mentioned in the ICCPR or ICESCR, although it is covered by 'other status' in the general non-discrimination clause of the two covenants.[6] The UDHR protects 'the right to security in the event of unemployment, sickness, *disability*, widowhood, old age or other lack of livelihood'.[7] This is however a different right which insures people against destitution and poverty. While enjoying a basic level of security is correlated to the right to work, it concerns entitlements to welfare benefits but not the possibility of employment itself.[8] It thus complements the right to work, but it should neither replace it nor be lost when being employed. As provided for by the UDHR, the right to work must be '*supplemented*, if necessary, by other means of social protection'.[9]

Although a change of perspective would only arrive much later, the consideration of disability with regard to work evolved gradually in the field of international human rights law. The way in which the CRPD would affirm the right of disabled people to work in Article 27 has roots that predate the Convention itself and is the result of a slow movement towards inclusive employment. The insurance of decent living conditions notwithstanding impairment has been replaced by an assurance that disability should not be a reason for impediments to accessing the labour market.

[2] CESCR Committee, *General Comment No 18: The Right to Work*, 6 February 2006, E/C.12/GC/18; CESCR Committee, *General Comment No 23: The Right to Just and Favourable Conditions of Work*, 27 April 2016, E/C.12/GC/23.

[3] B. Saul, D. Kinley and J. Mowbray, *The International Covenant on Economic, Social and Cultural Rights. Commentary, Cases, and Materials* (Oxford: Oxford University Press, 2014) 280.

[4] Article 8(3), ICCPR.

[5] Article 8, ICESCR; Article 22, ICCPR.

[6] Article 2(1), ICCPR; Article 2(2), ICESCR. This was confirmed later on by the CESCR Committee (CESCR Committee, *General Comment No 5: Persons with Disabilities*, 9 December 1994, E/1995/22, para 5).

[7] Article 25(1), UDHR (emphasis added).

[8] H. Collins, 'Is There a Right to Work?' in V. Mantouvalou (ed), *The Right to Work. Legal and Philosophical Perspectives* (Oxford: Hart Publishing, 2015) 17, 23.

[9] Article 23(3), UDHR (emphasis added).

The ILO has been a pioneer in this evolution. It had issued a recommendation relating to rehabilitation and vocational training in 1955.[10] A major milestone was then reached in 1983 when the organisation adopted Convention 159 on Vocational Rehabilitation and Employment (Disabled Persons) (ILO Convention 159).[11] ILO Convention 159 stipulates that rehabilitation must 'enable a disabled person to secure, retain and advance in suitable employment and thereby to further such person's integration or reintegration into society'.[12] While the emphasis lies on rehabilitation, States Parties must develop national policies to promote 'employment opportunities for disabled persons in the open labour market'.[13] ILO Convention 159 nevertheless frames disability from the medical perspective, which it sees as the consequence of 'a duly recognised physical or mental impairment' that presents an obstacle to 'suitable employment'.[14] Alongside this Convention, the ILO issued a recommendation providing for a series of measures to increase the employment of disabled people.[15] By stressing participation in the 'open labour market', it has been much ahead of its time despite its focus on rehabilitation and paved the way towards the right to work for disabled people. While the organisation has been influential on the right to work generally,[16] this has thus been the case particularly with respect to disability. It has continued to provide guidance on promoting employment opportunities for disabled people after the Convention was adopted.[17]

Another international instrument that has been crucial in advancing the right of disabled people to work is the Standard Rules for the Equalisation of Opportunities for Persons with Disabilities (Standard Rules). Adopted in 1993, the Standard Rules provide that disabled people should 'have equal opportunities for productive and gainful employment in the labour market'.[18] This wording testifies the new approach to dealing with disability with regard to work. While the Standard Rules were in continuity with ILO Convention 159, they highlight that 'States should actively support the integration of persons with disabilities into open employment'.[19] They also outline the steps that States should take towards this end, 'such as vocational training, incentive-oriented quota schemes, reserved or designated

[10] ILO, *Recommendation No 99 – Vocational Rehabilitation (Disabled)*, 22 June 1955.

[11] ILO, *Convention No 159 – Vocational Rehabilitation and Employment (Disabled Persons) Convention*, 20 June 1983.

[12] Articles 1(2), ILO Convention 159.

[13] Articles 3, ILO Convention 159. Note that ILO Convention 159 uses the term 'disabled people' in contrast to the CRPD and other international instruments.

[14] Article 1(1), ILO Convention 159.

[15] ILO, *Recommendation No 168 – Employment Promotion and Protection against Unemployment Convention*, 21 June 1988 (ILO Recommendation 168).

[16] Saul, Kinley and Mowbray, *The International Covenant on Economic, Social and Cultural Rights*, 277–8.

[17] ILO, *Managing Disability in the Workplace: An ILO Code of Practice* (Geneva: ILO, 2015); ILO, *Promoting Diversity and Inclusion through Workplace Adjustments: A Practical Guide* (Geneva: ILO, 2016).

[18] Rule 7, Standard Rules.

[19] Rule 7(2), Standard Rules.

employment … or other technical or financial assistance to enterprises employing workers with disabilities'.[20] Although they are non-legally binding, the Standard Rules are an attempt to move away from the emphasis placed upon rehabilitation by the ILO to focus instead on the provision of equal employment opportunities.

The Committee on Economic, Social and Cultural Rights (CESCR Committee) shortly hereafter issued its general comment on the situation of disabled people.[21] Referring to the Standard Rules, it advised that '[t]he integration of persons with disabilities into the regular labour market should be actively supported by States'.[22] It requested that 'artificial barriers to integration in general, and to employment in particular, be removed' while affirming States Parties' responsibility 'to ensure that disability is not used as an excuse for creating low standards of labour protection or for paying below minimum wages'.[23] It reiterated these recommendations later on in its general comment on the right to work.[24]

7.1.2 Article 27 of the CRPD

Disabled people remain disproportionately outside of the labour market. Despite the adoption of the CRPD, the situation does not show many signs of actual improvement. According to the Organisation for Economic Co-operation and Development (OECD), they still have twice the chance of being unemployed than non-disabled people.[25] When they are employed, they are more often subject to precarious contracts as well as part-time work and have more limited career prospects, especially insofar as they are intellectually disabled or have a mental health condition.[26] This affects women much more than men, as disabled women especially struggle with unequal working conditions.[27]

Article 27(1) of the CRPD provides that States Parties 'recognize the right of persons with disabilities to work … [which] includes the right to the opportunity to gain a living by work freely chosen or accepted in a labour market and work environment that is open, inclusive and accessible to persons with disabilities'. This provision is close to Article 6(1) of the ICESCR, except that it noticeably adds that disabled people should enjoy the right to work in 'a labour market … that is

[20] Ibid.
[21] CESCR Committee, *General Comment No 5: Persons with Disabilities*.
[22] Ibid, para 20.
[23] Ibid, paras 22 and 25.
[24] CESCR Committee, *General Comment No 18: The Right to Work*, para 17.
[25] OECD, *Sickness Disability and Work: Breaking the Barriers. A Synthesis of Findings across OECD Countries* (Paris: OECD, 2010) 23.
[26] ILO, *Decent Work for Persons with Disabilities: Promoting Rights in the Global Development Agenda* (Geneva: ILO, 2015) 64–6; World Health Organisation (WHO) and World Bank, *World Report on Disability* (Geneva: WHO, 2011) 237–8.
[27] ILO, *Decent Work for Persons with Disabilities*, 68.

open, inclusive and accessible'.[28] The CRPD therefore provides that disabled people should be able to participate in the 'open labour market'.

Discussions during the Convention's negotiation process essentially revolved around the question of the 'open labour market', including its meaning for the employment of disabled people. From this negotiation process, it can be inferred that the term refers to ordinary employment in opposition to segregated employment.[29] As indicated in the discussions' daily summaries, '[t]he [Ad Hoc] Committee expressed a general preference for States to recognise the importance of access by persons with disabilities to the open labour market, in order to empower and enable them to participate fully in society'.[30] This interpretation is in line with the previously cited international instruments. The term 'open labour market' is used in ILO Convention 159,[31] and both the Standard Rules and the CESCR Committee, in its general comment on the situation of disabled people, mix the terms 'open employment' and 'regular labour market' (in very similar sentences).[32] Still, the CRPD gives no indication as to what an 'open labour market' in which disabled people can participate entails for the States Parties. As seen in Chapter 6, this contrasts with an 'inclusive education system' to be developed for the realisation of the right to inclusive education.[33]

The CRPD subsequently addressed the barriers in the labour market but not in Article 27 itself. There are both physical and social barriers, both of which can create disadvantages for disabled people.

First, physical barriers are a serious obstacle to employment. In the words of the OHCHR, they are 'often among the main reasons why persons with disabilities are not employed'.[34] These barriers concern more than the workplace itself, but they are also to be found in other areas of life that may affect their employment. According to the CESCR Committee (referring to the ILO), 'it is very often the physical barriers that society has erected in areas such as transport, housing and the workplace which are . . . cited as the reason why persons with disabilities cannot be employed'.[35] The issue therefore must be seen in its totality, that is, as a matter of

[28] The reference to 'freely chosen or accepted' means that people should not be pushed into particular jobs, which can be especially relevant for disabled people and which relates to freedom from forced labour in Article 27(2) of the CRPD.

[29] M. Ventegodt Liisberg, 'Flexicurity and Employment of Persons with Disability in Europe in a Contemporary Disability Human Rights Perspective' in L. Waddington, G. Quinn and E. Flynn (eds), *European Yearbook of Disability Law* (Antwerp/Portland: Intersentia, 2013) 145, 149.

[30] Ad Hoc Committee, *Six Section Article 27 – Right to Work*, https://www.un.org/esa/socdev/enable/rights/ahcstata27ssrepchair.htm.

[31] Article 3, ILO Convention 159.

[32] Rule 7(2), Standard Rules; CESCR Committee, *General Comment No 5: Persons with Disabilities*, para 20.

[33] Article 24(1), CRPD.

[34] OHCHR, *Thematic Study on Work and Employment of Persons with Disabilities*, 17 December 2012, A/HRC/22/25, para 26.

[35] CESCR Committee, *General Comment No 5: Persons with Disabilities*, para 22. There is also a cross-reference in CESCR Committee, *General Comment No 18: The Right to Work*, para 12 (b)(ii).

accessibility related to society as a whole. The CRPD provides in this regard for the obligation 'to ensure to persons with disabilities access ... to the physical environment, to transportation [and] to information and communications' and extends this obligation explicitly to 'workplaces'.[36] The CRPD Committee likewise reckons that '[b]esides the physical accessibility of the workplace, persons with disabilities need accessible transport and support services to get to their workplaces'.[37]

This scope of application must be seen even more broadly. For instance, disabled people often struggle to get access to job interviews and work-related social events.[38] The result is a lack of social capital that is strongly needed for career advancement. As argued by Albin, the labour market must be transformed from within, which calls for more than mere physical accessibility.[39] Accessibility similarly applies to information. Referring to Article 9 of the Convention, the CRPD Committee provides that '[a]ll information pertaining to work, advertisements of job offers, selection processes and communication at the workplace that is part of the work process must be accessible'.[40]

Second, social barriers restrict access to the labour market by the prevalence of stereotypes and prejudices. Both in high income countries and in low income countries, disabled people are considered to be less productive than non-disabled people.[41] Seen as unfit for work, there are doubts as to whether these people are capable of doing the tasks assigned to them.[42] Consumers and co-workers also may have negative social attitudes towards disabledworkers, thereby further discouraging potential employers from hiring them.[43] This is especially the case with those who ask for particular adjustments to deal with mental health conditions.[44] While the physical barriers are a real obstacle to employment, the social barriers are equally, if not more, a significant impediment to developing 'a labour market ... that is open, inclusive and accessible'.[45] As pointed out by the OHCHR, 'it is evident that one of the core challenges lies in negative attitudes, stigma and stereotypes of persons with disabilities being in some way "unsuitable" to participation in working

[36] Article 9(1)(a), CRPD.

[37] CRPD Committee, *General comment No 2: Accessibility*, 11 April 2014, CRPD/C/GC/2, para 41.

[38] WHO and World Bank, *World Report on Disability*, 239.

[39] E. Albin, 'Universalising the Right to Work of Persons with Disabilities: An Equality and Dignity Based Approach' in Mantouvalou, *The Right to Work*, 61, 77–8.

[40] CRPD Committee, *General Comment No 2: Accessibility*, para 41.

[41] S. Bruyère and Sara Van Looy, 'Finding and Maintaining Employment Lessons from Workplace Nondiscrimination Measures in High-Income Countries' in J. Heymann, M. Stein and G. Moreno (eds), *Disability and Equity at Work* (New York: Oxford University Press, 2014) 42, 62; S. Mitra, 'Employment Challenges and Successes in Low- and Middle-Income Countries' in Heymann, Stein and Moreno, *Disability and Equity at Work*, 267, 277–9.

[42] Albin, 'Universalising the Right to Work of Persons with Disabilities', 66.

[43] L. Schur, D. Kruse and P. Blanck, *People with Disabilities. Sidelined or Mainstreamed?* (New York: Cambridge University Press, 2013) 70.

[44] P. Harpur, *Ableism at Work: Disablement and Hierarchies of Impairment* (Cambridge: Cambridge University Press, 2019) 151.

[45] Article 27(1), CRPD.

life'.[46] As a result, many disabled people do not even attempt to find gainful employment,[47] which means they are unregistered as job-seekers and unaccounted for in labour policies.[48]

The CRPD places particular emphasis on the need to combat stigma surrounding disabled people in the employment context. It provides for 'public awareness campaigns designed ... [t]o promote recognition of the skills, merits and abilities of persons with disabilities, and of their contributions to the workplace and the labour market'.[49] Given the deeply-entrenched assumption that disabled people do not possess those 'skills, merits and abilities', more attention could be drawn to awareness-raising as a way to '[p]romote employment opportunities ... for persons with disabilities', as required by the Convention.[50] At the same time, participation in the 'open labour market' by itself can help break down the stereotypes and prejudices, as it increases social interaction between disabled and non-disabled people and encourages diversity within the workplace itself.[51]

A further obstacle is that disabled people can lose part of their welfare benefits when entering into the labour market, which can be seen as administrative barriers. The CRPD Committee urges that they 'do not lose the benefit of disability allowances when they start work'.[52] This so-called 'benefit trap' provides them with an impossible choice, because they might need a higher income to cover extra costs associated with disability.[53] As mentioned earlier, the right to work and right to social security, which is protected too by the CRPD,[54] are two distinguished rights.

The remainder of Article 27 of the CRPD considers all aspects of the employment of disabled people. While it reformulates the right to work for this purpose, it contains a number of new elements. The Convention requires that States Parties '[p]rohibit discrimination on the basis of disability with regard to all matters concerning all forms of employment, including conditions of recruitment, hiring and employment' and that they '[p]rotect the rights of persons with disabilities ... to just and favourable conditions of work, including equal opportunities and equal remuneration for work of equal value, safe and healthy working conditions'.[55] The Convention thereby aims both at ending discrimination and at achieving substantive equality in the labour market. It also provides that States Parties must '[e]nable

46 OHCHR, *Thematic Study on Work and Employment of Persons with Disabilities*, para 67.

47 WHO and World Bank, *World Report on Disability*, 240.

48 OHCHR, *Thematic Study on Work and Employment of Persons with Disabilities*, para 53.

49 Article 8(2)(a)(iii), CRPD.

50 Article 27(1)(e), CRPD.

51 J. Heymann, M. Stein and G. Moreno, 'Disability, Employment, and Inclusion Worldwide' in Heymann, Stein and Moreno, *Disability and Equity at Work*, 1, 2.

52 CRPD Committee, *General Comment No 6: Equality and Non-discrimination*, 26 April 2018, CRPD/C/GC/6, para 67(c).

53 ILO, *Decent Work for Persons with Disabilities*, 144; WHO and World Bank, *World Report on Disability*, 237.

54 Article 28(2), CRPD.

55 Article 27(1)(a) and (b), CRPD.

persons with disabilities to have effective access to general technical and vocational guidance programmes, placement services and vocational and continuing training'.[56] As training offers disabled people the qualification required in order to be employed, the right to work has a close relationship with the obligation to ensure that they can 'access general tertiary education, vocational training, adult education and lifelong learning' in Article 24.[57] The CRPD requires that States Parties '[p]romote opportunities for self-employment, entrepreneurship, the development of cooperatives and starting one's own business'.[58] This concerns especially low-income countries, where self-employment might be the only option open to disabled people considering the very inaccessible labour markets.[59] The Convention also provides for the promotion of 'vocational and professional rehabilitation, job retention and return-to-work programmes'.[60] Rehabilitation was the focus for disabled people prior to this Convention, but it remains an essential aspect of their right to work and is addressed in Article 26, which explicitly refers to 'employment'.[61]

Furthermore, States Parties must '[p]romote the employment of persons with disabilities in the private sector through appropriate policies and measures, which may include affirmative action programmes, incentives and other measures'.[62] Such affirmative action can be diverse, but the most common one is quotas, which can be binding or not and attached to penalties in case of non-compliance. The CESCR Committee has urged States to have such quotas or to meet those they have set for themselves,[63] and the Standard Rules likewise recommends them.[64] Whether quotas really lead to inclusion nonetheless is questionable, as they may send the signal that disabled people are in fact less valuable workers.[65] Such quotas can result in stigma due to the impression they create that these people 'are hired solely on the basis of their disability'.[66] Even though they might be as ineffective, promotional measures have at least the merit of presenting a positive image of such people.

Finally, the CRPD establishes a duty to provide reasonable accommodation.[67] This duty plays an important role for the employment of disabled people. It is

56 Article 27(1)(d), CRPD.
57 Article 24(5), CRPD.
58 Article 27(1)(f), CRPD.
59 Schur, Kruse and Blanck, *People with Disabilities*, 62–4.
60 Article 27(1)(k), CRPD.
61 Article 26(1), CRPD.
62 Article 27(1)(h), CRPD.
63 Saul, Kinley and Mowbray, *The International Covenant on Economic, Social and Cultural Rights*, 305–6.
64 Rule 7(2), Standard Rules.
65 A. Sargeant, Radevich-Katsaroumpa and A. Innesti, '*Disability Quotas: Past* or *Future Policy*?' (2018) 39 *Economic and Industrial Democracy* 404, 414–15.
66 OHCHR, *Thematic Study on Work and Employment of Persons with Disabilities*, para 39.
67 Article 5(3), CRPD.

provided for not only by the Americans with Disabilities (Amendment) Act and but also by EU Directive 2000/78/EC on equal treatment in employment and occupation.[68] The Convention includes it amongst its general obligations.[69] The duty to provide reasonable accommodation 'in the workplace' is once more set out in Article 27,[70] while it also falls under the prohibition of discrimination stated in the same article.[71] Its fulfilment involves a large variety of measures, including making physical adaptations and other changes to working arrangements as well as the provision of specific equipment.[72] The CESCR Committee has similarly advised that disabled people 'not be denied reasonable accommodation, like workplace adjustments or flexible working arrangements'.[73] Although it has been shown that the cost of providing such accommodation is most of the time relatively low, employers continue to overestimate this cost and see it as a challenge to the employment of disabled people.[74]

7.1.3 The CRPD's New Emphasis

The right to work as provided for by the CRPD does not in essence diverge from the general right to work according to international human rights law. However, it has brought a new emphasis by endorsing an evolution that pursues inclusiveness rather than mere income replacement. The objective is participation in the 'open labour market', which must meet the different needs of disabled people. The Convention fails however to indicate what is in fact needed to make 'a labour market ... open, inclusive and accessible'.[75] By not elaborating on how to develop such an inclusive and accessible 'open labour market' and concentrating on the obstacles in this labour market, Article 27 does not reflect plainly the social model of disability. This is startling, especially since this model was coined precisely with reference to the very exclusion from work as a result of competitive market forces.[76]

[68] ADA Amendments Act. Pub. L. No 110–325, 42 Stat. § 12101, 25 September 2008; Article 5, Council Directive 2000/78/EC, Establishing a General Framework for Equal Treatment in Employment and Occupation, 2000 O.J. (L 303) 16. See also Rule 7(2), Standard Rules.

[69] Article 5(3), CRPD.

[70] Article 27(1)(i), CRPD.

[71] Article 27(1)(a), CRPD.

[72] ILO, *Managing Disability in the Workplace: An ILO Code of Practice* (Geneva: ILO, 2015); ILO, *Promoting Diversity and Inclusion through Workplace Adjustments: A Practical Guide* (Geneva: ILO, 2016).

[73] CESCR Committee, *General Comment No 23*, 27 April 2016, E/C.12/GC/23, para 47(b).

[74] Schur, Kruse and Blanck, *People with Disabilities*, 76–9; Heymann, Stein and Moreno, 'Disability, Employment, and Inclusion Worldwide', 6–7.

[75] Article 27(1), CRPD.

[76] L. Waddington, M. Priestley and B. Yalcin, 'Equality of Opportunity in Employment? Disability Rights and Active Labour Market Policies' in P. Blanck and E. Flynn (eds), *Routledge Handbook of Disability Law and Human Rights* (Oxon/New York: Routledge, 2017) 72, 74.

As mentioned earlier, the main point of contention has been the existence of sheltered workshops.[77] The sheltered workshops as a rule operate under different sets of rules and at lower remuneration for its workers.[78] There was no consensus on whether they should remain available to disabled people at the time of the CRPD's drafting. In its recommendation accompanying ILO Convention 159, the ILO advised that the measures 'to promote employment opportunities for disabled persons ... should include ... the establishment of various types of sheltered employment for disabled persons for whom access to open employment is not practicable'.[79] The Standard Rules also provide that if some 'needs cannot be met in open employment, small units of sheltered or supported employment may be an alternative'.[80] The CESCR Committee on the contrary considered that the right to work is 'not realized where the only real opportunity open to disabled workers is to work in so-called "sheltered" facilities under substandard conditions'.[81]

Given the disagreement on the matter between disabled people's organisations and the negotiating parties as well as the ILO which expressed its concerns for the '[l]ack of provision for alternative forms of employment' (in then Article 22),[82] the question was left unresolved. The Ad Hoc Committee eventually decided that it was preferable not to mention 'sheltered workshops' in the future convention. It concluded that '[t]he balance of views ... was that such settings were undesirable because of the potential for segregation from the community and their conditions of employment'.[83]

The result is that the CRPD neither supports nor bans sheltered workshops. As in the case of 'special schools', the term is not used in the Convention. The CRPD Committee has nonetheless asked several States Parties to reduce or eliminate their reliance on sheltered workshops in its concluding observations even though it has stopped short of providing how to move disabled people onto the labour market.[84] In its general comment on the right to just and favourable conditions of work, the CESCR Committee prescribed that 'workers with disabilities should not be segregated in sheltered workshops'.[85] The Human Rights Council (HRC) has taken a more cautious stance, by urging States to promote 'alternative approaches

[77] A. Broderick and D. Ferri, *International and European Disability Law and Policy: Text, Cases and Materials* (Cambridge: Cambridge University Press, 2019) 235–6.

[78] C. May-Simera, 'Reconsidering Sheltered Workshops in Light of the United Nations Convention on the Rights of Persons with Disabilities (2006)' (2018) 7 *Laws*, 4–5, https://www.mdpi.com/2075-471X/7/1/6.

[79] ILO Recommendation 168, para 11(b).

[80] Rule 7(7), Standard Rules.

[81] CESCR Committee, *General Comment No 5: Persons with Disabilities*, para 21.

[82] ILO, 'Draft Article 22 Right to Work. ILO Comments', Six Session of the Ad Hoc Committee, https://www.un.org/esa/socdev/enable/rights/documents/ahc6iloda22.doc.

[83] Ad Hoc Committee, *Six Section Article 27 – Right to Work*, https://www.un.org/esa/socdev/enable/rights/ahcstata27ssrepchair.htm.

[84] Harpur, *Ableism at Work*, 61–4.

[85] CESCR Committee, *General Comment No 23: The Right to Just and Favourable Conditions of Work*, para 47(c).

to sheltered employment schemes where such schemes are inconsistent with the Convention'.[86] Awaiting a general comment on the right of disabled people to work, uncertainty remains, which could actually have the effect of providing legitimacy to sheltered workshops.[87] What is certain is that such workshops can only be temporary and that their working conditions must respect the general right to work. As stated by the CESCR Committee, 'the right of everyone to the enjoyment of just and favourable conditions of work … applies to all disabled workers, whether they work in sheltered facilities or in the open labour market'.[88] In a similar vein, the CRPD prohibits discrimination 'concerning all forms of employment',[89] thus covering both sheltered and inclusive employment.

One solution in order to avoid segregated employment is the provision of supported employment. The CRPD does not mention it either, but its usefulness has been recognised for the employment of disabled people. Originating in the US, supported employment refers to various services that enable disabled people to work in companies.[90] It provides 'on-the-job training in a regular workplace',[91] through the use of specialised training, job coaches, assistive technology and so on.[92] The provision of supported employment can be a means to increase employment opportunities for disabled people. It avoids reliance on sheltered workshops, although it might actually benefit only those with less severe forms of impairment.[93] It may also sometimes lock disabled people into positions which prevent them from evolving in the labour market. It is therefore not just a matter of location but of the prevalence of different working conditions.[94] While supported employment seems preferable to segregated employment, the distinction between the two is indeed not always straightforward. The Standard Rules mention, in one stroke, 'small units of sheltered or supported employment', which they regard as an alternative to participation in the 'open labour market'.[95]

The difficulty in drawing the line shows the crux of the problem: there is a 'mismatch' in supply- and demand-sides. Disabled people tend to obtain skills that are not in demand and are unable to meet advertising criteria.[96] It starts with education in special schools, which does not prepare them for the labour market.

[86] HRC, *The Work and Employment of Persons with Disabilities*, 14 March 2013, A/HRC/22/L.4, para 5(b).

[87] May-Simera, 'Reconsidering Sheltered Workshops in Light of the United Nations Convention on the Rights of Persons with Disabilities (2006)', 13.

[88] CESCR Committee, *General Comment No 5: Persons with Disabilities*, para 25.

[89] Article 27(1)(a), CRPD.

[90] ILO, *Decent Work for Persons with Disabilities*, 74–5.

[91] OHCHR, *Thematic Study on Work and Employment of Persons with Disabilities*, para 17.

[92] WHO, *World Report on Disability*, 242.

[93] ILO, *Decent Work for Persons with Disabilities*, 74–80.

[94] Ventegodt Liisberg, 'Flexicurity and Employment of Persons with Disability in Europe in a Contemporary Disability Human Rights Perspective', 154–6.

[95] Rule 7(2), Standard Rules.

[96] ILO, *Decent Work for Persons with Disabilities*, 94 and 143; Schur, Kruse and Blanck, *People with Disabilities*, 69–70.

While anti-discrimination law might proscribe refusal to employ a disabled person who meets the criteria, it does not oblige anyone to provide her with the required qualification.[97]

In order to correct this 'mismatch', the forces of supply and demand must be considered as a whole in relation to the CRPD.[98] Attention has mainly gone to the supply-side, where precedence has been afforded to the perspective of disabled people.[99] Strategies to encourage the employers to adapt the labour market to these people's needs have been less examined, at least as yet. The lack of attention to the demand-side can be seen in the Convention, which is mostly concerned with how to empower disabled people but not how to create an inclusive and accessible 'open labour market'. Disabled people will not be able to use their skills without such a transformation, which explains the persistent need for sheltered workshops. The CRPD provides for 'appropriate policies and measures, which may include affirmative action programmes, incentives and other measures',[100] but it does not determine what kind of working arrangements could hasten the removal of all the barriers embedded in the labour market.

7.2 Implications for International Human Rights Law

7.2.1 The Universality of Work

Disabled people's right to work brings to the fore questions that pertain to more than a particular group of people. According to Albin, this right can be applied universally, that is, even to 'persons that are not considered to experience disability.'[101] It would therefore aim to remove any kind of barriers in the labour market.

The argument here is somewhat different. As argued in Chapter 4, any human beings will encounter issues related to disability over the course of their lives. The CRPD lays down the requirement that disability seen as a universal experience should not translate into disadvantage in the workplace. This does not mean that all individuals must actually enter the labour market, as the right to work is not an 'absolute and unconditional right to obtain employment'.[102] They should however be able to do so as any other people, which entails that States Parties 'take appropriate steps to safeguard this right' in accordance with the ICESCR.[103]

97 S. Bagenstos, 'The Future of Disability Law' (2004) 114 *Yale Law Journal* 1, 23.

98 M. Saleh and S. Bruyère, 'Leveraging Employer Practices in Global Regulatory Frameworks to Improve Employment Outcomes for People with Disabilities' (2018) 6 *Social Inclusion* 18, 19–20.

99 Bruyère and Van Looy, 'Finding and Maintaining Employment Lessons from Workplace Nondiscrimination Measures in High-Income Countries', 46.

100 Article 27(1)(h), CRPD.

101 Albin, 'Universalising the Right to Work of Persons with Disabilities', 62.

102 CESCR Committee, *General Comment No 18: The Right to Work*, para 6.

103 Article 6(1), ICESCR.

Article 27 of the Convention may prove useful to all those facing 'personal constraints' that reduce employment opportunities.[104] These include the elderly, the proportion of which has been growing in recent decades.[105] People suffering from various types of illnesses or mental health conditions are likewise concerned. In this regard, families of disabled people also encounter disability-related issues, as their care-taking functions may prevent them from being in employment.[106] The CRPD provides for flexibility in the workplace in a way that demonstrates sensitivity to human differences, so that both disabled and non-disabled people can obtain a better work-balance and maintain productivity simultaneously.[107] In order to make employment more inclusive, States Parties must therefore provide an environment that will allow all individuals to put their skills to use.

In order to realise the right to work, working arrangements should recognise the complexity of human diversity. Failure to do so has been detrimental to many individuals. As stated by the CESCR's Committee, 'work' in the sense of the ICESCR should be 'decent work'.[108] While this 'decent work' has mainly been related to working conditions,[109] it remains a distant goal if it does not factor in all sorts of disabilities.

This goal indeed cannot be reached by focusing solely on the particular needs of disabled people. It will only be achieved by integrating policy relating to disability into overall employment strategies rather than by providing responses which see disabled people as a discrete group of people.[110] Separate regimes hamper the creation of an inclusive and accessible 'open labour market' and limit the effects of any changes made towards that end. The labour market will continue to single out disabled people, regarding them as less capable than others. It has been said that the presence of disabled people can have a positive effect on working practices,[111] but this will not be achieved through adopting a group-based approach that considers disability in an isolated manner.

Anti-discrimination law has been the most widely used tool so far in guaranteeing equal employment opportunities for disabled people, particularly through the duty to provide reasonable accommodation. The CRPD has further

[104] Albin, 'Universalising the Right to Work of Persons with Disabilities', 64.

[105] S. Bruyère and B. Murray, 'The Human Rights of Workers with Disabilities' in J. Gross and L. Compa (eds), *Labor and Employment Relations: International and Domestic Perspectives* (Ithaca, NY: Cornell University Press, 2009) 213, 215.

[106] Inclusion Europe, *Children's Rights for all! Implementation of the United Nations Convention on the Rights of the Child for Children with Intellectual Disabilities* (Brussels: Inclusion Europe, 2011) 14, http://www.eenet.org.uk/resources/docs/6130.pdf.

[107] Schur, Kruse and Blanck, *People with Disabilities*, 51.

[108] CESCR Committee, *General Comment No 18: The Right to Work*, para 7.

[109] Coomans, 'Education and Work', 248.

[110] Bagenstos, 'The Future of Disability Law', 73.

[111] Saleh and Bruyère, 'Leveraging Employer Practices in Global Regulatory Frameworks to Improve Employment Outcomes for People with Disabilities', 24.

strengthened this duty by making the denial of reasonable accommodation a form of discrimination.[112] It explicitly reminds States of this duty in the context of employment.[113] The emphasis on the need for providing reasonable accommodation in cases of disability has thus given a new meaning to the right to work according to international human rights law. It compels States Parties to ensure that employers make adjustments to a disabled person's environment so that she can exercise her right to work on an equal basis with others.

The strong reliance on non-discrimination, however, has not brought with it any improvement in the employment of disabled people. Since reasonable accommodation is only made for the disabled person who requests it, it locates the source of the problem in that individual whose employment is regarded as an additional cost. The burden of accommodating the individual is also placed on a particular employer instead of on society as a whole.[114] Courts have in addition tended to limit this duty by focusing more on the continuing cost than on the overall benefits.[115] Although its fulfilment can enable disabled people to gain and retain employment, it does not by itself entail a transformation of the labour market.

The CRPD's move to provide for new legal tools so as to facilitate access to the labour market is therefore welcome. Such tools include not only accessibility and awareness-raising but also training and affirmative action. Notwithstanding its limited concern for the 'open labour market' as such, the Convention is actually dedicated to the removal of barriers that disability engenders for all.

Going further with the transformation of the labour market, disability brings to light aspects of the right to work that were previously ignored in the international human rights framework. While the ICESCR provides for 'the right of everyone to the enjoyment of just and favourable conditions of work',[116] it did not consider how to open up employment opportunities for those excluded from work. The CRPD has come to mean that 'there is an acknowledgement of specific requirements that need to be accommodated' towards this end.[117] The working population has to fit into the labour market by finding for itself the means to do so. However, the labour market too needs to reach out to the working population. The way to developing an inclusive and accessible 'open labour market' is not just to equip people with the requisite qualifications in order to enter the labour market but also to bring changes to the organisation of work by avoiding a 'one-size-fits-all' approach.

[112] Article 2, CRPD.
[113] Article 27(1)(i).
[114] Bagenstos, 'The Future of Disability Law', 54.
[115] Harpur, *Ableism at Work*, 139–40.
[116] Article 7, ICESCR.
[117] Bruyère and Murray, 'The Human Rights of Workers with Disabilities', 217.

7.2.2 Closing the Gap

The right to work is pivotal for human dignity. Work goes beyond earning a living: it gives people a sense of worth as well as the opportunity for social relations and chance of fulfilling themselves.[118] Lack of employment, therefore, not only causes economic insecurity but also accentuates one's marginalisation.

The underemployment of disabled people has been a loss for both the economy and for disabled people.[119] It has forced them to find other means to support themselves while depriving them of access to social security. If unemployed, disabled people have no choice but to rely on social services, which may push them further into poverty. Without work they remain disconnected from the labour market, with the problem only getting worse over time. Prolonged unemployment also reinforces the belief that disabled people are unfit for work.

Disability has barely featured in the debate on the right to work when compared with other grounds such as gender. The ICESCR provides that 'women [be] guaranteed conditions of work not inferior to those enjoyed by men, with equal pay for equal work'.[120] Although the CESCR Committee noted that 'equality applies to all workers without distinction based on race, ethnicity, nationality, migration or health status, disability, age, sexual orientation, gender identity or any other ground',[121] it has hardly addressed disability in relation to employment.[122] The consideration of disability when researching the question of employment relations likewise remains scant and still emphasizes various forms of rehabilitation.[123]

The CESCR Committee considers that the right to work's 'core obligations' include '[t]o ensure the right of access to employment, especially for disadvantaged and marginalized individuals and groups, permitting them to live a life of dignity.[124] This is however far from being done regarding those who are disabled. The HRC has stated that it is 'deeply concerned that many persons with disabilities in all regions continue to face significant obstacles in exercising their right to work'.[125] Given the multiple consequences for society, this right deserves to be more prioritised.

The ILO quite early took on the initiative to tackle the problem. ILO Convention 159 provides that States Parties '[promote] employment opportunities for disabled persons in the open labour market'.[126] This objective would be endorsed three

[118] Collins, 'Is There a Right to Work?', 35.

[119] Heymann, 'Disability, Employment, and Inclusion Worldwide', 4.

[120] Article 7(a)(i), ICESCR.

[121] CESCR Committee, *General Comment No 23: The Right to Just and Favourable Conditions of Work*, para 11 (footnote omitted).

[122] Saul, Kinley and Mowbray, *The International Covenant on Economic, Social and Cultural Rights*, 304.

[123] Bruyère and Murray, 'The Human Rights of Workers with Disabilities', 228.

[124] CESCR Committee, CESCR Committee, *General Comment No 18: The Right to Work*, para 31(a).

[125] HRC, *The Work and Employment of Persons with Disabilities*, Preamble.

[126] Articles 3, ILO Convention 159.

decades later by the CRPD. The latter's adoption not only confirmed the overall direction of the right of disabled people to work, but it is also in keeping with '[f]ull and effective participation and inclusion in society' (one of the Convention's general principles).[127] The CRPD thereby incorporated the ILO's vision into international human rights law. At the same time, it provided leverage to the ILO itself, which is now able to call upon international human rights law in the pursuit of its own standards.

The question can nonetheless be asked whether this objective is sustainable long term. While the labour market is getting tighter, it might be difficult to provide 'equal opportunities for productive and gainful employment' to all disabled people, as advised by the ICESCR Committee.[128] Disabled people's needs might sometimes be better met through other kinds of employment, especially since employment is still far from inclusive. As pointed out by Harpur, the simple closure of sheltered workshops might result in many disabled people working in precarious or unregulated jobs and losing whatever support they previously had.[129] The current economic context further increases the risk that those people might end up in even worse working conditions.

A deeper problem is that gainful employment is viewed as the ideal kind of employment, and it is not certain whether the ICESCR allows for another understanding of work.[130] The labour market has been based on the image of the individual who is always capable of working full time and productively,[131] but this does not reflect the reality of most people today. International human rights law thus disregards other ways of contributing to society, such as the provision of unpaid care which is still largely carried out by women. While the Covenant stipulates that States Parties must provide training 'to achieve ... full and productive employment',[132] it is open to question whether this is the only way to realise the right to work and whether it should be the aim under any circumstances. Redefining the notion of work, however, meets the challenge that capacity for gainful employment is now a requisite for the acquisition of social status. Those who are unable to undertake such kind of employment continue to be stigmatised in modern democracies, whatever the reason.

[127] Article 4(c), CRPD.

[128] CESCR Committee, *General Comment No 5: Persons with Disabilities*, para 22 (footnote omitted).

[129] Harpur, *Ableism at Work*, 67–73.

[130] Saul, Kinley and Mowbray, *The International Covenant on Economic, Social and Cultural Rights*, 281.

[131] Albin, 'Universalising the Right to Work of Persons with Disabilities', 83.

[132] Article 6(2), ICESCR.

8

Political Participation: An Ultimate Priority

This chapter examines the right to political participation. It exposes the persistent lack of protection of disabled people's political rights, including denial of the right to vote for those with cognitive impairments (8.1. The Right to Political Participation). It analyses what the CRPD requires in order for all disabled people to be able to exercise their voting rights and what it provides beyond the mere act of voting so as to encourage participation in 'the conduct of public affairs'. It goes on to explain why the inclusion of disabled people in political life is a matter for the whole population and why there is no reason for denying the right to vote to any particular group (8.2. Implications for International Human Rights Law). It also explores how to achieve political participation more broadly through real engagement in political activities.

8.1 The Right to Political Participation

8.1.1 Prior to the CRPD

The right to political participation has deep roots in international human rights law. Article 21(1) of the Universal Declaration of Human Rights (UDHR) states that '[e]veryone has the right to take part in the government of his country, directly or through freely chosen representatives'. Article 25(a) of the International Covenant on Civil and Political Rights (ICCPR) similarly provides that '[e]very citizen shall have the right and the opportunity . . . [t]o take part in the conduct of public affairs, directly or through freely chosen representatives'. Participation in 'the conduct of public affairs' plays a fundamental role in democratic societies. In its general comment on the right to participate in public affairs, the Human Rights Committee itself reckoned that 'Article 25 lies at the core of democratic government.'[1]

The political rights of disabled people were not well protected prior to the CRPD, and anomalies remain in international human rights law when it comes to such protection. The ICCPR's general anti-discrimination clause does not explicitly refer to 'disability'.[2] Nor has the Human Rights Committee confirmed that the

[1] Human Rights Committee, *General Comment No 25. Article 25: The Right to Participate in Public Affairs, Voting Rights and the Right to Equal Access to Public Service*, 12 July 1996, CCPR/C/21/Rev.1/Add.7, para 1.

[2] Article 2(1), ICCPR.

Disability in International Human Rights Law. Gauthier de Beco, Oxford University Press. © Gauthier de Beco 2021.
DOI: 10.1093/oso/9780198824503.003.0009

term 'other status' includes it.[3] What is more, the Human Rights Committee considers that political rights may be limited 'on grounds which are established by law and which are objective and reasonable', so that, '[f]or example, established mental incapacity may be a ground for denying a person the right to vote or to hold office'.[4] Although it advised that 'no distinctions are permitted between citizens' on any ground (without mentioning disability),[5] it concedes that a lower level of mental capacity can be a valid reason for depriving a person of her voting rights.[6] On the other hand, the Human Rights Committee stressed that it would be 'unreasonable to restrict the right to vote on the ground of physical disability'.[7]

As a result, no international instrument guaranteed the right of disabled people to political participation. There is no mention of such a right in the Standard Rules for the Equalisation of Opportunities for Persons with Disabilities (Standard Rules), and neither has it been recognised in any recommendation by the UN treaty bodies. The closest to it is probably the Vienna Declaration and Programme of Action (VDPA)'s reaffirmation that 'all human rights and fundamental freedoms … unreservedly include persons with disabilities' and that '[e]very person is born equal and has the same rights to … active participation in all aspects of society'.[8] The failure to affirm disabled people's right to political participation attests to the prevailing interpretation that it is possible to limit political rights on the basis of (intellectual) disability.

ICCPR allows for the limitation of political rights for other groups as well. This includes non-citizens, as can be seen in the Covenant's terminology (where the term 'everyone' in the UDHR is replaced by 'citizen'). Other groups who can be deprived of voting rights are individuals convicted of crimes – provided this is not happening through a blanket ban without any consideration for the circumstances –,[9] as well as children up to a certain age limit.[10] Women were previously often excluded from political life, exclusion which the Convention on the Elimination of All Forms of Discrimination against Women (CEDAW) has

[3] This is in contrast to the Committee on Economic, Social and Cultural Rights (CESCR Committee). See CESCR Committee, *General Comment No 5: Persons with Disabilities*, 9 December 1994, E/1995/22, para 5.

[4] Human Rights Committee, *General Comment No 25. Article 25*, para 4.

[5] Ibid, para 3. It referred to 'race, colour, sex, language, religion, political or other opinion, national or social origin, property, birth or other status' but, once more, not disability.

[6] The American Convention on Human Rights (ACHR) explicitly provides that political rights may be limited on the basis of an exhaustive number of grounds which include 'mental capacity' (Article 23(2), ACHR).

[7] Human Rights Committee, *General Comment No 25. Article 25*, para 10.

[8] World Conference on Human Rights, *Vienna Declaration and Programme of Action*, 25 June 1993, A/Conf.157/23, para 63.

[9] S. Joseph and M. Castan, *The International Covenant on Civil and Political Rights: Cases, Materials and Commentary* (Oxford University Press: Oxford, 3rd edn, 2013) 739–41. See also European Court of Human Rights, *Hirst vs United Kingdom (No 2)*, 6 October 2005, Appl No 74025/01, para 82.

[10] The ACHR allows States to set such restrictions on the grounds of 'age, nationality, residence, language, education, civil and mental capacity, or sentencing by a competent court in criminal proceedings' (Article 23(2), ACHR).

addressed. Article 7 of CEDAW requires that States Parties 'take all appropriate measures to eliminate discrimination against women in the political and public life of the country'. It grants 'women' (not just 'citizens') the right '[t]o vote in all elections and public referenda and to be eligible for election to all publicly elected bodies'.[11] The Committee on the Elimination of Discrimination against Women (CEDAW Committee) has given important guidance on the issue,[12] which sheds light on many of the questions to be resolved with regard to disability. While there is no general comment by the CRPD Committee on the right to political participation, at least as yet, the OHCHR has prepared a thematic study that offers some analysis of the right in question.[13]

The issue has recently attracted attention in the US where steps have been taken to facilitate the exercise of voting rights.[14] Several European organisations have also sought to enhance political participation for disabled people. As early as 1991, the Organisation for Security and Co-operation in Europe (OSCE) declared that disabled people should have the opportunity 'to participate fully in the life of their society'.[15] More recently, it has issued guidelines on how to ensure their participation in the whole electoral process.[16] In the EU, the Fundamental Rights Agency (FRA) has also developed human rights indicators relating to the right of disabled people to political participation in a report which highlighted the various barriers in political life.[17]

8.1.2 Article 29 of the CRPD

Disabled people face a number of obstacles to political participation. When it comes to voting, turnout in elections is much lower amongst them than amongst non-disabled people,[18] especially for those who are unemployed.[19] Polling stations

[11] Article 7(a), ICCPR.

[12] CEDAW Committee, *General Recommendation No 23: Political and Public Life*, 13 January 1997, A/52/38.

[13] OHCHR, *Thematic Study on Participation in Political and Public Life by Persons with Disabilities*, 21 December 2011, A/HRC/19/36.

[14] A. Johnson and S. Powell, 'Disability and Election Administration in the United States: Barriers and Improvements' (2020) 41 *Policy Studies* 249, 250; T. Matsubayashi and M. Ueda, 'Disability and Voting' (2014) 7 *Disability and Health Journal* 285, 285–6.

[15] OSCE, *Document of the Moscow Meeting of the Conference on the Human Dimension*, Moscow, 3 October 1991, para 41.2, https://www.osce.org/odihr/elections/14310?download=true.

[16] OSCE Office for Democratic Institutions and Human Rights, *Guidelines on Promoting the Political Participation of Persons with Disabilities* (Warsaw: OSCE, 2019).

[17] FRA, *The Right to Political Participation for Persons with Disabilities: Human Rights Indicators* (Vienna: FRA, 2014).

[18] L. Schur, 'Towards Inclusion: Political and Social Participation of People with Disabilities' in P. Blanck and E. Flynn (eds), *Routledge Handbook of Disability Law and Human Rights* (Oxon/New York: Routledge, 2017) 118, 126; L. Schur, D. Kruse and P. Blanck, *People with Disabilities. Sidelined or Mainstreamed?* (New York: Cambridge University Press, 2013) 104–5.

[19] Johnson and Powell, 'Disability and Election Administration in the United States', 261.

are often inaccessible while disabled people often lack access to electoral information. Removal of legal capacity can also deprive them of voting rights, because those under guardianship are as a rule denied the right to vote.[20] Such denial by itself not only affects the enjoyment of political rights but also sends the negative message that they are not supposed to take part in political life.[21] It further discourages disabled people from engaging in political activities, which, in turn, removes disability from the realm of public discourse.

Article 29 of the CRPD starts by announcing that 'States Parties shall guarantee to persons with disabilities political rights and the opportunity to enjoy them on an equal basis with others'. The Convention in this regard builds upon existing human rights treaties, although its reference to 'political rights' provides for a expansion to cover every matter related to the administration of government. In continuity withboth the ICCPR and CEDAW, Article 29(a) of the CRPD requires that States Parties '[e]nsure that persons with disabilities can effectively and fully participate in political and public life … directly or through freely chosen representatives'. The Convention thus borrows from CEDAW both the term 'persons' (rather than 'citizens' as in the ICCPR) as well as the term 'political and public life' to enlarge its scope of application as far as possible.

Voting has by far been the most prominent way of political participation in modern democracies. The OHCHR deems that '[t]he right to vote is arguably the most important political right'.[22] The CPRD provides that States Parties must ensure that 'voting procedures, facilities and materials are appropriate, accessible and easy to understand and use'.[23] This provision is related to Article 9, which concerns accessibility in general even if it does not refer to political participation itself. States Parties therefore must ensure that the entire voting procedure is accessible. This requires not only that they adopt general measures but also that they provide reasonable accommodation upon request by any disabled person.[24] Accessibility should allow disabled people to access polling stations, transport as well as electoral information, including party programmes and political candidates. As indicated by the CRPD Committee, it applies to 'political meetings and materials used and produced by political parties or individual candidates participating in public elections'.[25]

[20] M. Priestley et al, 'The Political Participation of Disabled People in Europe: Rights, Accessibility and Activism' (2016) 42 *Electoral Studies* 1, 4; J. Lord, M. Stein and J. Fiala-Butora, 'Facilitating an Equal Right to Vote for Persons with Disabilities' (2014) 6(1) *Journal of Human Rights Practice* 115, 125.

[21] Schur, Kruse and Blanck, *People with Disabilities*, 208.

[22] OHCHR, *Thematic Study on Participation in Political and Public Life by Persons with Disabilities*, para 7.

[23] Article 29(a)(i), CRPD.

[24] Article 5(3), CRPD.

[25] CRPD Committee, *General Comment No 2. Article 9: Accessibility*, 22 May 2014, CRPD/C/GC/2, para 43.

The Convention also protects 'the right of persons with disabilities to vote by secret ballot in elections and public referendums without intimidation'.[26] It thereby secures the right to a secret vote, as guaranteed by the ICCPR,[27] and reminds States Parties of the necessity to do so as part of any measures taken in order to realise the right to political participation. Training should be available so that officials responsible can also interact with disabled people and support them in polling stations.[28]

Hence, disability can no longer serve as a ground for exclusion from political life in international human rights law. The CRPD departs from the Human Rights Committee's interpretation of the right to political participation that has permitted States Parties to deprive of voting rights for people with cognitive impairments. By stipulating that this Convention aims 'to promote, protect and ensure the full and equal enjoyment of all human rights and fundamental freedoms by all persons with disabilities', its drafters clearly expressed their intention that there should be no differentiation between any kinds of disabilities.

In order to understand how States Parties ought to deal with deficits in mental capacity, the right to political participation must be read in conjunction with the right to legal capacity. Article 12(2) stipulates that 'States Parties shall recognize that persons with disabilities enjoy legal capacity on an equal basis with others in all aspects of life'. This includes political participation, as indicated by the term 'all aspects of life'. As seen in Chapter 5, the CRPD does not tolerate any restrictions on legal capacity. There should indeed be no removal of legal capacity depriving disabled people of their voting rights. States Parties should grant them 'legal agency' so as to allow them to make decisions by themselves. As stated by the CRPD Committee, 'a person's decision-making ability cannot be a justification for any exclusion of persons with disabilities from exercising their political rights'.[29] In the *Zsolt Bujdosó vs Hungary* case, which concerned removal from the electoral register of disabled people placed under guardianship, the Committee provided that 'Article 29 does not foresee any reasonable restriction, nor does it allow any exception for any group of persons with disabilities'.[30] Although the State Party had changed its national legislation by requiring an individualised assessment of people's voting capacity, it ruled that such practice amounted to a violation of the Convention. While the European Court of Human Rights had condemned a blanket ban on voting for all those subject to guardianship systems,[31] the CRPD

[26] Article 29(a)(ii), CRPD.

[27] Article 25(b), ICCPR.

[28] OSCE Office for Democratic Institutions and Human Rights, *Guidelines on Promoting the Political Participation of Persons with Disabilities*, 39; OHCHR, *Thematic Study on Participation in Political and Public Life by Persons with Disabilities*, 52–3.

[29] CRPD Committee, *General Comment No 1. Article 12: Equal Recognition Before the Law*, 19 May 2014, CRPD/C/GC/1, para 48.

[30] CRPD Committee, *Zsolt Bujdosó and five others v Hungary*, 20 September 2013, CRPD/C/10/D/4/2011, para 9.4.

[31] European Court of Human Rights, *Alajos Kiss v Hungary*, 20 May 2010, Appl No 38832/06, paras 42–3.

Committee went a step further by ruling that the Convention does not tolerate whatever form of restriction.

Instead, Article 12(3) of the CRPD stipulates that States Parties must offer disabled people 'the support they may require in exercising their legal capacity'.[32] The right to political participation entails that all of them have access to the entire electoral process. Although the Convention itself does not establish the link between the right to legal capacity and right to political participation, the nexus is made by the obligation to guarantee that disabled people can express their 'will ... [by] where necessary, at their request, allowing assistance in voting by a person of their own choice'.[33] There should therefore be some form of support provided so that those who are disabled can exercise their voting rights. The CRPD Committee has confirmed this interpretation by requiring that States Parties uphold their right to vote 'with ... support, where desired, in the exercise of their legal capacity',[34] thereby making this link between the two rights.

8.1.3 The CRPD's New Emphasis

The CRPD emphasises the necessity to promote the participation of disabled people in 'the conduct of public affairs'. It provides that States Parties should offer them 'the right and the *opportunity* to enjoy [political rights] on an equal basis with others'.[35] This imposes on the States Parties 'the adoption of positive measures' which provide disabled people with such an 'opportunity'.[36] The Convention in this way adds a socio-economic dimension to the right to political participation. While the CRPD has blurred the distinction between civil and political and economic and social rights,[37] the way it has done so is particularly visible in relation to political participation.

Although political rights may be limited on the basis of disability according to the Human Rights Committee, the CRPD prevents States Parties from actually doing so. As explained by the OHCHR, the Convention has produced changes in the 'legal landscape' that put in question the Committee's position that (intellectual) disability can be a motive for restricting the right to vote.[38] It calls for a

[32] Article 12(3), CRPD.
[33] Article 29(a)(iii), CRPD.
[34] CRPD Committee, *General Comment No 1. Article 12*, CRPD/C/GC/1, para 49.
[35] Article 29, CRPD (emphasis added).
[36] OHCHR, *Thematic Study on Participation in Political and Public Life by Persons with Disabilities*, para 15.
[37] G. de Beco, 'The Indivisibility of Human Rights and the Convention on the Rights of Persons with Disabilities' (2019) 68 *International & Comparative Law Quarterly* 141, 133–4.
[38] OHCHR, *Thematic Study on Participation in Political and Public Life by Persons with Disabilities*, para 28.

revision of that position and, thereby, avoiding the deprivation of voting rights as a means to exclude disabled people from political life.

What is required is the provision of support tailored to the diverse needs of disabled people. Despite its statement to the contrary, such an interpretation could be deduced from the Human Rights Committee's general comment on the right to political participation in order to reconcile the two human rights treaties (ICCPR and CRPD). While the Committee refers to independent '[a]ssistance to the disabled (sic)' – by which it means those who are physically disabled –,[39] people who are intellectually disabled to may depend on such assistance for the enjoyment of their political rights. As mentioned earlier, the CRPD provides that they should receive 'assistance in voting by a person of their own choice' if so requested.[40] A rigorous account of assistance in the terms of the Human Rights Committee would lead to providing assistance to all disabled people, instead of distinguishing between different categories of disability. This interpretation of the right to political participation would give true meaning to the 'universal and equal suffrage', as intended by the ICCPR,[41] by enabling all individuals to exercise their voting rights.

One way of achieving this is to promote alternatives to voting in person at a polling station. Turnout amongst disabled people indeed is greater in those States that arrange for distance voting (such as voting by email).[42] However, the CRPD does not just seek to promote alternatives like these; its goal is to ensure that the electoral process is made accessible as a whole. While offering distance voting could be one possible option, it cannot be regarded as a substitute for voting in person and thereby become the default option for the actual right to vote, especially since distance voting does not appear to be the preference of disabled people.[43] The right to political participation entails a review of the voting procedure in order to allow these people to 'effectively and fully participate in political and public life'.[44] While it has been argued that international human rights law is not concerned with marginalised groups' disempowerment which hinders political participation,[45] States now must reach out to them so as to ensure the full exercise of their voting rights.

The CRPD also stresses the need for going further than securing the right to vote in order to realise the right to political participation. This Convention recognises the fact that political life is not just about turnout in elections. Article 29(b) provides that States Parties must '[p]romote actively an environment in which persons with disabilities can effectively and fully participate in the conduct of public affairs'.

39 Human Rights Committee, *General Comment No 25. Article 25*, para 20.
40 Article 29(a)(iii), CRPD.
41 Article 25(b), ICCPR.
42 Matsubayashi and Ueda, 'Disability and Voting', 289.
43 Schur, 'Towards Inclusion: Political and Social Participation of People with Disabilities', 126.
44 Article 29(a), ICCPR.
45 Joseph and Castan, *The International Covenant on Civil and Political Rights*, 751–2.

This provision mirrors the right '[t]o participate in the formulation of government policy and the implementation thereof' set out in CEDAW.[46]

The term 'the conduct of public affairs' comes from Article 25 of the ICCPR. It was replaced by 'political and public life' in Article 29(a) which protects the right to vote, while it is used in Article 29(b) which concerns political participation more broadly. The Human Rights Committee indicated that the term '[t]he conduct of public affairs ... covers all aspects of public administration, and the formulation and implementation of policy at international, national, regional and local levels'.[47] As far as the CRPD is concerned, the OHCHR extended this wording by specifying that it 'also covers participation in public debates and peaceful demonstrations'.[48] The CEDAW Committee further considers that it 'includes many aspects of civil society, including ... trade unions, professional or industry associations, women's organizations, community-based organizations and other organizations concerned with public and political life'.[49]

The reference to 'the conduct of public affairs' signals the importance of the ability to take part in political life. It can be understood as contribution to decision-making processes in various forums, such as political gatherings, consultations and meetings, and social media, such as Twitter and Facebook, all of which can inform discussions on new policies. It therefore relates to all activities that can affect government, regardless of reach or location, and is not just concerned with any representative legislative bodies. Such 'direct participation' has been overshadowed by 'indirect participation' which takes place by means of regular elections. By focusing attention to the participation of disabled people in 'the conduct of public affairs' separately from their right to vote, the CRPD has brought a new emphasis on the right to political participation which was not discernible in the field of international human rights law.

'Direct participation' calls for the creation of conditions that foster inclusion in political life. Noteworthy is that the CRPD starts by requires that States Parties '[p]romote actively an environment in which persons with disabilities can effectively and fully participate in the conduct of public affairs'.[50] Not only does the Convention thereby confirm that realising the right to political participation depends on modifications to the 'environment' itself but also that international human rights law is no longer silent in the face of the disempowerment suffered by marginalised groups.

[46] Article 7(b), CEDAW.

[47] Human Rights Committee, *General Comment No 25. Article 25*, para 5. Note that the CEDAW Committee has adopted the same definition for 'political and public life', thereby adding confusion between the two terms ('the conduct of public affairs' and 'political and public life') (CEDAW Committee, *General Recommendation No 23*, para 3).

[48] OHCHR, *Thematic Study on Participation in Political and Public Life by Persons with Disabilities*, para 9.

[49] CEDAW Committee, *General Recommendation No 23: Political and Public Life*, para 5.

[50] Article 29(b), CRPD.

Article 29(b) of the CRPD subsequently sets out what this 'environment' must contain in order to ensure that disabled people 'can effectively and fully participate in the conduct of public affairs'. On the one hand, the Convention provides for '[p]articipation in non-governmental organizations and associations concerned with the public and political life of the country, and in the activities and administration of political parties'.[51] This entails that States Parties allow disabled people to play a role in both governmental and non-governmental organisations. The CRPD partly replicates CEDAW as far as civil society is concerned.[52] In addition, it makes explicit what the CEDAW Committee has advised regarding gender in terms of fair representation of political parties by the phrase 'the activities and administration of political parties'.[53] On the other hand, the Convention provides for '[f]orming and joining organizations of persons with disabilities to represent persons with disabilities'.[54] This is also something international human rights law had not acknowledged in the past, although it had been advocated by the Standard Rules.[55] The CPRD draws particular attention to the issue in Article 4(3), which requires that States Parties 'closely consult with and actively involve persons with disabilities … through their representative organizations' (which will be discussed in Chapter 9). As highlighted by the CRPD Committee, this requirement is instrumental to the right to political participation.[56] It nonetheless depends in the first place on the very possibility of '[f]orming and joining organizations of persons with disabilities to represent persons with disabilities'.[57] In other words, the requirement to 'closely consult with and actively involve persons with disabilities' is not only instrumental but also contingent upon the right to political participation.

8.2 Implications for International Human Rights Law

8.2.1 The Universality of Political Participation

The CRPD protects the right to political participation in a way which concurrently upgrades this right more generally. In line with the present book's argument that disability should be seen as a universal experience, the focus on disability as part of every matter related to the administration of government may yield benefits for the whole population. This view underscores the need for a 'universalist model of

[51] Article 29(b)(i), CRPD.
[52] Article 7(c), CEDAW.
[53] CEDAW Committee, *General Recommendation No 23: Political and Public Life*, paras 32–3.
[54] Article 29(b)(ii), CRPD.
[55] Rule 18(1), Standard Rules.
[56] CRPD Committee, *General Comment No 7: The Participation of Persons with Disabilities, including Children with Disabilities, through their Representative Organizations, in the Implementation and Monitoring of the Convention*, 9 November 2018, CRPD/C/GC/7, para 30.
[57] Article 29(b)(ii), CRPD.

disability', which acknowledges that anyone will experience disability sooner or later.[58] This may be older people, as well as all those who face obstacles to political participation because of the lack of some of the required skills, whether of literacy or of language, or because of any personal circumstances such as illness, accident and transport issues.

The ICCPR stipulates that people have 'the right and *the opportunity* ... [t]o take part in the conduct of public affairs',[59] and the CRPD provides so in similar terms. The Human Rights Committee itself provided that '[p]ositive measures should be taken to overcome specific difficulties, such as illiteracy, language barriers, poverty, or impediments to freedom of movement which prevent persons entitled to vote from exercising their rights effectively'.[60] It thus underlined the obstacles for particular groups of people and recognised the necessity to alleviate them in order to render the electoral process accessible. The 'positive measures' enumerated demonstrate that such obstacles cannot be associated solely with one of these groups as they overlap partly with those faced by other groups. Interestingly, attention is also given to factors that relate to decision-making skills but not when prompted by (intellectual) disability. The Human Rights Committee advised that '[s]pecific methods, such as photographs and symbols, should be adopted to ensure that illiterate voters have adequate information on which to base their choice'.[61] No such methods are recommended concerning deficits in mental capacity, which 'may be a ground for denying a person the right to vote or to hold office'.[62] This is indeed what the CRPD rectifies by affirming 'the right and opportunity ... to vote and be elected, inter alia, by ... allowing assistance in voting by a person of their own choice'.[63]

The continued stigma attached to deficits in mental capacity is confirmed by the different degree of political participation between groups of disabled people. Turnout in elections remains very low for those with cognitive impairments while it is as high for those with sensory impairments as it is for non-disabled people.[64] The fact is that most countries exclude those who are subject to guardianship systems either automatically or following the individual assessment of their voting capacity. The question therefore is: why are only they denied their right to vote or required to undergo such individual assessment?

The reason behind this bias can be seen in the emphasis laid on the absence of manipulation in the electoral process. As indicated by the Human Rights Committee, people 'must be free to vote ... without undue influence or coercion of

[58] Schur, Kruse and Blanck, *People with Disabilities*, 99–100.
[59] Article 25(a), ICCPR (emphasis added).
[60] Human Rights Committee, *General Comment No 25. Article 25*, para 12.
[61] Ibid.
[62] Ibid, para 4.
[63] Article 27(a)(iii), CRPD.
[64] L. Schur and M. Adya, 'Sidelined or Mainstreamed? Political Participation and Attitudes of People with Disabilities in the United States' (2013) 94 *Social Science Quarterly* 811, 831–2.

any kind which may distort or inhibit the free expression of the elector's will'.[65] The existence of 'undue influence' is then employed as argument to restrict the right to vote on the ground of (intellectual) disability, as the ones concerned are presumed to be oftenunder 'undue influence'. Nothing however indicates that these people are more easily manipulated than others, and fears in this regard should not lead to such presumption against them but rather to improved access to education and electoral information.[66] There is no reason to believe that those with cognitive impairments would have their choice particularly undermined.[67] Influence is just inherent to any electoral process. It is a vital part of political life that should be respected by government, although it should be open to scrutiny by members of the public and the media.

The CRPD also shows concern for the issue in relation to legal capacity. Article 12 makes reference to 'undue influence' with respect to the need for safeguards in 'measures relating to the exercise of legal capacity'.[68] As explained in chapter 5, there can however be difficulties in ascertaining whether such measures result in 'undue influence'. While the context is different with regard to political participation because it concerns measures to support the exercise of voting rights, the question here again is this: what precisely is 'undue influence'? Voters seek advice from people around them, including in families and communities. They may be misled or confused as a consequence, but this has nothing to do with disability.

As can be seen from the analysis, the right to political participation as initially conceived in international human rights law did not aim at actual inclusion in political life. This resulted in limited efforts to realise disabled people's political rights, which has been a significant shortcoming of democracy. The CEDAW Committee declared that '[s]ocieties in which women are excluded from public life and decision-making cannot be described as democratic'.[69] It added that '[w]omen's full participation is essential not only for their empowerment but also for the advancement of society as a whole'.[70] What can be said of women holds true for disabled people. The participation of disabled people in 'the conduct of public affairs', or rather the lack thereof, is a question that touches upon the entire population. It moreover appears that disabled people are in general highly in favour of human rights and are sympathetic to State regulation and healthcare provision.[71]

[65] Human Rights Committee, *General Comment No 25. Article 25*, para 19.

[66] J. Fiala-Butora, M. Stein and J. Lord, 'The Democratic Life of the Union: Toward Equal Voting Participation for Europeans with Disabilities' (2014) 55 *Harvard International Law Journal* 71, 86–8.

[67] M. Redley et al, 'The Voting Rights of Adults with Intellectual Disabilities: Reflections on the Arguments, and Situation in Kenya and England and Wales' (2012) 56 *Journal of Intellectual Disability Research* 1026, 1028.

[68] Article 12(4), CRPD.

[69] CEDAW Committee, *General Recommendation No 23: Political and Public Life*, para 14.

[70] Ibid, para 17.

[71] Schur, Kruse and Blanck, *People with Disabilities* 114; Schur and Adya, 'Sidelined or Mainstreamed?', 834–5.

The implementation of their right to political participation could thus have positive effects on the entire organisation of society.

The way forward is to work on a more representative political class. The CRPD stipulates that States Parties should encourage the participation of disabled people 'in the activities and administration of political parties'.[72] This participation could make political programmes more sensitive to human diversity and provide a platform for voices that are less likely to be heard in public discourse. In the CEDAW Committee's words, '[p]olicies developed and decisions made by men alone reflect only part of human experience and potential',[73] and this could also be said about disability. The failure to include disabled people in political life inevitably leads to the pursuit of narrower political goals, thereby obscuring issues that all human beings might be exposed to during their lifetime.

8.2.2 Closing the Gap

The participation of disabled people in 'the conduct of public affairs' has attracted little attention to date. The result is that disabled people remain largely excluded from political life. It leads to them being ever more isolated, which, in turn, reduces the availability of resources they need for the purpose of political participation.[74] As disabled people need to mobilise such resources in order to cope with their impairments, their capacity to contribute to deciding-making processes is much more limited than that of others. This reinforces the view that disabled people are not full members of society and incapable of contributing to the 'public good'.

In order to provide disabled people with 'the right and the *opportunity* to enjoy [political rights] on an equal basis with others',[75] States should encourage them to express their opinion in decision-making processes. Political participation is not just about voting, especially for those whose challenges are not so often discussed in electoral campaigns. Disabled people are less likely to vote for this reason, but they are eager to contact politicians and join demonstrations in order to raise matters affecting them.[76] The resentment associated with prejudices about disability fosters a belief that acting together will be more effective, and this creates an incentive for engaging in collective mobilisation.[77] Although disabled people can be reluctant to identify with a group that is still stigmatised,[78] they might consider that

[72] Article 29(b)(i), CRPD.

[73] CEDAW Committee, *General Recommendation No 23: Political and Public Life*, para 13.

[74] Schur, 'Towards Inclusion: Political and Social Participation of People with Disabilities', 124; Schur, Kruse and Blanck, *People with Disabilities*, 116.

[75] Article 29, CRPD (emphasis added).

[76] M. Mattila and A. Papageorgiou, 'Disability, Perceived Discrimination and Political Participation' (2017) 38 *International Political Science Review* 505, 513 and 516.

[77] Ibid, 515.

[78] Schur, Kruse and Blanck, *People with Disabilities*, 94.

when they act together they might have a greater influence on political agendas than through exercising their voting rights individually and in isolation.

Hence, there is a need to shift focus away from 'indirect participation' to 'direct participation' if disabled people are to 'effectively and fully participate in the conduct of public affairs', as provided for by the CRPD.[79] Too much attention has gone to the act of voting at the expense of other ways of taking part in political life. While the ICCPR offers States Parties the choice to fulfil the right to political participation 'directly *or* through freely chosen representatives',[80] the reality is that marginalised groups of people rely more on 'direct participation' if they are to enjoy their political rights. Traditionally, it has been considered that there is no obligation to guarantee 'direct participation',[81] but the time has perhaps come to move on and place 'direct participation' on an equal footing with 'indirect participation' (thus transforming 'or' into 'and' in the different human rights treaties). While the CRPD reiterates that States Parties can do either, as do both the ICCPR and CEDAW, many of its provisions aim at inclusion in political life.

Thus, it is not enough to regard 'direct participation' as an option to be tolerated alongside the regular organisation of elections. States must achieve political participation more broadly through stimulating real engagement in political activities. They should do so both by making public events accessible to disabled people and by recognising the need for their actual involvement. As younger generations display greater willingness to take part in political life than older generations,[82] there is an opportunity here to widen political participation in the future.

This being said, the way forward should not be limited to realising the right to political participation itself. Because the root of the problem lies in the isolation of disabled people as well as the resulting unavailability of resources, inclusion itself should be nurtured as a means to empower them. The right to political participation, therefore, is not only an aspect of '[f]ull and effective participation and inclusion in society' (which is one of the CRPD's general principles).[83] 'Full and effective participation and inclusion in society' in general is crucial to make headway with the exercise of that right as such, as it provides for an environment wherein individuals can take part in political life and reverses the trend whereby marginalisation prevents them from doing so. Being both the means and the end of inclusion, the political participation of disabled people marks the culmination of efforts in implementing the CRPD.

It is therefore through all the Convention rights, that is, both civil and political and economic and social rights, that the right to political participation can be

[79] Article 29(b), CRPD.
[80] Article 25(a), ICCPR (emphasis added).
[81] Joseph and Castan, *The International Covenant on Civil and Political Rights*, 737.
[82] Schur, 'Towards Inclusion: Political and Social Participation of People with Disabilities', 123; Schur, Kruse and Blanck, *People with Disabilities*, 112.
[83] Article 3(c), CRPD.

fulfilled. On the one hand, low levels of education and high levels of unemployment significantly reduce the enjoyment of political rights.[84] Economic and social rights are essential to make political participation more of a reality. As a matter of fact, disabled people who are in employment appear to be as active politically as non-disabled people.[85] As stressed in Chapter 7, this confirms that work is not just about earning a living for it provides individuals with the resources, in terms of funding, time and social relations, which are needed to organise and participate. On the other hand, the right to political participation is connected to other civil and political rights. Its very realisation depends upon both the freedom of expression and the freedom of association. As indicated by the Human Rights Committee, the right to political participation entails respect for 'freedom to engage in political activity individually or through political parties and other organizations, freedom to debate public affairs, to hold peaceful demonstrations and ... to advertise political ideas'.[86] States Parties should proactively safeguard those freedoms, and this further underscores the interrelationship between both sets of rights throughout the CRPD.[87] States Parties should not only let disabled people participate in 'the conduct of public affairs' but also enable them to do so. In the words of the OHCHR, 'mere passivity on the part of the State' does not meet the requirements set by Article 29 of the Convention.[88]

[84] Schur and Adya, 'Sidelined or Mainstreamed?', 836; Schur, 'Towards Inclusion: Political and Social Participation of People with Disabilities', 124–5.

[85] Schur, Kruse and Blanck, *People with Disabilities*, 110.

[86] Human Rights Committee, *General Comment No 25. Article 25*, para 25.

[87] de Beco, 'The Indivisibility of Human Rights and the Convention on the Rights of Persons with Disabilities', 153–4.

[88] OHCHR, *Thematic Study on Participation in Political and Public Life by Persons with Disabilities*, para 16.

III

IMPLEMENTATION: FROM RIGHTS TO REALITY

9

Participation: 'Nothing About Us Without Us'

This chapter focuses on the participation of disabled people. It starts by looking at the way in which disabled people organisations (DPOs) joined forces in the CRPD's negotiation process and disabled people managed to infuse their claims into the Convention, thereby accelerating the formation of the disability rights movement (9.1. Participation of Disabled People in the Negotiation Process). It then turns to the domestic level examining the obligation to consult disabled people 'through their representative organizations', including the requirements of such consultations, and the necessity of facilitating the participation of disabled people in the implementation of the Convention (9.2. Participation of Disabled People in the Implementation of the CRPD). It also explores the broader implications of 'Nothing about us without us' for international human rights law with regard to the involvement of civil society organisations (9.3. Participation in International Human Rights Law).

9.1 Participation of Disabled People in the Negotiation Process

Disabled people were mostly absent from the elaboration of international instruments on disability prior to the CRPD. In those international instruments that did address disability, they were regarded more as recipients of welfare than as subjects of rights. A change in perspective was precipitated in 2002 when the General Assembly decided to launch negotiations on a 'comprehensive and integral international convention to promote and protect the rights and dignity of persons with disabilities'.[1] The resulting human rights treaty would transform the view of disability in the field of international human rights law.

Civil society actually took part in the elaboration of the new convention to a degree never done before.[2] A contrasting example – witnessed by the present

[1] GA, *Comprehensive and Integral International Convention to Promote and Protect the Rights and Dignity of Persons with Disabilities*, 26 February 2002, A/RES/56/168.

[2] R. Kayess and P. French, 'Out of Darkness into Light? Introducing the Convention on the Rights of Persons with Disabilities' (2008) 8 *Human Rights Law Review* 1, 3–4; A. Kanter, *The Development of Disability Rights under International Law. From Charity to Human Rights* (Abingdon: Routledge, 2015) 40.

Disability in International Human Rights Law. Gauthier de Beco, Oxford University Press. © Gauthier de Beco 2021.
DOI: 10.1093/oso/9780198824503.003.0010

author–[3] is the Optional Protocol to the Convention on the Rights of the Child on a communications procedure (OP3-CRC) adopted in 2011, where NGOs were largely excluded from the negotiation process, as governmental delegations decided to discuss the draft behind closed doors in order to avoid opposition.[4] Another such example is the project of a Convention on the Rights of Older Persons. Despite the establishment of an UN Open-Ended Working Group on Ageing (OEWGA) with the mandate to examine 'proposals for an international legal instrument to promote and protect the rights and dignity of older persons',[5] this project is currently on hold. In comparison with disability, the lack of an elderly rights movement, which could defend the interests of old people, is one reason that explains the challenge.[6] It is a particular characteristic of the CRPD that its drafting has involved so closely its beneficiaries, and this has given the Convention extensive symbolic power in the eyes of those beneficiaries.

The negotiation process was thus quite open, especially in view of the fact that disabled people had hitherto been largelyinvisible in the international framework of human rights. Governmental delegations were keen to use disabled people's expertise given that they had limited knowledge on issues related to disability.[7] Disabled people had the opportunity to share their lived experience with the negotiators in furtherance of this end. It helped that the General Assembly ruled that any organisation could apply for accreditation to participate in the sessions regardless of its consultative status with the UN.[8] The latter had granted just seven organisations such a status so far, which formed together the International Disability Alliance (IDA), a restricted and exclusive group of DPOs which came to dominate the scene.[9] The lobbying for this change in procedural rules led to a multitude of DPOs that were not part of the IDA joining in the drafting of the CRPD. Mainstream NGOs, like Amnesty International and Human Rights Watch, likewise expressed their approval for the drafting although their actual participation remained minimal.[10] Whether they were reluctant to do so do or whether the

[3] The author represented Belgium in all the sessions of the Working Group on OP3-CRC in his capacity of Legal Adviser at the Belgian Ministry of Justice.

[4] G. de Beco, 'The Optional Protocol to the Convention on the Rights of the Child on a Communications Procedure: Good News?' (2013) 13 *Human Rights Law Review* 367, 387.

[5] GA, *Towards a Comprehensive and Integral International Legal Instrument to Promote and Protect the Rights and Dignity of Older Persons*, 20 December 2012, A/RES/67/139.

[6] J. Sciubba, 'Securing Rights in the 21st Century: A Comparison of the Disability and Older Persons' Rights Convention' (2016) 15 *Journal of Human Rights* 533, 538–9.

[7] A. Herro, 'The Pre-negotiation of UN Human Rights Treaties: The Case of the Convention on the Rights of Persons with Disabilities' (2019) 24 *International Negotiation* 240, 250.

[8] G. Quinn, 'Disability and Human Rights: A New Field in the United Nations' in K. Krause and M. Scheinin (eds), *International Protection of Human Rights: A Textbook* (Turku: Åbo Akademi University-Institute for Human Rights, 2009) 247, 256.

[9] The seven organisations were represented in the Expert Panel established by the Standard Rules on the Equalization of Opportunities for Persons with Disabilities (Standard Rules).

[10] J. Lord, 'Disability Rights and the Human Rights Mainstream: Reluctant Gate-Crashers?' in B. Clifford (ed), *The International Struggle for New Human Rights* (Philadelphia: University of Pennsylvania Press, 2008) 83, 90.

DPOs were unwilling to engage with them is subject to interpretation. Other actors involved were national human rights institutions (NHRIs), academics and the European Union (which subsequently became a 'State Party' to the CRPD).

The International Disability Caucus (IDC) played a major role in facilitating the participation of disabled people in the negotiation process. The IDC was a large international network of DPOs, including national, regional and international organisations, as well as a number of NGOs concerned with disabled people, which expanded considerably as discussions moved forward.[11] Under the leadership of the DPOs, it came to coordinate their action and to intervene on behalf of them thanks to intensive consultations and mutual agreement on the common position. Under the motto 'Nothing about us without us', disabled people could, at last, speak out in a united voice.

The Ad Hoc Committee, which was charged with the task of elaborating the new convention by the General Assembly, met eight times between 2002 and 2006 (the Economic and Social Council (ECOSOC) acting as its Secretariat in New York). At its second meeting, it set up a Working Group in order to prepare a draft text for the future convention. DPOs were represented in this Working Group alongside governmental delegations with whom they were on an equal footing. While the number of DPOs was initially restricted to the aforementioned seven organisations that were part of the IDA, States would expand the number by eventually nominating twelve of them through the addition of five regional organisations so as to ensure a broader representation.[12] Many prominent activists of the disability rights movement were thus allowed to provide input in the discussions, which largely drew upon ideas emanating from disabled people themselves. The lack of an accessible venue for disabled people meant that they had to place themselves in the room next to governmental delegations where they could have free exchanges of ideas with the officials on the proposals that were on the table.[13] Some of the prominent activists even assumed positions on those government delegations as advisors and, in certain instances, as head of delegation.

In this way, 'Nothing about us without us' came to shape the debate on the future convention. The formation of a large coalition in fact started as a result of Mexico's proposal to launch the negotiation process, an initiative which took civil society very much by surprise.[14] The establishment of an Ad Hoc Committee compelled

[11] S. Tromel, 'Personal Perspective on the Drafting History of the United Nations Convention on the Rights of Persons with Disabilities' in G. Quinn and L. Waddington (eds), *European Yearbook of Disability Law* (Antwerp: Intersentia, 2009) 115, 117–18.

[12] J. Lord, 'NGO Participation In Human Rights Law And Process: Latest Developments in The Effort to Develop An International Treaty On The Rights Of People With Disabilities' (2004) 10 *ILSA Journal of International & Comparative Law* 311, 315.

[13] J. Lord, 'Mirror Mirror, Mirror on the Wall: Voice Accountability and NGOs in Human Rights Standard Setting' (2004) 5 *Seton Hall Journal of Diplomacy and International Relations* 93, 96.

[14] Lord, 'NGO Participation in Human Rights Law and Process', 313; Herro, 'The Pre-negotiation of UN Human Rights Treaties', 254–5.

the DPOs to join forces with a view to maximising their impact on the deliberations in New York. Retrospectively, the opportunity to participate in the negotiation process has proven transformative for this nascent disability rights movement. It created not only a real momentum but also a sense of ownership on the part of disabled people that would persist long after the entry into force of the CRPD. The drafting also gave new direction to many organisations involved, which added the protection of human rights to their own mandate and sometimes changed their name in order to align themselves with the Convention's objectives.[15]

The manner in which DPOs have exerted their influence is visible throughout the Convention. As seen in Chapter 5, the contested footnote to Article 12, declaring legal capacity solely as a 'capacity for rights' in certain UN official languages, was withdrawn after fierce opposition.[16] The provision of 'alternative forms of education' in Article 24, where there was no other option available, was similarly put aside.[17] While the Convention does not say so in plain language, it definitely supports arguments against the maintenance of separate regimes or segregated settings for disabled people (like guardianship systems and special schools). While there was discordance between the DPOs which had to make trade-offs to reach consensus, the fact that they succeeded in making such compromises by itself substantially increased their clout.

While 'Nothing about us without us' has been a reality indeed, the question is whether representativity has characterised this negotiation process all the way through. In order to understand the problem, it is worth reiterating that disability can manifest itself in an infinite number of ways, so that those who are disabled do not form a heterogeneous group. DPOs for this reason have most of the time focused their attention on particular kinds of impairments, whereas umbrella organisations are more recent phenomena. As a result, the feelings of collective identity have been relatively weak and the different interests of disabled people have not always coincided but sometimes been in opposition to each other.

As mentioned in Chapter 4, the CRPD has catered for the inherent plurality of disability in some respects, but the project remains incomplete. Some organisations have had more weight than others during the Convention's negotiation process. The extent of their influence often depended on the organisational strength and bargaining power of the individual DPOs. While the IDC managed to build consensus, it did not completely resolve disagreement and remained to an extent under the control of the IDA.[18] The result is that not all groups of disabled people

[15] Lord, 'Disability Rights and the Human Rights Mainstream', 91.

[16] A. Dhanda, 'Legal Capacity in the Disability Rights Convention: Stranglehold of the Past or Lodestar for the Future?' (2007) 34 *Syracuse Journal of International Law and Commerce* 429, 454–5.

[17] G. de Beco, 'Comprehensive Legal Analysis of Article 24 of the Convention on the Rights of Persons with Disabilities' in G. de Beco, J. Lord and S. Quinlivan (eds), *The Right to Inclusive Education in International Human Rights Law* (Cambridge: Cambridge University Press, 2019) 58, 65–6.

[18] M. Sabatello, 'The New Diplomacy' in M. Sabatello and M. Schulze (eds), *Human Rights & Disability Advocacy* (Philadelphia: University of Pennsylvania Press 2013) 238, 248.

were represented equally, which is why the CRPD may seem to privilege certain categories of disabilities over others.

The World Blind Union (WBU), World Federation of the Deaf (WFD) and Deafblind International (DbI) noticeably distanced themselves from the general position. For instance, they raised serious doubts about the goal of inclusive education, which they considered as an attempt to impose assimilation in mainstream settings.[19] Sharing a distinct identity associated with 'Deaf culture', those who are deaf told of their particular negative experiences of inclusive education. They defended the possibility of providing education in special schools, where deaf children can have the ability to maintain social relations and communicate in their own language with their peers.[20] The CRPD consequently stipulates that disabled people 'in particular children, who are blind, deaf or deafblind, [should be educated] ... in environments which maximize academic and social development',[21] which has been interpreted as a 'sensory exception' to the goal of inclusive education.[22] Following the pressure of the relevant organisations, the negotiators reconfigured the text of the Convention in quite ambiguous terms with a view to reflecting the wishes of the 'Deaf community'. There is still contention in this regard as the CRPD Committee has adopted a different interpretation of the abovementioned provision. This interpretation has been criticised by scholars who refer to Article 24's drafting history in order to defend the reservation of spaces for deaf children in the education system.[23]

Another organisation which pushed its demands during the CRPD's negotiation process and ultimately within the text itself is the World Network of Users and Survivors of Psychiatry (WNUSP). Reckoning that any forced treatment is a violation of human rights, the WNUSP advocated for the full closure of institutions and banning of all coercive and involuntary measures, whatever the conditions under which they are carried out or the reasons behind them, including protection against self-harm or harm to others. Just as happened with the WBU, WFD and the DbI, it was particularly those '[s]ingle issue' organisations which represented extremely marginalised groups that were successful in garnering support for their strong views.[24] Other organisations with different aims were somewhat silenced

[19] WBU, WFD and DbI, 'Article 17 Statement on Inclusive Education for Persons who are Deaf, Blind and Deafblind: The Rationale for Choice in Education', https://static.un.org/esa/socdev/enable/rights/ahcstata24sevscomments.htm#multi.

[20] R. Kayess and J. Green, 'Today's Lesson is on Diversity: A Reflection on Inclusive Education' in P. Blanck and E. Flynn (eds), *Routledge Handbook of Disability Law and Human Rights* (London: Routledge, 2016) 53, 66.

[21] Article 24(3)(c), CRPD.

[22] J. Murray, M. De Meulder and D. le Maire, 'An Education in Sign Language as a Human Right?: The Sensory Exception in the Legislative History and Ongoing Interpretation of Article 24 of the UN Convention on the Rights of Persons with Disabilities' (2018) 40 *Human Rights Quarterly* 37, 45–6.

[23] J. Murray et al, 'Intersectional Inclusion for Deaf Learners: Moving beyond General Comment No. 4 on Article 24 of the United Nations Convention on the Rights of Persons with Disabilities' (2020) 24 *International Journal of Inclusive Education* 691, 694–5.

[24] Lord, 'Mirror Mirror, Mirror on the Wall', 103.

as a consequence. For people with cognitive impairments, for instance, respect for autonomy might overshadow the importance of social relations in exercising their freedoms.[25] As highlighted by Meyers, the risk in gearing DPOs' efforts towards advocacy is to lose sight of other priorities, which may matter more for their members, in order to align themselves with a larger agenda.[26] Input has moreover been limited from the very stakeholders to whom the CRPD is directed, such as mental health services and education systems. While the negotiation process has been one of the most participative in the whole of international human rights law, the varying degrees of representativity might turn out to be a source of resistance when considering the practical consequences of meeting the ensuing legal obligations.

Intersectionality raised similar issues concerning the heterogeneity of disabled people. As mentioned in Chapter 4, the CRPD draws particular attention to intra-group differences. While it has done so more than any previous human rights treaty, it does not offer all groups of disabled people the same level of consideration. It overlooks the specific forms of disadvantage faced by disabled LGBT people, while it makes no reference at all to 'sexual orientation' (not even in the Preamble).[27] Similarly, the negotiators displayed little enthusiasm for mentioning indigenous disabled people despite repeated requests to do so from some DPOs,[28] even if the term 'indigenous' narrowly found its way into the Preamble.[29] The Convention also gives scant attention to the elderly, with no more than two references to 'old age', despite the increasing proportion of old people in today's population and the close relationship between disability and old age.[30] In contrast, disabled women and children are well protected by the CRPD. The question, once more, is how it comes that some groups of disabled people have had their voice heard in the discussions and others not. One explanation as to why they were able to obtain higher gains is that their rights were already specially protected by other human rights treaties (like the CEDAW and the CRC) and that their concerns were already high on the international agenda. Compared with LGBT and indigenous disabled people, disabled children and women could call upon such human rights treaties prior to the CRPD. With the Convention's adoption, they can now lean even more on international human rights law.[31]

[25] K. Johnson, 'The UN Convention on the Rights of Persons with Disabilities: A Framework for Ethical and Inclusive Practice?' (2013) 7 *Ethics & Social Welfare* 218, 226–7.

[26] S. Meyers, 'NGO-Ization and Human Rights Law: The CRPD's Civil Society Mandate' (2016) 5 *Laws 1*, 6–7.

[27] G. de Beco, 'Intersectionality and Disability in International Human Rights Law' (2020) 24 *International Journal of Human Rights* 593, 605–6.

[28] P. Harpur, 'Indigenous Persons with Disabilities and the Convention on the Rights of Persons with Disabilities. An Identity without a Home?' (2018) 7 *International Human Rights Law Review* 165, 179–80.

[29] Preamble(p), CRPD.

[30] Articles 25(b) and 28(2)(b), CRPD.

[31] de Beco, 'Intersectionality and Disability in International Human Rights Law', 607.

9.2 Participation of Disabled People in the Implementation of the CRPD

The CRPD itself has integrated the manner in which disabled people participated in its negotiation process. Providing for the participation of disabled people is a fundamental requirement in implementing the Convention. It obliges States Parties to give due consideration to these people's views when adopting policies relating to disability. This is probably the true and real expression of the motto 'Nothing about us without us', because it is at the national level that this Convention will meet its test of truth. The right to participate in decision-making processes is also crucial to achieve the shift from seeing disabled people as mere objects of charity to regarding them as holders of rights.

Article 4(3) of the CRPD stipulates that in 'decision-making processes concerning issues relating to persons with disabilities, States Parties shall closely consult with and actively involve persons with disabilities ... through their representative organisations'. This provision attests to DPOs' international standing which sprung out of the negotiation process and paved the way for the disability rights movement's consolidation. Article 4(3) strengthens 'participatory rights' and recognizes the expertise of disabled people themselves.[32] While it accords with the spirit of this Convention, there was a similar sort of requirement in the Standard Rules.[33] It was nonetheless key to have the Convention stress it once again given disabled people's exclusion from political life in the past.

No other human rights treaty provides for such an obligation to reach out to civil society. As mentioned in Chapter 8, the CRPD requires that States Parties encourage participation in 'the conduct of public affairs' through the '[f]orming and joining organizations of persons with disabilities to represent persons with disabilities'.[34] Article 4(3) goes a step further by obliging States Parties to turn to those organisations in order to give disabled people the opportunity to express their opinions wherever their rights are at stake. According to the CRPD Committee, the kind of issues on which they should be consulted are wide and cover 'the full range of legislative, administrative and other measures that may directly or indirectly impact the rights of persons with disabilities'.[35] Although it is linked to the right to political participation, this obligation is something new in the field of international human rights law. Its importance is attested not only by the recurring reference to 'Nothing about us without us' in domestic debates but also by a General Comment

[32] M. Sabatello, 'A Short History of the International Disability Rights Movement' in Sabatello and Schulze, *Human Rights & Disability Advocacy* 13, 23.

[33] Rule 18(2), Standard Rules.

[34] Article 29(b)(ii), CRPD.

[35] Ibid, para 18.

on the participation of disabled people in the implementation of the Convention from the CRPD Committee (which is its last general comment to date).[36]

States Parties must consult disabled people 'through their representative organisations', that is, through the organisations *of* disabled people (abbreviated DPOs). These organisations are different to those that are *for* disabled people, whose function is to defend the latter's interests or offer them different kinds of services. In the words of the CRPD Committee, it concerns 'those that are led, directed and governed by persons with disabilities'.[37] There are naturally different types of DPOs, including umbrella organisations, cross-disability organisations, self-advocacy groups or organisations of families with disabled people.[38] What crucially matters is that they are effectively run by disabled people, which of course does not prevent other people from being part of them.

As highlighted by the CRPD Committee, it is also essential that the consultations take place 'in a meaningful and timely manner'.[39] In order to do so, States Parties must foster an environment that enables DPOs to actually engage in conversations. The participation of disabled people if it is to be fruitful is contingent upon the allocation of resources and availability of expertise.[40] Participation entails allowing the DPOs to exert real influence over the debate. The States Parties must act transparently by offering these organisations access to the available information and inviting them to the meetings, while leaving enough time for them to prepare their responses to any proposals. The reality is that they often feel that decisions have been made in advance, with the holding of such meetings being only 'pro forma' in order to satisfy procedural requirements.[41] It is crucial however that the opinion of disabled people is taken seriously by government. The latter should not only answer the questions such people may have but also give enough weight to their arguments and adjust any decisions accordingly. In the words of the CRPD Committee, States Parties should provide 'an explicit explanation ... of the findings, considerations and reasoning of decisions on how their views were considered and why'.[42]

The CRPD in fact has confirmed and consolidated existing practice in many jurisdictions. The consultation of disabled people 'through their representative

[36] CRPD Committee, *General Comment No 7: The Participation of Persons with Disabilities, including Children with Disabilities, through their Representative Organizations, in the Implementation and Monitoring of the Convention*, 9 November 2018, CRPD/C/GC/7.

[37] Ibid, para 11.

[38] Ibid, para 12.

[39] Ibid, para 21.

[40] G. de Beco and A. Hoefmans, 'National Structures for the Implementation and Monitoring of the UN Convention on the Rights of Persons with Disabilities' in G. de Beco (ed), *Article 33 of the UN Convention on the Rights of Persons with Disabilities: National Structures for the Implementation and Monitoring of the Convention* (Leiden/Boston: Martinus Nijhoff Publishers, 2013) 11, 58–9.

[41] L. Löve, R. Traustadóttir and J. Rice, 'Achieving Disability Equality: Empowering Disabled People to Take the Lead' (2018) 6 *Social Inclusion* 1, 6.

[42] CRPD Committee, *General Comment No 7*, para 23.

organizations' often occurs through national advisory councils attached to (national or regional) public departments. While such councils existed prior to the CRPD, they can now facilitate the participation of disabled people in the implementation of the Convention.[43] They usually consist of DPO as well as ministerial representatives and provide advice on the adoption of policies relating to disability.[44] Although the national advisory councils are not decision-making bodies, they represent a useful channel of communication between government and civil society.

The requirement to consult disabled people 'through their representative organisations' extends to assessing whether States Parties are progressing in the realisation of the CRPD rights. Article 33(3) provides that '[c]ivil society, in particular persons with disabilities and their representative organizations, shall be involved and participate fully in the monitoring process'. While this provision is connected to the obligation provided for by Article 4(3) of the Convention, it does not relate to the Convention's implementation as such but to the monitoring of this implementation. Article 33(3) covers the classic monitoring function of civil society *vis-à-vis* the government. It encompasses not just DPOs even though it concerns 'in particular persons with disabilities and their representative organizations'. Article 33(3) has therefore not only a broader reach (which includes 'persons with disabilities' themselves) but also a stronger terminology than Article 4(3), referring to 'full participation' rather than mere consultation.

In monitoring the implementation of the CRPD, the DPOs may join other forces. They can do so in umbrella organisations, but they may also work through independent mechanisms in which DPOs should be represented alongside other civil society organisations, as will be seen Chapter 10. Disabled people must also be able to participate in their own right both by engaging in advocacy and campaigns and by undertaking independent reviews. It is necessary for that purpose that they be given the means to 'be involved and participate fully in the monitoring process'.[45] In order to enhance their capacity to do so, States Parties should support disabled people by allocating resources to DPOs in addition to, and not as a replacement of, those put in place in line with Article 4(3).[46] A delicate exercise will be to ensure that they reach those organisations that defend less powerful groups. States Parties should make provision to ensure that all disabled people are actually included whether or not the major DPOs are present. As provided by the CRPD Committee, they should 'actively involve and consult the full range of persons with

[43] de Beco and Hoefmans, 'National Structures for the Implementation and Monitoring of the UN Convention on the Rights of Persons with Disabilities', 60–1.

[44] G. de Beco, 'Article 33 of the UN Convention on the Rights of Persons with Disabilities: Practice and Evaluation' in L. Waddington, G. Quinn and E. Flynn (eds), *European Yearbook of Disability Law. Volume 5* (Antwerp: Intersentia, 2014) 9, 14–15.

[45] Article 33(3), CRPD.

[46] CRPD Committee, *General Comment No 7*, para 39.

disabilities including organizations of women with disabilities, older persons with disabilities, children with disabilities, persons with psychosocial disabilities and persons with intellectual disabilities'.[47]

One particular instance where such monitoring can take place is the State reporting process before the CRPD Committee. DPOs may submit a 'shadow report' or contribute to a collective one that is prepared by a broader alliance.[48] In order to be able to draft such a 'shadow report', they must be able to compile data on the discharge of State Party's legal obligations under the CRPD. The DPOs will therefore allow the Committee to check the accuracy of the information provided in the State report.

Moving further on in the State reporting process, it is crucial that the CRPD Committee itself includes disabled people in its membership. The motto 'Nothing about us without us' is especially relevant for this Committee whose mandate it is to evaluate compliance with the CRPD. The latter stipulates that, in the nomination of its members, States Parties should give 'consideration ... to equitable geographical distribution, representation of the different forms of civilization and of the principal legal systems, balanced gender representation and participation of *experts with disabilities*'.[49] Disability is thus a factor to be taken into consideration with regard to this nomination. The Convention moreover encourages the States Parties to seek input by the DPOs in the selection process along the lines of Article 4(3).[50]

Disabled people have actually made up the vast majority of the CRPD Committee's members up to until now.[51] Many of those who helped draft the CRPD came to be in charge of making recommendations to States Parties concerning the steps to be taken in order to meet their legal obligations. Many of the Committee's members are associated with national and regional DPOs or are part of the grassroots movements of their country of origin. Their presence is essential not only to ensure the Committee's legitimacy in disabled people's eyes but also to gain first-hand information on the situation on the ground. It is also in keeping with the need for appreciating and valuing these people's expertise whenever advice is provided on disability-related issues.

Whether there is a need for having an overwhelming 'participation of experts with disabilities' in the membership is nonetheless debatable. The CRPD refers to other criteria as well, such as 'equitable geographical distribution ... [and]

[47] CRPD Committee, *General Comment No 5. Article 19: Living Independently and Being Included in the Community*, 29 August 2017, CRPD/C/GC/5, para 70.

[48] de Beco and Hoefmans, 'National Structures for the Implementation and Monitoring of the UN Convention on the Rights of Persons with Disabilities', 61–2.

[49] Article 34(5), CRPD.

[50] Article 34(4), CRPD. A call for reserving membership to disabled people or requiring that its chairperson be disabled however was unsuccessful (M. Stein and J. Lord, 'Monitoring the Convention on the Rights of Persons with Disabilities: Innovations, Lost Opportunities, and Future Potential' (2010) 32 *Human Rights Quarterly* 689, 695 fn 26).

[51] The list is available here: https://www.ohchr.org/EN/HRBodies/CRPD/Pages/Membership.aspx.

balanced gender representation',[52] which have been an issue with regard to the CRPD Committee. The Committee has expressed its concerns about this issue at a time when only one amongst its members (18 in total) was a woman.[53] What is more, it may be argued that for a treaty body to be efficient a broad spectrum of knowledge relating to the subject matter is essential, which entails not only familiarity with different policy areas but also the ability to work with different disciplines. The handling of communications, as set out in the Optional Protocol to the Convention, for instance, requires essential legal skills. The question is why has identity received such a high level of priority over the other criteria.

Although such concerns do not take away the advantages of the 'participation of experts with disabilities', it may create a sense of partiality and a feeling that the CRPD Committee's opinions are too one-sided. Being composed of the most prominent activists of the disability rights movement, this Committee has essentially partnered up with civil society organisations in a departure from most other treaty bodies which tend to collaborate with governments with a view to multiplying best practices globally.[54] The Committee then may be regarded more as a lobbying than as an expert body. This makes it harder for it to act as a mediator between the various stakeholders and to use forms of language that could encourage subsequent follow-up. Although it would be wrong to conclude that the views of the CRPD Committee are pushing the Convention to its extreme for that reason, its membership can result in opinions regarding its provisions that are considered as far removed from the reality of government.

9.3 Participation in International Human Rights Law

'Nothing about us without us' has implications for the whole of international human rights law. It confirms the active role that civil society should play in the development of international (human rights) law. Never had the UN endorsed this role in such an explicit manner though. The participation of disabled people in the CRPD's negotiation process therefore serves as an example of how to listen to the people in the elaboration of international instruments.

Citizens have actually a limited degree of control in the conduct of international affairs and are not really represented by States at the international level.[55] Once

[52] Article 34(5), CRPD.

[53] CRPD Committee, 'Achieving gender balance and equitable geographical representation in the elections of members of the Committee', Adopted during the Committee's seventeenth session (20 March–12 April 2017), https://www.ohchr.org/Documents/HRBodies/CRPD/Statements/FINAL0504.docx.

[54] J. Craigie et al, 'Legal Capacity Mental Capacity and Supported Decision-Making: Report from a Panel Event' (2019) 62 *International Journal of Law and Psychiatry* 160, 165.

[55] S. Besson and J. Marti, 'Legitimate Actors of International Law-Making: Towards a Theory of International Democratic Representation' (2018) 9 *Jurisprudence* 504, 516–17.

a government has been elected, it enjoys extensive freedom on its course of action, without or only rarely being held accountable for its positions. There is a gap in legitimacy, which is why the involvement of civil society organisations is so important. As it would be impractical for all constituents to represent themselves in the international arena, their interests need to be protected by such organisations.[56] States must therefore ensure that these organisations can be involved through the joining of their efforts to mobilise and their emergence as a counterweight to power.

Disabled people indeed managed to infuse many of their claims into the CRPD. This is a remarkable achievement, especially since there was as yet no coherent disability rights movement. The impact civil society has had on these deliberations remains a unique phenomenon in the field of international human rights law.

Several conditions facilitated the participation of disabled people in the Convention's negotiation process. One of them was the decision mentioned earlier by the General Assembly to drop the requirement of enjoying consultative status with the UN.[57] The pressure by civil society organisations to gain more access to the table resulted in an opening for many DPOs to get in. Another was their capability to organize themselves quickly at the very start of the negotiation process by overcoming disagreement among themselves and establishing a large coalition so quickly.[58] The IDC's role again was crucial for enabling them to form a single front in the discussions.

The question nonetheless remains whether this achieves a genuine representation of the citizens internationally. Civil society organisations also may not be representative. Some groups mattered a lot more than others in the drafting of the CRPD, so that the latter may prove particularly favourable to some categories of disability. The reality is that not all civil society organisations have the same capacity to influence the outcome.[59] It is therefore necessary to keep participation in check, as done by the States when they decided to adapt the procedural rules in order to enlarge access to more and more DPOs.

The involvement of civil society organisations is not some kind of passive engagement where governments allow them to have their say only when so requested. As noted by Peters, 'participatory rights are at least on the halfway point between merely having rights and making law, and blur the line between law-producers and bystanders'.[60] Never has this been truer than with the CRPD, the drafting of which led to a quasi-total blurring of any such line. Both physically and sometimes in the

[56] N. Maisley, 'The International Right of Rights? Article 25(a) of the ICCPR as a Human Right to Take Part in International Law-Making' (2017) 28 *European Journal of International Law* 89, 108.

[57] Quinn, 'Disability and Human Rights', 256.

[58] Sciubba, 'Securing Rights in the 21st Century', 538–9.

[59] Besson and Marti, 'Legitimate Actors of International Law-Making', 527–8.

[60] A. Peters, 'Membership in the Global Constitutional Community' in J. Klabbers, A. Peters and G. Ulfstein (eds), *The Constitutionalization of International Law* (Oxford: Oxford University Press, 2009) 155, 160.

technical sense, disabled people were inside governmental delegations whilst the Ad Hoc Committee progressed with its work.[61] This has been positive not only in terms of legitimacy, but also because governments tend largely to concentrate on matters of deliberation rather than drawing on expertise.[62] By tapping on the life-experience of disabled people, the governmental delegations could increase their knowledge of the range of issues to be dealt with in the new convention.

This being said, States accept the proposals under consideration and eventually adhere to the international instrument which imposes legal obligations on them. While they are responsible for making the choices, they are free to have civil society organisations involved. Civil society has a 'voice' but not 'a vote' in the international arena, since it is the States that are charged with international (human rights) law making.[63] Whether this 'voice' is incorporated or not in the final text actually depends on whether and how far the better argument can prevail in any discussions.[64] The CRPD's negotiation process actually allowed this to happen in contrast to that of other human rights treaties (like OP3-CRC). In the view of de Burca, Keohane and Sabel, by establishing a set of interim goals and providing for a flexible procedure with broader objectives, this Convention qualifies as 'experimentalist'.[65] It stands out as an example of collaboration between government and civil society, thereby enhancing the position of non-state actors in international (human rights) law. There is nonetheless a good chance that it may not be replicated any time soon, since there is no appetite currently for adopting more human rights treaties and any initiatives towards this end have had a limited success so far.

Turning to the domestic level, international human rights law has recognised the right to be consulted in decision-making processes. The CRC explicitly guarantees such right by providing to 'the child who is capable of forming ... her own views the right to express those views freely in all matters affecting the child'.[66] The right of the child to be heard was not only unknown prior to this Convention but has also become one of its most influential provisions in the entire field of international human rights law.[67] Testament to its prominence is that CRC Committee has listed it amongst the four general principles of the Convention.

The CRPD expands upon that right, but its wording differs in essential ways. It does not refer to matters affecting a 'disabled person' but rather to 'issues relating to *persons with disabilities*'.[68] This wording is stronger because the right to

61 Tromel, 'Personal Perspective on the Drafting History', 117–18.
62 Besson and Marti, 'Legitimate Actors of International Law-Making', 519–20.
63 Peters, 'Membership in the Global Constitutional Community', 237.
64 Maisley, 'The International Right of Rights?', 111.
65 G. de Burca, R. Keohane and C. Sabel, 'New Modes of Pluralist Global Governance' (2013) 45 *New York University Journal of International Law & Politics* 723, 743 and 754–6.
66 Article 12(1), CRC.
67 L. Lundy, J. Tobin and A. Parkes, 'Article 12: The Right to Respect for the Views of the Child' in J. Tobin (ed), *The UN Convention on the Rights of the Child. A Commentary* (Oxford: Oxford University Press, 2019) 397, 398–9.
68 Article 4(3), CRPD (emphasis added).

be consulted in decision-making processes does not pertain to the situation of a particular individual but to that of the group as a whole whether the issues relate specifically or not to this group. The Preamble even considers that States Parties should consult disabled people 'in decision-making processes about policies and programmes, *including* those directly concerning them'.[69] The CRPD thus establishes 'participatory rights' in general even if it does foremost pertain to policies relating to disability.

The CRPD makes a further distinction with regard to disabled children. It does not limit the right of the child to be heard only to those 'capable of forming [their] own views', which limitation is present in the CRC.[70] Even if the latter requires finding out how the child could express herself rather than imposing an adult perspective to the right,[71] this limitation may be used as a motive for imposing restrictions on consultations because of disability. The CRPD does not simply omit it but on the contrary specifies that disabled children should 'be provided with disability and age-appropriate assistance to realize that right',[72] thereby reflecting the need for achieving 'supported decision-making' as a way to strive for autonomy. As a result, the right of the child to be heard is not conditional on the assessment of coming to understand what is precisely at stake. The question nonetheless remains whether this assessment is still part of the CRC's requirements. The resulting discrepancy between the two human rights treaties at least pleads in favour of relaxing the condition that the child must be 'capable of forming her own views' before exercising the right in question.[73]

Human rights bodies have confirmed the right to be consulted in decision-making processes. In its General Comment on the right to the highest attainable standard of health, the CESCR Committee declared that '[t]he right of individuals and groups to participate in decision-making processes . . . must be an integral component of any policy, programme or strategy developed to discharge governmental obligation'.[74] It furthermore reckoned that 'the participation of the population in all health-related decision-making at the community, national and international levels' is essential with regard to the realisation of the right to health.[75] In relation to a new night-flight policy at Heathrow Airport, the European Court of Human Rights also considered that 'it would have been open to [the plaintiffs] to make any representations they felt appropriate ... [and] [h]ad any representations not been taken into account, they could have challenged subsequent decisions, or the

[69] Preamble(o), CRPD (emphasis added).
[70] Article 12(1), CRC.
[71] Lundy, Tobin and Parkes, 'Article 12: The Right to Respect for the Views of the Child', 402.
[72] Article 7(3), CRPD.
[73] Article 12(1), CRC.
[74] CESCR Committee, *General Comment No 14: The Right to the Highest Attainable Standard of Health*, 11 August 2000, E/C.12/2000/4, para 54.
[75] Ibid, para 11.

scheme itself, in the courts'.[76] These considerations show the importance assigned to civil society organisations' involvement, and failure to allow for this involvement can amount to a violation of the right to be consulted in decision-making processes.

For 'participatory rights' like those to be protected, States must still be able to regulate citizens' representation. Such regulation is necessary in order to protect them from unequal power relationships between civil society organisations.[77] It involves verifying that those organisations that are at the table do represent those on whose behalf they purportedly speak and that they take into account all people's interests. From a non-discrimination perspective, States therefore should provide support to the organisations that defend more marginalised groups even if this might sometimes result in conflict with the freedom of association.[78] The CRPD reveals the need for such interventions so that these groups can contribute to any debate on issues that may be relevant to them.

[76] European Court of Human Rights, *Hatton and others v United Kingdom*, 8 July 2003, Appl No 36022/97, para 128.

[77] M. Walzer, 'The Civil Society Argument' in C. Mouffe (ed), *Dimensions of Radical Democracy. Pluralism, Citizenship, Community* (London/New York: Verso, 1992) 89, 104.

[78] M. McMurry, 'Applying Human Rights to Enable Participation' (2019) 23 *International Journal of Human Rights* 1049, 1056–9.

10
Monitoring: The Role of Independent Mechanisms

This chapter concerns the role of independent mechanisms. It explains what are national human rights institutions (NHRIs) as well as the fundamental principles that should guide these institutions, as set out in the Paris Principles (10.1. National Human Rights Institutions (NHRIs)). It then examines the requirement to set up a 'framework including one or more independent mechanism' in accordance with the CRPD as well as the way in which such mechanisms relate to the said Principles and all the possibilities open to States Parties regarding this framework (10.2. Framework including One or More Independent Mechanisms). It finishes by exploring what the reference to the Paris Principles has come to mean for NHRIs and what the Convention reveals in the field of international human rights law through its elaborate monitoring system (10.3. Lessons for International Human Rights Law).

10.1 National Human Rights Institutions (NHRIs)

The idea of establishing NHRIs dates back to the very beginnings of the UN. In 1946, the Economic and Social Council (ECOSOC) invited States to set up 'local human rights committees . . . to collaborate with them in furthering the work of the Commission on Human Rights' (now Human Rights Council).[1] Several of them did so, starting with the French *Commission nationale consultative des droits de l'homme* (CNCDH) in 1947. ECOSOC also continued to encourage the creation of NHRIs.[2] The next significant step took place in 1978 when the Commission on Human Rights convened a 'Seminar on National and Local Institutions for the Promotion and Protection of Human Rights'.[3] This seminar culminated in a set of guidelines on the structure and functioning of NHRIs, which were acknowledged by the General Assembly.[4]

[1] ECOSOC, Resolution 2/9, 21 June 1946, para 5.

[2] ECOSOC, Resolution 772 B (XXX), 25 July 1960; ECOSOC, Resolution 888 F (XXXIV), 24 July 1962.

[3] UN, Seminar on National and Local Institutions for the Promotion and Protection of Human Rights, 18–29 September 1978, ST/HR/SER.A/2.

[4] GA, Resolution 33/46, 14 December 1978, A/RES/33/46.

Disability in International Human Rights Law. Gauthier de Beco, Oxford University Press. © Gauthier de Beco 2021.
DOI: 10.1093/oso/9780198824503.003.0011

In 1991, the NHRIs gathered at their first International Workshop in Paris at the invitation of the CNCDH. This International Workshop saw the drafting of the 'Principles relating to the status and functioning of national institutions for the protection and promotion of human rights', commonly named the 'Paris Principles'. Both the Commission on Human Rights and the General Assembly subsequently endorsed the Paris Principles.[5] The Vienna Declaration and Programme of Action (VDPA) promoted 'the establishment and strengthening of [NHRIs] having regard to the [Paris Principles],[6] and a number of treaty bodies issued general comments that likewise recommended doing so.[7] The Paris Principles are still considered to be the minimum standards for NHRIs at the international level.

According to the Paris Principles, NHRIs have three main functions: to provide advice to governments; to contribute to the promotion of human rights and; to handle complaints on alleged violations of human rights. Activities include the examination of both legislation and practice, the conduct of general inquiries and the dissemination of information on human rights treaties. NHRIs not only generate debate on issues related to human rights, but they can also set up local desks to direct individuals to other bodies. Quasi-judicial powers allowing these institutions to settle disputes are optional under the Paris Principles.

In addition to outlining the responsibilities, composition and working methods of NHRIs, the Paris Principles emphasise two fundamental principles: independence and pluralism.

First, independence requires that NHRIs be free from governmental interference. While these institutions were created by States, they must be able to work independently. Hence, the Paris Principles provide that their mandate must be established 'by a constitutional or legislative text'.[8] With this requirement fulfilled, it will be impossible for government to turn them down should they raise criticism against it. Furthermore, NHRIs should be allowed to choose their own staff members and define their priorities.[9] They must also have enough funding in order to pursue their day-to-day activities without being subject to governmental oversight.

[5] Commission on Human rights, Resolution 1992/54, 3 March 1992, E/CN.4/RES/1992/54; GA, Resolution 48/134, 20 December 1993, A/RES/48/134. The Paris Principles outline the responsibilities, composition and working methods of NHRIs in the following headings: A. Competence and responsibilities; B. Composition and guarantees of independence and pluralism; C. Methods of operation; and D. Additional principles concerning the status of commissions with quasi-jurisdictional competence.

[6] World Conference on Human Rights, *Vienna Declaration and Programme of Action*, 25 June 1993, A/Conf.157/23, Part I, para 36.

[7] Committee on the Rights of the Child (CRC Committee), *General Comment No 2: The Role of Independent National Human Rights Institutions in the Promotion and Protection of the Rights of the Child*, 15 November 2002, CRC/GC/2002/2; Committee on Economic, Social and Cultural Rights (CESCR Committee), *General Comment No 10: The Role of National Human Rights Institutions in the Protection of Economic, Social and Cultural Rights*, 10 December 1998, HRI/GEN/Rev.7; Committee on the Elimination of Racial Discrimination (CERD Committee), *General Recommendation No 17: Establishment of National Institutions to Facilitate Implementation of the Convention*, 25 March 1993, A/48/18.

[8] A(2), Competence and responsibilities, Paris Principles.

[9] B(2), Composition and guarantees of independence and pluralism, Paris Principles.

Second, pluralism relates to civil society organisations' involvement. The Paris Principles require that the appointment procedure guarantee 'the pluralist representation of the social forces (of civilian society) involved in the promotion and protection of human rights'.[10] In addition, they mention a series of actors that have to be represented in a NHRI:

(a) Non-governmental organisations responsible for human rights and efforts to combat racial discrimination, trade unions, concerned social and professional organizations, for example, associations of lawyers, doctors, journalists and eminent scientists;
(b) Trends in philosophical or religious thought;
(c) Universities and qualified experts;
(d) Parliament and;
(e) Government departments (if these are included, their representatives should participate in the deliberations only in an advisory capacity).[11]

Representativity is essential for any NHRI, because it allows the national institution to liaise with organisations that have strong links with the entire population and reflect the various groups that compose the community. In order to do so, it must secure a balanced presence of men and women, and, where applicable, ethnic, religious and linguistic minorities.[12] Ministerial representatives should be included, especially since they will be the recipients of its recommendations, though only 'in an advisory capacity'.

The major actor which should be represented in NHRIs are non-governmental organisations (NGOs). The latter are indeed the first ones to be mentioned in the list cited above. Both of them (NHRIs and NGOs) can benefit from this relationship. While NHRIs may help NGOs to channel their demands to the various levels of government, NGOs increase their capacity to gain knowledge of the situation on the ground. Although representativity can take many forms, these organisations should be able to enter into discussions without being co-opted by the NHRI. They should be allowed to express divergent opinions and keep the option of withdrawing from the discussions. They need to hold NHRIs accountable if these institutions fail to maintain their independence. As indicated in the Paris Principles, it is important to also involve other civil society organisations, such as 'trade unions, concerned social and professional organisations … [as well as] trends in

[10] B(1), Composition and guarantees of independence and pluralism, Paris Principles.

[11] Ibid.

[12] B. Lindsnaes and L. Lindholt, 'National Human Rights Institutions – Standard Setting and Achievements' in B. Lindsnaes, L. Lindholt and K. Yigen (eds), *National Human Rights Institutions. Articles and Working Papers: Input into the Discussions on the Establishment and Development of the Functions of National Human Rights Institutions* (Copenhagen: The Danish Centre of Human Rights, 2000) 1, 20.

philosophical or religious thought ... and qualified experts'.[13] These organisations too are concerned with the implementation of human rights treaties even if more incidentally.

In order to be equipped with an international network, NHRIs created the International Coordinating Committee of National Institutions for the Promotion and Protection of Human Rights (ICC) in 1993.[14] The ICC facilitates the worldwide cooperation of such institutions and is responsible for their interaction with UN agencies. The OHCHR provides the necessary support through its National Institutions and Regional Mechanisms Section (NIRMS) which serves as the ICC's secretariat. The ICC has acquired an international position thanks to its engagement in global policy making with regard to NHRIs.[15] It has appointed a representative in Geneva who assists in liaising between its members and the treaty bodies (which are based in Geneva), a move which has further increased its visibility.

Since its inception, the ICC set out to verify that NHRIs comply with the Paris Principles.[16] In order to determine which of them qualify, it established a Sub-Committee on Accreditation (SCA) in 2002. The SCA compiles a list of those institutions that comply, do not fully comply or do not comply with the Paris Principles, which are granted 'A-Status', 'B-Status' or 'C-Status', respectively. This peer review is unique in its genre, not only because accreditation gives legitimacy to the NHRI but also because compliance with the Paris Principles actually depends on the State that created it in the first place. Only the NHRIs that are granted 'A-Status' are full member of the ICC.[17] They are also allowed to participate in their own name in the sessions of the HRC.[18] In order to provide an interpretation of the Paris Principles, the SCA has issued General Observations which are regularly updated.[19]

The ICC (which had hitherto no legal personality) has more recently been renamed the Global Alliance of National Human Rights Institutions (GANHRI).[20] GANHRI is registered as a non-profit organisation under Swiss Law and has a Bureau to fulfil its tasks in collaboration with the OHCHR.

[13] B(1), Composition and guarantees of independence and pluralism, Paris Principles.

[14] This international network is composed of four regional networks: the Network of NHRIs in the Americas; the Asia-Pacific Forum of NHRIs; the Network of African NHRIs and; the European Group of NHRIs.

[15] See A.-M. Garrido and B. Kofod Olsen, 'Coordination of the Work of NHRIs – From Liaison to Joint Achievements', in R.F. Jørgensen and K. Slavensky (eds), *Implementing Human Rights. Essays in Honour of Morten Kjaerum* (Copenhagen: Danish Institute for Human Rights, 2007) 190.

[16] M. Brodie, 'Progressing Norm Socialisation: Why Membership Matters. The Impact of the Accreditation Process of the International Coordinating Committee of National Institutions for the Promotion and Protection of Human Rights' (2011) 80 *Nordic Journal of International Law* 143, 153–4.

[17] Article 1, GANHRI Statute.

[18] GA, *Human Rights Council*, 3 April 2006, A/RES/60/251, para 11. This is also provided for in the HRC Rules of Procedure (HRC, *Institution-building of the United Nations Human Rights Council*, 18 June 2007, A/HRC/RES/5/1, para 7 (b)).

[19] SCA, *General Observations*, Adopted by the GANHRI Bureau in Geneva on 21 February 2018, https://nhri.ohchr.org/EN/AboutUs/GANHRIAccreditation/General%20Observations%201/AR_General%20Observations_adopted_21.02.2018_vf.pdf (General Observations).

[20] See https://ganhri.org.

10.2 Framework Including One or More Independent Mechanisms

The CRPD devotes particular attention to monitoring mechanisms as no other human rights treaty has done to date. It was negotiated at a time when the UN planned to reform the treaty body system, so the Convention's drafters decided to suspend the creation of a new treaty body. With this in mind, there were proposals to oblige States Parties to have not only focal points but also independent mechanisms in their jurisdiction. The Ad Hoc Committee eventually decided to provide for both national and international monitoring mechanisms in the new convention.

The CRPD itself testifies that NHRIs were key to shaping its content.[21] These institutions took an active part in the discussions while collaborating with DPOs. They suggested that for the purpose of monitoring the Convention's implementation States Parties appoint bodies in line with the Paris Principles and – rather innovatively – that they elaborate a national action plan as an essential element for this purpose.[22] This was in fact not the first time that a human rights treaty would refer to the said Principles.[23] The Optional Protocol to the Convention against Torture and other Cruel, Inhuman or Degrading Treatment or Punishment (OPCAT) set a precedent by stipulating that the States Parties must 'designate or establish … one or several independent national preventive mechanisms for the prevention of torture' (national preventive mechanisms).[24] It also requires that '[w]hen establishing [such] mechanisms, [they] shall give due consideration to the [Paris Principles].[25]

Article 33(2) of the CRPD provides that States Parties set up 'a framework, including one or more independent mechanisms, as appropriate, to promote, protect and monitor implementation of the … Convention' (independent mechanisms). The independent mechanisms have therefore three tasks: promotion, protection and monitoring. These tasks are indeed very similar to the functions of NHRIs. As far as those mechanisms are concerned, however, they pertain exclusively to the CRPD, so it is worth considering in greater detail what is expected of them.

[21] A. Byrnes 'The Role of National Human Rights Institutions' in M. Sabatello and M. Schulze (eds), *Human Rights & Disability Advocacy* (Philadelphia: University of Pennsylvania Press 2013) 222, 234.

[22] G. Quinn, 'Resisting the "Temptation of Elegance": Can the Convention on the Rights of Persons with Disabilities Socialise States to Right Behaviour?' in O. Arnardóttir and G. Quinn (eds), *The UN Convention on the Rights of Persons with Disabilities. European and Scandinavian Perspectives* (London/Boston: Martinus Nijhoff Publishers, 2009) 215, 247; M. Stein and J. Lord, 'Monitoring the Convention on the Rights of Persons with Disabilities: Innovations, Lost Opportunities, and Future Potential' (2010) 32 *Human Rights Quarterly* 689, 702).

[23] Other proposals included a treaty body that would work closely with DPOs as well as a global disability rights advocate (Quinn, 'Resisting the "Temptation of Elegance"', 249; Stein and Lord, 'Monitoring the Convention on the Rights of Persons with Disabilities', 701–2).

[24] Articles 17, OPCAT.

[25] Articles 18(4), OPCAT.

The first task is to raise awareness of the Convention by disseminating materials and organising events. The independent mechanisms should foster acceptance of the values underlying the Convention. This task entails offering training to all those whose actions could affect the life of disabled people. It is worth noting though that promotion is not the sole responsibility of these mechanisms. Article 8 of the CRPD requires that States Parties combat stereotypes and prejudices by taking measures such as 'public awareness campaigns'.[26] Disabled people's organisations (DPOs) also do so in order to achieve their goals. As promotion straddles the competences of multiple actors, the independent mechanisms should not pursue promotion in isolation but rather be entrusted with providing its direction and identifying gaps.

The second task relates to dispute settlement through mediation or legal action in the name of victims. It generally takes place by assisting a disabled person in obtaining a legally-binding decision. It may also involve intervening as *amicus curiae* before the courts. In this regard, the CRPD has created an inconsistency in international human rights law, because the Paris Principles regard quasi-judicial powers as optional. While some NHRIs do focus on protection, it might be unwise to expand their mandate to include such powers given the additional workload it might generate for them. There are also other bodies such as equality bodies or ombudsmen that are already discharging this mandate and are best placed to continue doing so.

The third task is assessing progress in the realisation of all CRPD rights. While the term 'monitoring' is not used as such in the Paris Principles, it is explicitly mentioned in Article 33(2) of the Convention. Monitoring involves both making recommendations to governments to adopt new or change existing legislation and assessing the impact of policies on the enjoyment of human rights. The Paris Principles allow NHRIs to do so either on demand or on their own initiative.[27] The task can be fulfilled in a variety of ways, including the elaboration of general reports, the examination of particular human rights violations and the elaboration of strategies to prevent such violations. It includes collecting data on the implementation of the CRPD, as foreseen in the Convention.[28]

Article 33(2) of the Convention specifies that '[w]hen designating or establishing [an independent] mechanism, States Parties shall take into account the [Paris Principles]'. The independent mechanisms thus ought to conform to the requirements of the two fundamental principles discussed earlier (independence and pluralism). The use of the Paris Principles as criteria for determining the suitability of such mechanisms has altered the scope of the Paris Principles, since it results in

[26] Article 8(2)(a), CRPD.
[27] C(a), Methods of operation, Paris Principles.
[28] Article 31, CRPD.

their abstraction from the mandate of NHRIs.[29] It requires the adaptation of these Principles to the objectives of the CRPD. The CRPD Committee has shed light on the matter by elaborating guidelines on their designation or establishment as an annex to its Rules of Procedure, which also consider the relationship of the independent mechanisms with the Committee itself.[30]

With regard to independence, not many changes are needed in order to meet the Paris Principles. Independent mechanisms should be free from governmental interference akin to NHRIs. One particular point of attention is that an NHRI, if appointed, should move away from an individual model towards a social model of disability in its general approach to dealing with disability. Problems are more likely to occur if the role is given to bodies other than NHRIs, such as national advisory councils. As explained in Chapter 9, the latter existed before the CRPD was adopted,[31] but it is difficult to equate them with the independent mechanisms in the sense of Article 33(2). While national advisory councils enable States Parties to consult disabled people 'through their representative organisations',[32] they cannot be designated as independent mechanisms as they include ministerial representatives. The CRPD Committee has confirmed that they 'should not be involved or in any manner take part in the activities of the monitoring framework'.[33]

Pluralism raises more challenges with regard to the independent mechanisms. The question is who can actually represent 'the social forces (of civilian society) involved in the promotion and protection of human rights' in relation to the CRPD.[34] While NGOs are the best placed to guarantee pluralism for NHRIs, DPOs are the organisations closest to disabled people. According to the CRPD Committee, the 'framework should ensure the full involvement and participation of persons with disabilities and their representative organizations in all areas of its work'.[35] These organisations can be involved through representation on the executive board or membership in a disability-specific committee whilst maintaining ongoing partnerships with the independent mechanism.[36] It is worth pointing out also that

[29] G. de Beco, 'Article 33 (2) of the UN Convention on the Rights of Persons with Disabilities. Another Role for National Human Rights Institutions?' (2011) 29 *Netherlands Quarterly of Human Rights* 84, 93.

[30] CRPD Committee, *Rules of Procedure. Annex: Guidelines on Independent Monitoring Frameworks and their Participation in the Work of the Committee on the Rights of Persons with Disabilities*, 10 October 2016, CRPD/C/1/Rev.1 (Rules of Procedure (Annex)).

[31] G. de Beco, 'Article 33 of the UN Convention on the Rights of Persons with Disabilities: Practice and Evaluation' in L. Waddington, G. Quinn and E. Flynn (eds), *European Yearbook of Disability Law. Volume 5* (Antwerp: Intersentia, 2014) 9, 14–15.

[32] Article 4(3), CRPD.

[33] Para 22, CRPD Committee Rules of Procedure (Annex).

[34] B(1), Composition and guarantees of independence and pluralism, Paris Principles.

[35] Para 20, CRPD Committee Rules of Procedure (Annex).

[36] It appears that almost all the NHRIs appointed are involving DPOs (Canadian Human Rights Commission (CHRC) and GANHRI, *Survey. National Human Rights Institutions and the Convention on the Rights of Persons with Disabilities* (Ottaway; Geneva: GANHRI, 2019) 18–19; https://ganhri.org/wp-content/uploads/2020/08/CHRC_rapport_survey_WEB_fev_2020_final_NEW_-_EN_FINAL-ua.pdf).

civil society in the Paris Principles is broader than '[c]ivil society' as referred to in Article 33(3) of the Convention. The independent mechanisms must therefore include other civil society organisations, such as organisations *for* disabled people (in addition to public departments 'in an advisory capacity').[37] In this way, they can provide a forum where the DPOs have the chance not only to express their concerns to government but also to exchange views with the relevant organisations.

Article 33(2) of the CRPD requires that States Parties set up 'a *framework*, including one or more independent mechanisms' (emphasis added). Such a 'framework' is needed in order to ensure that the independent mechanisms taken together form a coherent whole, as it would be counterproductive for them to operate otherwise.[38] These mechanisms should not only exhibit some kind of coherence, but also one of them must take the lead. This point is of course irrelevant if there is only one independent mechanism.

Fulfilling the requirement to set up 'a framework, including one or more independent mechanisms', is one of the first efforts that States Parties should pursue upon the ratification of the CRPD, for it will lay down the practical conditions of the Convention's implementation.[39] In the words of Lagoutte, domestication by way of the 'institutional localisation of human rights' will be conducive to accelerating the translation of international commitments into changes on the ground.[40] The CRPD Committee likewise considered that '[t]he designation or establishment of the independent monitoring framework should be done at the earliest possible opportunity after the entry into force of the Convention'.[41] States Parties should arrange for setting up this framework without much delay and, indeed, provide it with the capacity to 'promote, protect and monitor implementation of the ... Convention'.[42]

The States Parties have nonetheless much flexibility in doing all this, which the term 'as appropriate' in Article 33(2) underscores. One the one hand, a State Party can limit the framework to a unique body that would play the role of independent mechanisms on its own or it can opt for dividing the role of independent mechanisms between a number of bodies. This option can be especially useful in federal

[37] B(1), Composition and guarantees of independence and pluralism, Paris Principles.

[38] G. de Beco and A. Hoefmans, 'National Structures for the Implementation and Monitoring of the UN Convention on the Rights of Persons with Disabilities' in G. de Beco (ed), *Article 33 of the UN Convention on the Rights of Persons with Disabilities: National Structures for the Implementation and Monitoring of the Convention* (Leiden/Boston: Martinus Nijhoff Publishers, 2013) 11, 52.

[39] Article 33(2), CRPD.

[40] S. Lagoutte, 'The Role of State Actors within the National Human Rights System' (2019) 37 *Nordic Journal of Human Rights* 177, 193.

[41] CRPD Committee, *General Comment No 7: The Participation of Persons with Disabilities, including Children with Disabilities, through their Representative Organizations, in the Implementation and Monitoring of the Convention*, 9 November 2018, CRPD/C/GC/7, para 8. Article 17 of OPCAT requires that States Parties 'designate or establish [national preventive mechanisms] at the latest one year after the entry into force of the ... Protocol', but this was not replicated in the CRPD.

[42] Article 33(2), CRPD.

States, where regional bodies would collaborate with regional DPOs. It is also possible to share the tasks outlined in the CRPD between different bodies according to their competences. On the other hand, a State Party could rely on the bodies that are already in place in its jurisdiction, provided that they meet the conditions laid down in the Convention, but it may prefer to have a new independent mechanism should there not be any that are capable of this. In practice, the 'framework, including one or more independent mechanisms' has thus taken a variety of forms which can be adapted to the constitutional structure of the States Parties.[43]

The possibility of designating or establishing 'one or more independent mechanisms' has led to one of the most controversial aspects of Article 33(2), namely whether each of these bodies that are part of the framework must be independent within the meaning of the Paris Principles. A literal reading of the CRPD suggests that this has not to be like this, since the Convention refers to a framework '*including* one or more independent mechanisms' (which implies that there might be other kinds of bodies in the framework).[44] While the Spanish version of the text contradicts such a reading,[45] it makes more sense that this framework solely consists of independent mechanisms.[46] The contrary might result in a double standard, with some of the tasks being carried out by independent mechanisms and other ones not. There may be other kind of bodies executing these tasks outside the framework, as long as there are some that do so in an independent manner within this framework. In the same way, the CRPD Committee reckons that 'all mechanisms are required to be independent from the executive branch and at least one of them must be compliant with the Paris Principles'.[47] Where the borderline lies between being 'independent from the executive' and being 'compliant with the Paris Principles', however, remains open to question.

10.3 Lessons for International Human Rights Law

The obligation to designate or establish independent mechanisms has significance for to the entire application of human rights treaties. While VDPA acknowledged the need for creating NHRIs,[48] the Paris Principles by themselves were not legally binding. Not only had they been adopted by those they were themselves

[43] de Beco, 'Article 33 of the UN Convention on the Rights of Persons with Disabilities. Practice and Evaluation', 33–5.
[44] Article 33(2), CRPD (emphasis added).
[45] It uses the phrase '*un marco,* que constará de *uno o varios mecanismos independientes*' (a framework, *made up of* one or more independent mechanisms). The six official UN languages are Arabic, Chinese, English, French, Russian and Spanish.
[46] de Beco, Article 33(2) of the UN Convention on the Rights of Persons with Disabilities. Another Role for National Human Rights Institutions?, 94.
[47] CRPD Committee, *General Comment No 7,* para 14.
[48] World Conference on Human Rights, *Vienna Declaration and Programme of Action*, Part I, para 36.

governing, that is, the NHRIs, but also no human rights treaty referred to them as yet. With first OPCAT and then the CRPD, this is no longer true as States Parties are required to act 'with due consideration to' and 'taking into account' the very same Principles.[49] Despite their loose wording, the two human rights treaties have offered NHRIs – indirectly by referring to the Paris Principles – a legal basis, which spurs debate on the status of such institutions under international human rights law. Regarding the CRPD, this legal basis is moreover not enshrined in an optional protocol, as is the case with OPCAT, but in the main international instrument.

One point of discussion is whether the reference to the Paris Principles presupposes that States Parties give the role of independent mechanisms to NHRIs. There are good arguments in favour of this. The tasks outlined in the CRPD are clearly falling within the mandate of NHRIs.[50] Earlier versions of Article 33(2), which provided more details about such tasks, testify that the independent mechanisms were modelled on these institutions.[51] This contrasts with the tasks outlined in OPCAT, which are more targeted and require specific kinds of expertise. The independent mechanisms are in charge of monitoring the CRPD's implementation as a whole, just as NHRIs have been doing with other human rights treaties. As declared by Quinn, 'the default setting lies in favour of [NHRIs]',[52] so they should have the best pedigree to become independent mechanisms.

This means that if a State Party has a NHRI with 'A-Status', the minimum requirement is to designate it and give it a leading position in the framework. The national institution can even be this framework alone while provision is made to involve DPOs and other relevant organisations. The CRPD Committee advises that States Parties 'appoint their Paris Principles-compliant [NHRI] as the monitoring framework or the [independent] mechanism forming part of the monitoring framework'.[53] Considering the reference to the Paris Principles, it would indeed be hard to exclude this 'Paris Principles-compliant NHRI' from the framework (if one does exist). If none exists, the CPRD could encourage States Parties to create such a 'Paris Principles-compliant NHRI' even though they have no obligation to do so. The 'Paris Principles-compliant NHRI' then would play the role of independent mechanisms at the same time.

What is certain is that any national institution appointed will have to give particular attention to the CRPD. A State Party somehow has to ensure that its 'Paris Principles-compliant NHRI' gives priority to carrying out those tasks outlined in the Convention. There are practical consequences in doing so, since this might

[49] Article 33(2), CRPD; 18(4), OPCAT.

[50] G. de Beco and R. Murray, *Commentary on the Paris Principles on National Human Rights Institutions* (Cambridge: Cambridge University Press, 2014) 27.

[51] M. Raley, 'The Drafting of Article 33 of the Convention on the Rights of Persons with Disabilities: the Creation of a Novel Mechanism' (2016) 20 *The International Journal of Human Rights* 138, 146–7.

[52] Quinn, 'Resisting the "Temptation of Elegance"', 130.

[53] CRPD Committee, *General Comment No 7*, para 17.

not only affect its independence but also lead to a drain on resources. NHRIs may therefore face constraints following their expanded mandate, unless they receive additional funding. According to a survey conducted by the Canadian Human Rights Commission (CHRC) and GANHRI, less than half of these institutions are provided such additional funding *as* independent mechanisms.[54] The Paris Principles however stipulate that an NHRI should have the resources 'in order to be independent of the Government and not be subject to financial control which might affect its independence'.[55]

Notwithstanding the additional funding, NHRIs whose State have ratified the CRPD will need to devote more energy to disabled people. The Convention has offered these institutions a stronger leg to stand on when it comes to disability. This begs the question not only as to why international human rights law does not offer other groups of people the same treatment but also how can one bring Article 33(2) into tune with the requirement that '[a NHRI] shall be given as broad a mandate as possible' that is anchored in 'a constitutional or legislative text'.[56] The independent mechanisms also are expected to have quasi-judicial powers, while the Paris Principles consider this as optional. When given the role of independent mechanisms, the national institution will undeniably experience an imbalance in its mandate.

On the other hand, the way in which the CRPD enumerates the tasks (promotion, protection and monitoring) reveals new insights into the very mandate of NHRIs. The Convention does not just recall what they do in general but reflects also perhaps better what they are expected to accomplish 30 years after they – then a much smaller number – drafted the Paris Principles. While the latter focus on 'monitoring' (which term they do not mention), the optional character of the quasi-judicial powers is no longer in keeping with current reality. Protection is now seen as an essential tool for NHRIs even though it was afforded less importance at that time.[57] The CPRD has thus provided an update of the mandate of NHRIs, which can be applied across the entire range of human rights treaties.

Another point of discussion is the possibility to have more than one independent mechanism in Article 32(2). This point of discussion can be taken on an even wider level. An NHRI is in principle a single entity. Would it be possible for several bodies to fulfil the mandate of NHRIs by *mutatis mutandis* constituting a 'framework'? The idea would particularly address the context where States are already equipped with bodies that have this mandate albeit to a limited extent but which have no such NHRI as yet.

[54] CHRC and GANHRI, *Survey*, 16.

[55] B(1), Composition and guarantees of independence and pluralism, Paris Principles.

[56] A(2), Competence and responsibilities, Paris Principles.

[57] de Beco and Murray, *Commentary on the Paris Principles on National Human Rights Institutions*, 112. It appears that most NHRIs have now complaints handling as part of their mandate (CHRC and GANHRI, *Survey*, 22).

There are in fact NHRIs with more limited mandates, the establishment of which seems to have been the preference of certain treaty bodies. Although the CRC itself is silent on the matter, the Committee on the Rights of the Child has recommended the creation of NHRIs for 'the ... monitoring of implementation of the [CRC]'.[58] The Committee on the Elimination of Racial Discrimination similarly has encouraged the creation of NHRIs in order '[t]o promote respect for the enjoyment of human rights without any discrimination, as ... set out in ... the International Convention on the Elimination of All Forms of Racial Discrimination'.[59] Equality bodies and ombudsmen already ensure compliance with anti-discrimination legislation, although there has in some places been a trend to merge them with NHRIs.[60] Rather than establishing an all-encompassing NHRI, States could therefore divide the mandate amongst a number of bodies subject to what they have available.

The advantage of such an arrangement is that it allows for the consideration of vulnerable groups and of thematic issues. It prevents the focus on them getting lost in a broader agenda but instead allows the concentration of expertise in different bodies. However, the question could be asked how many such bodies would be needed for the purpose and whether the multiplicity of such bodies may not undermine the indivisibility of human rights.[61] Also, this may not be the most cost-effective way forward, since it could lead to competition for resources and duplication between the different bodies. It is also at odds with the Paris Principles, which were not really designed for this scenario. It is therefore important that States work out how these bodies all collectively comply with the Paris Principles by forming a coherent whole. A similar discussion has been taking place with regard to national human rights action plans (NHRAPs). It has been noted that while a global NHRAP is often the most feasible option, having specific national action plans could sometimes prove more effective.[62]

The CRPD thus provides for a richer domestic human rights architecture in comparison with previous human rights treaties. It attaches particular responsibilities to each of the actors that are concerned by its implementation. Article 33(1) of the Convention requires that States Parties 'designate one or more focal points within government for matters relating to the implementation of the ... Convention'. The designation of such focal points can help them towards the centralisation of decision-making and to increase the accountability of government.[63] Thereafter,

[58] CRC Committee, *General Comment No 2*, para 2.

[59] CERD Committee, *General Recommendation No 17*, para 1(a).

[60] O'Cinneide and N. Crowther, *Bridging the Divide: Integrating the Functions of National Equality Bodies and National Human Rights Institutions in the European Union*' (2019) 1 *Juridikum: Zeitschrift für Kritik – Recht – Gesellschaft* 210, 217.

[61] R. Carver, 'One NHRI or Many? How Many Institutions Does It Take to Protect Human Rights? – Lessons from the European Experience' (2011) 3 *Journal of Human Rights Practice* 1, 11.

[62] A. Chalabi, *National Human Rights Action Planning* (Oxford: Oxford University Press, 2018) 98–100.

[63] de Beco and Hoefmans, 'National Structures for the Implementation and Monitoring of the UN Convention on the Rights of Persons with Disabilities', 23.

the CRPD introduces a dual monitoring system through both the setting up of 'a framework, including one or more independent mechanisms,' and the participation of disabled people 'in the monitoring process'.[64] It can be said that a 'national human rights system' like this allows for a swift integration of human rights treaties into national policies.[65]

The CRPD affords civil society a dominant role in this dual monitoring system. Participation is not only essential according to the Paris Principles but is also a stand-alone requirement under the Convention. It should take place through the inclusion of DPOs in the independent mechanisms as well as the building of their capacity to monitor the implementation of the Convention. As discussed in Chapter 9, States Parties are required to consult disabled people 'through their representative organizations' in any decision-making processes.[66] This 'multi-level involvement of civil society', which is a landmark of the Convention, provides the DPOs with much opportunity to engage with government at various levels.[67] The demands that this 'multilevel involvement' entails may nonetheless place a heavy burden on these organisations.[68] While choices have to be made, its success will inevitably vary according to the resources at their disposal.

This dual monitoring system is then accompanied by a traditional international monitoring mechanism. As the UN reflected upon the reform of the treaty body system, the CRPD's drafters delayed discussing the features of the CRPD Committee, which in the end would resemble very much those of the other treaty bodies.[69] The interaction of the national and international monitoring mechanisms, which the Convention maintains, still attests to the '[e]xperimentalist' nature of this Convention.[70] In the terms of Arduin, the independent mechanisms and disabled people share regulatory functions as 'state regulator' and 'internal civil regulator', respectively, while the CRPD Committee is the 'external meta-regulator'.[71] The Convention thereby comprises a tripartite structure of implementation that should alleviate the burden of this Committee and increase reliance on the 'national human rights system'.

For such a tripartite structure to work, it is necessary – in Arduin's terminology – that the 'external meta-regulator' focuses on evaluating the performance of the 'internal civil regulator'. The problem is that this function is scattered over a

[64] Article 33(2) and (3), CRPD.

[65] Lagoutte, 'The Role of State Actors within the National Human Rights System', 191.

[66] Article 4(3), CRPD.

[67] de Beco and Hoefmans, 'National Structures for the Implementation and Monitoring of the UN Convention on the Rights of Persons with Disabilities', 59.

[68] S. Lorion, 'A Model for National Human Rights Systems? New Governance and the Convention on the Rights of Persons with Disabilities' (2019) 37 *Nordic Journal of Human Rights* 234, 256.

[69] Stein and Lord, 'Monitoring the Convention on the Rights of Persons with Disabilities', 692–4.

[70] G. de Burca, R. Keohane and C. Sabel, 'New Modes of Pluralist Global Governance' (2013) 45 *New York University Journal of International Law & Politics* 723, 760.

[71] S. Arduin, 'Taking Metaregulation to the United Nations Human Rights Treaty Regime: The Case of the Convention on the Rights of Persons with Disabilities' (2019) 41 *Law & Policy* 411, 424.

number of actors. *Quis custodiet ipsos custodes*? The Subcommittee on Prevention of Torture and Other Cruel, Inhuman or Degrading Treatment or Punishment (SPT) has the mandate not only to '[v]isit the places [of detention]' but also to '[m]ake recommendations … with a view to strengthening the capacity … of the national preventive mechanisms'.[72] Nothing is provided in this regard concerning the CRPD Committee. From its mandate, it can however be implied that this Committee should act in a similar way with regard to the independent mechanisms designated or established under the CRPD. It has already engaged with them in the State reporting process and even beyond. While both treaty bodies (SPT and CRPD Committee) have responsibility for determining the suitability of those mechanisms (national preventive mechanisms and independent mechanisms),[73] the responsibility for accrediting the NHRIs lies with the SCA.[74] There is therefore a need for ensuring that they proceed consistently in accordance with their respective mandate. Without co-ordination, it will be difficult to set a clear course of action on how to improve the actual functioning of the mechanisms in question.

[72] Article 11(1)(a) and (b)(iv), OCPAT.

[73] Both the CRPD Committee and the SPT have provided guidelines on the designation or establishment of independent mechanisms and national preventive mechanism, respectively. See CRPD Committee Rules of Procedure (Annex); SPT, *Guidelines on National Preventive Mechanisms*, 9 December 2010, CAT/OP/12/5.

[74] de Beco and Murray, *Commentary on the Paris Principles on National Human Rights Institutions*, 29.

11

Conclusion: From the Margins to the Centre

This chapter is the conclusion. It gives an overview of the context of the present book and outlines its main findings (11.1. Context and Main Findings). It examines the various issues treated in this book and recaps them in the form of a short summary of the chapters which form Parts I (Concepts), II (Standards) and III (Implementation). It then takes another look at the aim to make disability an integral part of international human rights law (11.2. Integrating Disability into International Human Rights Law). The chapter explains the shift in addressing disability from a scattering of welfare policies to a focus on non-discrimination the limitations of which the idea of the dis-abled subject allows to break through. It finally addresses how to capitalise on the adoption of the CRPD by uniting the entire human rights community.

11.1 Context and Main Findings

In a 2002 study that would serve as an impetus for adopting the first legally binding international instrument on disability, Quinn and Degener set out to explore the way 'to make the rights that are available to all persons directly relevant to people with disabilities'.[1] Commenting on the fact that disabled people had been largely invisible in the international human rights framework, they advocated in favour of a legally binding international instrument in order 'to accelerate the mainstreaming of disability in the six [human rights treaties]'.[2] This legal instrument, the CRPD, would see the light of day in 2006 after a negotiation process involving more civil society organisations than ever before.

At the time of writing this book, 182 States have ratified the Convention,[3] which has led to a new wave of academic scholarship as well as a large body of advice coming from the CRPD Committee. As argued throughout the book, not only has the Convention strengthened human rights protection for disabled people, but it has also enriched the notion of human rights itself by tailoring existing rights to their specific situation. Although the issue of disability attracted some interest,

[1] G. Quinn and T. Degener, *The Current Use and Future Potential of United Nations Human Rights Instruments in the Context of Disability* (Geneva: UN, 2002) 28.
[2] Ibid, 295.
[3] See https://treaties.un.org/Pages/ViewDetails.aspx?src=TREATY&mtdsg_no=IV-15&chapter=4&clang=_en.

Disability in International Human Rights Law. Gauthier de Beco, Oxford University Press. © Gauthier de Beco 2021.
DOI: 10.1093/oso/9780198824503.003.0012

only now has it begun to receive the consideration it really deserves. The question is: what has international human rights law gained from the new elements in the CRPD? While there has been much focus on the way in which the Convention protects the rights of disabled people, its significance for the whole field of international human rights law is very much under-researched.

The present book explores some of the innovations the CRPD has introduced in the field of international human rights law. For the purpose of this exploration, it developes a theoretical framework which explicitly integrates disability into international human rights law while offering an analysis of a number of particular rights and considering the implementation of human rights treaties. It not only engages with relevant literature across several disciplines but also uses the recommendations of treaty bodies and reports of UN agencies as well as disabled people's organisations (DPOs).

Taking the International Year of Disabled Persons in 1981 as the starting point,[4] Chapter 1 retraces the steps towards the CRPD's adoption following Mexico's proposal to elaborate a 'comprehensive and integral international convention to promote and protect the rights and dignity of persons with disabilities'.[5] International instruments up to then had regarded disability as a question of welfare albeit to a lesser degree in the Standard Rules for the Equalisation of Opportunities for Persons with Disabilities (Standard Rules).[6] The Convention on the Rights of the Child (CRC) was a turning point in international human rights law, not only because it explicitly referred to 'disability' in its general non-discrimination clause but also because it contained a separate article on disabled children.[7] There are other ways in which the CRC shares resemblances with the CRPD. Both human rights treaties focus on grounds other than the ones that characterise people who fall within their remit, namely age and disability. They bridge civil and political as well as economic and social rights. The CRPD goes a step further by developing the principle of substantive equality as much as the Convention embraces the concept of 'inclusive equality'.[8] It specifically expands the prohibition of discrimination on the basis of disability by stressing that the failure to provide reasonable accommodation is itself a form of discrimination.[9]

Chapter 2 presents different models of disability as a preliminary step to exploring the Convention's own understanding of disability. Rather than viewing disability through a medicalised perspective the social model sees disability as

[4] GA, *International Year of Disabled Persons*, 8 December 1981, A/RES/36/77.

[5] GA, *Comprehensive and Integral International Convention to Promote and Protect the Rights and Dignity of Persons with Disabilities*, 26 February 2002, A/RES/56/168.

[6] GA, *Standard Rules for the Equalisation of Opportunities for Persons with Disabilities*, 20 December 1993, A/RES/48/96.

[7] Articles 2 and 23, CRC.

[8] CRPD Committee, *General Comment No 6: Equality and Non-discrimination*, 26 April 2018, CRPD/C/GC/6, para 11.

[9] Article 2, CRPD.

a product of social organisation. While the social model has been a real breakthrough for the disability rights movement, it has also faced criticism, which continues to spur the debate on the concept of disability. Since the social model is found right across the CRPD,[10] it acts as a lens on disability throughout the present book. The manner in which the Convention approaches disability has had repercussions for the entire field of international human rights law. Disability has been brought more into the mainstream even though there remain significant variations between treaty bodies. Taking stock of the Convention, some of these bodies have actually started to alter their views of disability by moving towards the social model. Academic literature on international human rights law, however, very much lags behind this shift. Beyond international human rights law, UN agencies themselves have, albeit to varying degrees, paid greater attention to disabled people since the CRPD was adopted, with the Sustainable Development Goals likewise following suit.

Chapter 3 investigates what theories of justice are most relevant to the inclusion of disabled people. It begins both by questioning the ideal of independence and by highlighting the shortcomings of social contract theory with regard to disability. Rawls' Theory of Justice presupposes that the parties to the social contract are capable of a 'conception of the good',[11] which means that those who are not capable of this have the status of 'outliers'.[12] While potential solutions remain uncertain, it is worth exploring alternatives to the social contract theory. Capabilities theory can be useful to include disabled people, especially since it takes into account personal, social and environmental factors in the conversion of resources into capabilities. Despite this theory's sensitivity to human differences, the fixed minimum threshold level of capabilities that Nussbaum sets for all unfortunately penalises disabled people. Turning to recognition theory, Fraser's principle of 'participatory parity' is well suited to address disability with its objective of the pursuit of an equal social status,[13] but the achievement of this 'participatory parity' requires further elaboration. A combination of both the capabilities theory and the recognition theory may provide a way forward. While inclusion would be the preferred route for achieving actual human functionings, the strengthening of capabilities would help determine how to actually allocate resources in order to bring this about.

[10] R. Kayess and P. French, 'Out of Darkness into Light? Introducing the Convention on the Rights of Persons with Disabilities' (2008) 8 *Human Rights Law Review* 1, 21; P. Bartlett, 'The United Nations Convention on the Rights of Persons with Disabilities and Mental Health Law' (2012) 75 *Modern Law Review* 752, 758–61; P. Harpur, 'Embracing the New Disability Rights Paradigm: The Importance of the Convention on the Rights of Persons with Disabilities' (2012) 27 *Disability & Society* 1, 3–4.

[11] J. Rawls, *Political Liberalism* (New York: Columbia University Press, 1993) 19.

[12] A. Silvers and L. Francis, 'Justice through Trust: Disability and the "Outlier Problem" in Social Contract Theory' (2005) 116 *Ethics* 40, 46.

[13] N. Fraser and A. Honneth, *Redistribution or Recognition? A Political-Philosophical Exchange* (London/New York: Verso, 2003) 34–7.

Chapter 4 challenges the alleged neutrality of the legal subject in the field of international human rights law. The ideal of 'able-bodiedness', as it emerges from the characterisation of the notion of personhood as capacity for normative agency,[14] has led to discounting the numerous possibilities of human variety. Departing from this ideal, the CRPD advances the vision of the embodied legal subject through its consideration for both intra-group and extra-group differences. Although it could have gone further with respect to some categories of disability, it calls into question the model shaped by the normativity of the average human being which has served as the basis for demarcating the very concept of human rights. The advantages of placing disabled people at the heart of international human rights law are made even plainer with the introduction of the idea of the dis-abled subject. Resting on Fineman's vulnerability theory, the dis-abled subject takes its point of departure from the fact that disability cannot be associated with a particular group of people only, thereby lending support to the argument that disability is a constant and universal experience of all human beings.[15] By shifting the focus from the side of 'rights' to the side of the 'human' in the notion of human rights, the idea of dis-abled subject takes on a universal approach that regards disability as a constant and universal experience of all human beings even though this approach does not at all dispense with referring to identities. By distinguishing the concept from the group, it identifies the holders of rights in a way that may more emphatically live up to the universality of human rights.

Chapter 5 examines the right to legal capacity. There was no such right for disabled people in international human rights law prior to the CRPD (5.1. The Right to Legal Capacity). The International Covenant on Civil and Political Rights (ICCPR) allows the imposition of restrictions on legal capacity as a response to deficits in mental capacity. The CRPD not only recognises this right but also prescribes that support must be given for the exercise of legal capacity. By affirming that the right to equal recognition before the law includes not only 'legal standing' but also 'legal agency', Article 12 guarantees that disabled people retain their ability to exercise rights and duties in spite of strong disagreements on the matter during the Convention's negotiation process. This has consequences for the whole field of international human rights law (5.2. Implications for International Human Rights Law). The reality is that everyone relies on others for proper decision-making and indeed may sometimes need 'supported decision-making'. To achieve the actual enjoyment of the right to legal capacity demands both the strengthening of existing social relationships and the expansion of whatever support is available through family and friendship. One may ask further why there should be any different treatment between disabled and non-disabled people in matters of legal capacity

[14] J. Griffin, *On Human Rights* (Oxford: Oxford University Press, 2008) 33–7.

[15] I. Zola, 'Toward the Necessary Universalizing of a Disability Policy' (1989) 67 *The Milbank Quarterly* 401, 420.

since everybody has the propensity to make 'bad' decisions. It remains to be seen though whether there is not too great an emphasis on the respect for one's 'will and preferences', which has also led to inconsistencies in international human rights law with regard to disabled children.

Chapter 6 examines the right to education. While human rights treaties generally protect the right to education, what they entail for the education of disabled people has been unclear (6.1. The Right to Education). Byincorporating the goal of inclusive education into international human rights law, the CRPD has endorsedd the right to inclusive education. It further provides what ought to be done in order to bring about inclusive education. Article 24 starts by requiring that States Parties establish an 'inclusive education system' to enable disabled people to be effectively educated alongside all other children, a requirement which does not necessarily disavow the maintenance of special schools. The Convention also takes into account the interests of deaf, blind or deaf-blind people. It is nevertheless impossible to develop such an 'inclusive education system' exclusively for disabled children, since this would depend on the categorisation of pupils and since it might overlook the needs of other children (6.2. Implications for International Human Rights Law). Efforts to pursue inclusiveness should pertain to all children alike notwithstanding disability-specific aspects attached to the right to inclusive education. By focusing on actual participation in the general education system, the CRPD has placed a new emphasis on the right to education which stresses the need for transforming the education system itself. The right to inclusive education calls for greater regard for human differences in the delivery of education although difficulties remain in attempting to translate this vision into reality.

Chapter 7 examines the right to work. While disability was regarded as an obstacle to employment, much progress has been made after the Universal Declaration of Human Rights (UDHR). It was the ILO that took the lead here by promoting participation in the 'open labour market', which set the tone for the CRPD (7.1. The Right to Work). The latter considers both physical and social barriers for disabled people and emphasises the need for equal treatment in the different aspects of their employment. Whether sheltered workshops must remain available is still a matter of debate though. Also undefined is what ought to be done in order to create an inclusive and accessible 'open labour market'. In light of this, the universal experience of disability throws into relief the importance of recognising the sheer complexity of human diversity in the organisation of work (7.2. Implications for International Human Rights Law). By requiring measures going beyond non-discrimination, the CRPD is not only a stepping stone towards the adoption of new legal tools for increasing access to the labour market but also questions the exclusive focus on gainful employment in international human rights law.

Chapter 8 deals with the right to political participation. Since the ICCPR allows for the limitation of political rights, the Human Rights Committee conceded that (intellectual) disability may lead to a deprivation of voting rights (8.1. Right to Political Participation). Article 29 of the CRPD by contrast guarantees access to the entire electoral process by providing that deficits in mental capacity should not lead to such deprivation but rather trigger the provision of support in order to enable disabled people to exercise their voting rights. By encouraging participation in 'the conduct of public affairs', the CRPD moreover stresses that the right to political participation is not just about securing the right to vote. It involves realising this right by enabling people to express their opinion in decision-making processes. The right to political participation, as proclaimed in the Convention, thus raises new issues in the field of international human rights law, and its enjoyment has the potential to expand the range of political goals and see a more representative political class (8.2. Implications for International Human Rights Law). It directs a shift in focus away from 'indirect participation' to 'direct participation' by fostering an environment wherein individuals can actually take part in political life.

Chapter 9 addresses the participation of disabled people. Armed with the motto 'Nothing about us without us', DPOs joined forces in the CRPD's negotiation process through the medium of the International Disability Caucus (IDC) (9.1. Participation of Disabled People in the Negotiation Process). The question however remains as to the full representativity of disabled people through which all of them could find their voices equally. Participation trickled down in the direction of domestic affairs as the Convention requires that States Parties consult disabled people 'through their representative organisations' (9.2. Participation of Disabled People in the Implementation of the CRPD). In order to fulfil this requirement, States Parties must do more than just give DPOs the possibility to express their concerns. They must also foster an environment which enables such organisations to exert real influence over the debate, whether in coalition or on their own. While the State remains in charge of international (human rights) law making, the involvement of civil society organisations can compensate for governments' lack of accountability in the international arena (9.3. Participation in International Human Rights Law). The CRPD in this way recognises 'participatory rights', which entails the strengthening of capacity to monitor its implementation particularly by the organisations that defend more marginalised groups of people.

Chapter 10 focuses on monitoring mechanisms. States have established national human rights institutions (NHRIs) in order to monitor the implementation of human rights treaties (10.1. National Human Rights Institutions (NHRIs)). The Paris Principles, which are the minimum standards for NHRIs, not only focus on two fundamental principles, namely independence and pluralism, but also outline these institutions' main functions. Article 32(2) of the CRPD stipulates that States Parties must designate or establish independent mechanisms in line with the said Principles (10.2. Framework including One or More Independent Mechanisms). The Paris Principles therefore need to be adapted to the objectives of the Convention so as to meet the requirements of the two fundamental principles. States Parties do have flexibility for this purpose though, since they must set up 'a framework including one or more independent mechanisms'. Through the reference to the Paris Principles, the CRPD has indirectly afforded a legal basis to the NHRIs, which has repercussions for such institutions in terms of both ascertaining their mandate and defining their structure (10.3. Lessons for International Human Rights Law). Providing for both national and international monitoring mechanisms, the Convention contains a tripartite structure of implementation which can be conducive to reinforcing the function of 'national human rights systems'.

11.2 Integrating Disability into International Human Rights Law

The welfarist approach to dealing with disability has long dominated the field of international human rights law. It is revealing in this regard that the UDHR guarantees 'the right to security in the event of in the event of unemployment, sickness, *disability*, widowhood, old age or other lack of livelihood in circumstances beyond his control',[16] which places disability only within the remit of social protection. The focus on non-discrimination supplanted this welfarist approach with the purpose of offering equal treatment to disabled people. Disability was added to the list of prohibited grounds in general non-discrimination clauses, first implicitly, in the International Covenant on Economic and Social Rights (ICESCR) and the ICCPR, as confirmed by the Committee on Economic, Social and Cultural Rights (CESCR) (CESCR Committee),[17] and then explicitly, in the CRC.[18] The CESCR Committee further provided that the lack of reasonable accommodation amounts to discrimination on the basis of disability.[19]

While disability had entered the field of international human rights law, disabled people needed more than such general non-discrimination clauses if they were to be able to the enjoy their human rights. Anti-discrimination law may eliminate barriers in a given context, but it does not aim at alleviating all those that are embedded in society.[20] The duty to provide reasonable accommodation is not only triggered on the request of a particular individual, but it is also directed solely to this or that individual. In contrast to the social model of disability, it locates the problem in the individual. Although the prohibition of discrimination on the basis of disability – through duty to provide reasonable accommodation – can lead to adjustments to the environment for the sake of a disabled person, it does not

[16] Article 25(1), UDHR (emphasis added).

[17] CESCR Committee, *General Comment No 5: Persons with Disabilities*, 9 December 1994, E/1995/22, para 5.

[18] Article 2, CRC.

[19] CESCR Committee, *General Comment No. 5*, para 15.

[20] P. Harpur, *Ableism at Work: Disablement and Hierarchies of Impairment* (Cambridge: Cambridge University Press, 2019) 29.

have the power to modify this environment for its own sake. Its purpose is to help disabled people fit into the pre-existing environment rather than challenging the structures that put them at a higher level of disadvantage in the first place.[21]

The consequence is that the non-discrimination norm is of limited use for inclusion into society. According to Goldschmidt, '[t]his may be due to the fact that a general, seemingly neutral, normative framework reflects only the perspective of dominant groups, and thereby cannot guarantee equal human rights to all'.[22] The supposed neutrality of the legal subject narrows down the reach of the prohibition of discriminationoften precisely to the detriment of those who are in greater need of human rights protection. This legal subject erects a 'norm' that reflects the model shaped by the normativity of the average human being to which all individuals have to conform.

The problem is that anti-discrimination law relies on identities in order to delimit its scope. While doing so enables States to respond to certain manifestations of vulnerability, there are inherent limitations in advancing this kind of essentialism. The latter culminates in a group-based approach by associating a particular characteristic to a certain group of people and in this way restricting membership of the said group. With regard to disability, this inevitably means that some people with impairments will be excluded according to the criteria applied in order to qualify. In the words of Satz, anti-discrimination law recognises '[disabled people] as a protected class rather than viewing disability as an aspect of the human experience'.[23] As explained in Chapter 4, the dis-abled subject moves away from the group-based approach by separating both the concept and the group from each other. While the dis-abled subject does not altogether reject the use of identities for taking effective action, it is based on the consideration that disability concerns every single individual. It does not correlate disability with a particular identity but highlights the fact that disability is a universal experience and therefore calls for a large set of differentiated responses.

Anti-discrimination law furthermore overlooks the role of welfare policies in improving the life of disabled people.[24] By incorporating the welfarist approach into its rights-based approach, the CRPD recognises the need for welfare, inasmuch as it is required to secure the real enjoyment of human rights. Unlike the International Convention on the Elimination of All Forms of Racial Discrimination (ICERD) and the Convention on the Elimination of All Forms of Discrimination against Women (CEDAW), it is not simply an anti-discrimination treaty. By proclaiming

[21] A. Broderick, *The United Nations Convention on the Rights of Persons with Disabilities* (Mortsel: Intersentia, 2015) 72.

[22] J. Goldschmidt, 'New Perspectives on Equality: Towards Transformative Justice through the Disability Convention?' (2017) 35 *Nordic Journal of Human Rights* 1, 2.

[23] A. Satz, 'Disability, Vulnerability, and Fragmented Protections' in A. Kanter and B. Ferri (eds), *Righting Education Wrongs* (Syracuse: Syracuse University Press, 2013) 265, 272. See also A. Satz, 'Disability, Vulnerability, and the Limits of Antidiscrimination' (2008) 83 *Washington Law Review* 513.

[24] S. Bagenstos, 'The Future of Disability Law' (2004) 114 *Yale Law Journal* 1, 4.

a full catalogue of civil, political, economic, social and cultural rights, it is a proper human rights treaty in the same vein as the CRC. The CRPD has however absorbed the non-discrimination norm by merging the prohibition of discrimination with a number of measures for its implementation.[25] As seen in Part II, the prohibition of discrimination is not only amongst the legal obligations but is also reiterated throughout the Convention. This creates a tension given that the group-based approach still remains present in this Convention with all the difficulties it brings with regard to reaching its objectives. What is more, non-discriminationcontinues to be the major focus of States Parties, especially since it involves the duty to provide reasonable accommodation and since it is enacted in anti-discrimination law as part of their national legislation, thereby risking losing the very benefits afforded by the CRPD.

In order to research disability as an integral part of international human rights law, there is a need for appreciating the universal experience of disability, as laid out in relation to the dis-abled subject in Chapter 4. In the words of Siebers, the 'human-rights discourse will never break free from the ideology of ability until it includes disability as a defining characteristic of human beings'.[26] This requires not only the acknowledgement of human beings' interdependency but also that adaptations to social arrangements are essential to foster actual participation in society. Drawing on the vulnerability theory, the dis-abled subject isused as a means to underscore the State's responsibility towards anyone experiencing issues related to disability over the course of life.

While the CRPD's general principles include the 'acceptance of persons with disabilities as part of human diversity',[27] it would be better if it was 'disability' rather than 'persons with disabilities' that had to be accepted 'as part of human diversity'. This affirmation has been slow in coming in international human rights law which has tended to espouse a disembodied conception of the legal subject. The consideration of disability challenges the 'abstractionism' that delineated the concept of human rights in a way that brushed aside the full range of human diversity.[28]

The dis-abled subject is premised on a recognition that disability stands for a characteristic associated with so many kinds of impairment. In the words of Stein, 'the disability dynamic ... has the potential for responding to individual need over group-based identity'.[29] The heterogeneity of the group, due to 'the diversity of persons with disabilities', which the Convention's Preamble indeed recognises,[30]

[25] S. Tromel, 'Personal Perspective on the Drafting History of the United Nations Convention on the Rights of Persons with Disabilities' in G. Quinn and L. Waddington (eds), *European Yearbook of Disability Law* (Antwerp: Intersentia, 2009) 115, 118.

[26] T. Siebers, *Disability Theory* (Ann Arbor: University of Michigan Press, 2008) 178.

[27] Article 3(d), CRPD.

[28] A. Grear, '"Framing the Project" of International Human Rights Law: Reflections on the Dysfunctional "Family" of the Universal Declaration' in C. Gearty and C. Douzinas (eds), *The Cambridge Companion to Human Rights Law* (Cambridge: Cambridge University Press, 2013) 17, 32.

[29] M. Stein, 'Disability Human Rights' (2007) 95 *California Law Review* 75, 113.

[30] Preamble(i), CRPD.

declines even further from uniformity when factoring in the consequences of disability's intersection with other characteristics such as gender and age. The result is not only that relations within the overall group are permanently in flux, but also that there is little or no use in a uniform application of human rights treaties for all disabled people.

The notion of human rights has been based on the existing paradigm of the able-bodied individual. This ideal of 'able-bodiedness' has neglected many aspects of the lived experience of human beings and has left the barriers engendered by society mostly undetectable. This problem had not claimed much attention in international human rights law before the CRPD was adopted. What is now needed in order to remedy this problem is to depart from the focus on group-identities. The Convention has given the impetus to grant human diversity its proper place by restoring the vision of the embodied legal subject. This does not entail the creation of separate regimes for a particular group but rather a re-formulation of human rights that can better accommodate the wide range of human differences.

At the same time, the invisibility of disabled people in the international human rights framework has to be confronted. As with any other group-specific human rights treaty,[31] the very adoption of the CRPD shows that disabled people have needs and face obstacles that were not accounted for in previous human rights treaties. This leads to a paradox: the CRPD supersedes the group-based approach which itself radiates from the prohibition of discrimination, although it still provides for such prohibition both in general and with regard to its particular rights. By concentrating on race and gender discrimination, the ICERD and CEDAW in turn follow this group-based approach in its entirety. While disability has been a missing piece of the human rights puzzle, the CRPD brings a fresh perspective to the field of international human rights law by broadening the sense of humanity enshrined within the notion of human rights.

As repeatedly pointed out during the negotiation process, the CRPD's drafters were not aiming so much to create new rights but rather to apply all human rights to disabled people. The Convention has therefore been conceived as an 'implementation convention'. The realisation of the Convention's rights would require a thorough knowledge of how other human rights treaties protect the same rights and indeed how treaty bodies themselves interpret the same rights. Retrospectively, it cannot be said that the negotiators just worked on an 'implementation convention', a tactical concession which might have re-assured some of the governmental delegations present in New York. While the CRPD does not provide for any new rights, it sheds new light on the very notion of human rights. As seen throughout the present book, the Convention has added substance to that notion as it changed, adapted and extended the meaning of human rights through addressing obstacles

[31] Grear, '"Framing the Project" of International Human Rights Law', 29.

that had been left overlooked by previous human rights treaties. 15 years after the Convention was adopted the time has come to ask what lessons can be drawn from this Convention for the whole field of international human rights law.

In their study, Quinn and Degener reckoned that a new convention would 'not undermine but underpin the protections provided in the existing six human rights treaties'.[32] The CRPD has actually done far more than that. By gaining a deeper insight into its transformative effect on the entire field of international human rights law, the book laid bare the way in which 'the idea of disability challenges many of the ordinary conceptions of rights'.[33] By allowing the concept of human rights to incorporate into itself the multifarious possibilities of human variety and re-defining the rights-holders in order to allow for the different forms of embodiment, the disability subject is helping to generate a more humane and true dimension to the notion of universality.

Disability, as a universal experience, can come about for a variety of reasons. The way States should address it is by alleviating the various barriers that hinder participation in society. As illustrated in the analysis of different rights in Part II, the alleviation of such barriers entails the creation of an environment wherein all individuals can flourish by learning, working and participating in political life in addition to exercising their legal capacity as full members of society. The Convention thus regards the interdependency of human beings as a cornerstone for securing the enjoyment of human rights. This interdependency not only tempers the individualism that has marked the field of international human rights law but also leads more than ever before to the blurring of both civil and political and economic and social rights.[34] It is reflected in the opinions of the CRPD Committee, which has regularly stressed 'the interdependence and interrelatedness of both categories of human rights' to the States Parties.[35]

How to bring reality more into alignment with the Convention undeniably remains a major challenge.[36] Efforts to meet this challenge have mostly been confined to DPOs and their allies who are eager to monitor its actual implementation. In the meantime, disability largely remains the concern of a limited number of specialists. In order to make it an integral part of international human rights law, it is imperative to build stronger partnerships within the human rights community. While the disability rights movement has tapped into international human rights

[32] Quinn and Degener, *The Current Use and Future Potential of United Nations Human Rights Instruments in the Context of Disability*, 297.

[33] F. Mégret, 'The Disabilities Convention: Towards a Holistic Concept of Rights' (2008) 12 *International Journal of Human Rights* 261, 262.

[34] G. de Beco, 'The Indivisibility of Human Rights and the Convention on the Rights of Persons with Disabilities' (2019) 68 *International & Comparative Law Quarterly* 141, 155–6.

[35] T. Degener, '10 years of Convention on the Rights of Persons with Disabilities' (2017) 35 *Netherlands Quarterly of Human Rights* 152, 154.

[36] L. Series, 'Disability and Human Rights' in N. Watson and S. Vehmas (eds), *Routledge Handbook of Disability Studies* (London: Routledge, 2nd edn, 2019) 72, 83.

law, the CRPD has not yet acted as a proper catalyst for improving human rights protection in general. Human rights experts need to show greater awareness of the advantages to be obtained from familiarising themselves with the new stipulations of the Convention.[37] They should no longer relegate disability to the fringes of the human rights domain but regard it as an essential and intrinsic part of it.

Such a move may very well lead to a two-way conflict. One the one hand, there is the challenge posed by some human rights treaties allowing the limitation of human rights as a result of impairment, as is the case with the ICCPR. This means that it will be difficult for treaty bodies to acquiesce unreservedly to the CRPD Committee's opinions. On the other hand, reconciling their respective recommendations could undermine the CRPD's ambitions because of the discrepancies that derive from the existing normative gap. With the Convention a new vision of the 'human' attached to the very notion of human rights has nevertheless emerged, a vision which has repercussions for evaluating the way in which social institutions have been configured until now.

The solution to closing this normative gap lies in constructing a dialogue of the treaty bodies with all the human rights experts, and not just with those interested disability. The dialogue should provide for the mapping of a broad research agenda where disability is finally regarded as a 'universal feature of the human condition'.[38] One entry point for this purpose is the Convention's general principles which could act as the common denominator for narrowing conflicts between the different human rights treaties and for building bridges across the human rights community. Noteworthy in this regard is the fact that most of the Convention's general principles are readily applicable to any group of people. As stressed throughout the book, '[e]quality of opportunity', '[a]ccessibility', not to mention '[e]quality between men and women', are important not just for disabled people but for all individuals.[39] These are aims which have been on the human rights agenda for decades and which the CRPD has brought to greater prominence.

In the absence of meaningful action, disability is not likely to get the attention it deserves. Rather than bringing it into the mainstream, international human rights law in that case would remain tied with a disembodied conception of the legal subject, thereby entrenching many people into a position of 'outliers'. In order to avoid this, it is important to explore all available avenues for accommodating human differences through recognising that disability is indeed a central aspect of the human experience. Such accommodation requires fostering an environment that enables all individuals to exercise their human rights. It should generate structures

[37] A. Dhanda, 'Constructing a new Human Rights Lexicon: Convention on the Rights of Persons with Disabilities' (2008) 5 *International Journal on Human Rights* 43, 55.

[38] J. Bickenbach, 'Minority Rights or Universal Participation: The Politics of Disablement' in M. Jones and L. Basser Mark (eds), *Disability, Divers-Ability and Legal Change* (The Hague: Martinus Nijhoff Publishers 1999) 101, 112.

[39] Article 3(e), (f) and (g), CRPD.

allowing for the achievement of decision making, the outreach of the learning experience, the flexibility of working arrangements as well as the broadening of political participation. It is through a universal approach like this that human rights will carry any real meaning for disabled people.

The task that lies ahead therefore is to ensure that the full range of human rights benefits all groups of people, with no limitations placed on any particular group, as well as to explore strategies for responding to specific needs arising from certain manifestations of vulnerability. This may even involve having to abandon sooner or later the use of disability as a ground for adopting the measures required to meet such needs. However, before any of this happens, it will still be necessary to increase awareness of disability when defining who are the beneficiaries of human rights protection. This is one of the reasons why the CRPD is holding on to its normative gap-filling mission.

Bibliography

Albin, E., 'Universalising the *Right to Work* of Persons with Disabilities: An Equality and Dignity Based Approach' in V. Mantouvalou (ed), *The Right to Work. Legal and Philosophical Perspectives* (Oxford: Hart Publishing, 2015) 61–85.

Arajävi, P., 'UN CRPD and the Human Rights of Persons with Disabilities' in J. Kumpuvuori and M. Scheinin (eds), *United Nations Convention on the Rights of Persons with Disabilities – Multidisciplinary Perspectives* (Helsinki: The Center for Human Rights of Persons with Disabilities in Finland, 2012) 34–51.

Arduin, S., 'Taking Metaregulation to the United Nations Human Rights Treaty Regime: The Case of the Convention on the Rights of Persons with Disabilities' (2019) 41 (4) *Law & Policy* 411–31.

Arnardóttir, O., 'A Future of Multidimensional Disadvantage Equality?' in O. Arnardóttir and G. Quinn (eds), *The UN Convention on the Rights of Persons with Disabilities. European and Scandinavian Perspectives* (London/Boston: Martinus Nijhoff Publishers, 2009) 41–65.

Arneil, B., 'Disability, Self Image, and Modern Political Theory' (2009) 27 (2) *Political Theory* 218–42.

Arneil, B., 'Disability in Political Theory versus International Practice: Redefining Equality and Freedom' in B. Arneil and J. Hirschmann (eds), *Disability and Political Theory* (Cambridge: Cambridge University Press, 2017) 20–42.

Arstein-Kerslake, A., *Restoring Voice to People with Cognitive Disabilities: Realizing the Right to Equal Recognition before the Law* (Cambridge: Cambridge University Press, 2017).

Arstein-Kerslake, A., 'An Empowering Dependency: Exploring Support for the Exercise of Legal Capacity' (2016) 18 (1) *Scandinavian Journal of Disability Research* 77–92.

Arstein-Kerslake, A. and Flynn, E., 'The Right to Legal Agency: Domination, Disability and the Protections of Article 12 of the Convention on the Rights of Persons with Disabilities' (2014) 10 (1) *International Journal of Law in Context* 22–38.

Bagenstos, S., 'The Future of Disability Law' (2004) 114 (1) *Yale Law Journal* 1–84.

Barclay, L., 'Disability, Respect and Justice' (2010) 27 (2) *Journal of Applied Philosophy* 154–71, 161–3.

Barclay, L., 'Natural Deficiency or Social Oppression? The Capabilities Approach to Justice for People with Disabilities' (2012) 9 (4) *Journal of Moral Philosophy* 500–20.

Barnes, E., *The Minority Body. A Theory of Disability* (Oxford: Oxford University Press, 2016).

Bartlett, P., 'The United Nations Convention on the Rights of Persons with Disabilities and Mental Health Law' (2012) 75 (5) *Modern Law Review* 752–78.

Battersbury, S., 'Language Justice for Sign Language Peoples: The UN Convention on the Rights of Persons with Disabilities' (2012) 11 *Language Policy* 253–72.

Becker, L., 'Reciprocity, Justice and Disability' (2005) 116 (1) *Ethics* 9–39.

Besson, S. and Marti, J.L., 'Legitimate Actors of International Law-Making: Towards a Theory of International Democratic Representation' (2018) 9 (3) *Jurisprudence* 504–40.

Bickenbach, J., 'Minority Rights or Universal Participation: The Politics of Disablement' in M. Jones and L. Basser Mark (eds), *Disability, Divers-Ability and Legal Change* (The Hague: Martinus Nijhoff Publishers, 1999) 101–15.

Bickenbach, J., Rubinelli, S. and Stucki, G., 'Being a Person with Disabilities or Experiencing Disability: Two Perspectives on the Social Response to Disability' (2017) 49 (7) *Journal of Rehabilitation Medicine* 543–9.

Broderick, A., *The Long and Winding Road to Equality and Inclusion for Persons with Disabilities. The United Nations Convention on the Rights of Persons with Disabilities* (Mortsel: Intersentia, 2015).

Broderick, A., 'Of Rights and Obligations: The Birth of Accessibility' (2020) 24 (4) *International Journal of Human Rights* 393–413.

Brolan, C., 'A Word of Caution: Human Rights, Disability, and Implementation of the Post-2015 Sustainable Development Goals' (2016) 5 *Laws* 1–18; available at: https://www.mdpi.com/2075-471X/5/2/22.

Bruyère, S. and Van Looy, S., 'Finding and Maintaining Employment Lessons from Workplace Nondiscrimination Measures in High-Income Countries' in J. Heymann, M. Stein and G. Moreno (eds), *Disability and Equity at Work* (New York: Oxford University Press, 2014) 42–70.

Bruyère, S. and Murray, B., 'The Human Rights of Workers with Disabilities' in J. Gross and L. Compa (eds), *Labor and Employment Relations: International and Domestic Perspectives* (Ithaca, NY: Cornell University Press, 2009) 213–33.

Burchardt, T., 'Capabilities and Disability: The Capabilities Framework and the Social Model of Disability' (2004) 19 (7) *Disability & Society* 735–51.

Byrne, B., 'Minding the Gap? Children with Disabilities and the United Nations Convention on the Rights of Persons with Disabilities' in M. Freeman (ed), *Law and Childhood Studies* (Oxford: Oxford University Press, 2012) 419–37.

Byrne, B., 'Hidden Contradictions and Conditionality: Conceptualisations of Inclusive Education in International Human Rights Law' (2013) 28 (2) *Disability & Society* 232–44.

Byrne, B., 'Dis-Equality: Exploring the Juxtaposition of Disability and Equality' (2018) 6 (1) *Social Inclusion* 9–17.

Byrne, B., 'Article 23. Children with Disabilities' in J. Tobin (ed), *The UN Convention on the Rights of the Child. A Commentary* (Oxford: Oxford University Press, 2019) 856–901.

Byrne, P., *Philosophical and Ethical Problems in Mental Handicap* (Basingstoke: Macmillan Press, 2000).

Calder, G., 'Disability and Misrecognition' in S. Thompson and M. Yar (eds), *The Politics of Misrecognition* (Aldershot: Ashgate, 2011) 105–25.

Carlson, L. and Kittay, E., 'Introduction: Rethinking Philosophical Presumptions in Light of Cognitive Disability' (2009) 40 (3–4) *Metaphilosophy* 307–30.

Carver, R., 'One NHRI or Many? How Many Institutions Does It Take to Protect Human Rights? – Lessons from the European Experience' (2011) 3 (1) *Journal of Human Rights Practice* 1–24.

Celik, E., 'The Role of the CRPD in Rethinking the Subject of Human Rights' (2017) 21 (7) *International Journal of Human Rights* 933–55.

Chalabi, A., *National Human Rights Action Planning* (Oxford: Oxford University Press, 2018).

Clough, B., 'Disability and Vulnerability: Challenging the Capacity/Incapacity Binary' (2017) 16 (3) *Social Policy & Society* 469–81.

Collins, H., 'Discrimination, Equality and Social Inclusion' (2003) 66 (1) *Modern Law Review* 16–43.

Collins, H., 'Social Inclusion: A Better Approach to Equality Issues?' (2005) 14 (3) *Transnational Law and Contemporary Problems* 897–918.

Connors, C. and Stalkers, K, 'Children's Experiences of Disability: Pointers to a Social Model of Childhood Disability' (2007) 22 (1) *Disability & Society* 19–33.

Courtis, C. and Tobin, J., 'Article 28. The Right to Education' in J. Tobin (ed), *The UN Convention on the Rights of the Child. A Commentary* (Oxford: Oxford University Press, 2019) 1056–115.

Craigie, J. et al, 'Legal Capacity Mental Capacity and Supported Decision-Making: Report from a Panel Event' (2019) 62 *International Journal of Law and Psychiatry* 160–8.

Danermark, B. and Gellerstedt, L., 'Social Justice: Redistribution and Recognition – A Non-reductionist Perspective on Disability (2004) 19 (4) *Disability and Society* 339–53.

de Beco, G., 'Article 33 (2) of the UN Convention on the Rights of Persons with Disabilities. Another Role for National Human Rights Institutions?' (2011) 29 (1) *Netherlands Quarterly of Huma*

de Beco, G., 'The Right to Inclusive Education According to Article 24 of the UN Convention on the Rights of Persons with Disabilities: Background, Requirements and (Remaining) Questions' (2014) 32 (3) *Netherlands Quarterly of Human Rights* 263–87.

de Beco, G., 'Transition to Inclusive Education Systems According to the Convention on the Rights of Persons with Disabilities' (2016) 34 (1) *Nordic Journal of Human Rights* 40–59.

de Beco, G., 'The Right to Inclusive Education: Why is There so much Opposition to its Implementation?' (2018) 14 (3) *International Journal of Law in Context* 396–415.

de Beco, G., 'Comprehensive Legal Analysis of Article 24 of the Convention on the Rights of Persons with Disabilities' in G. de Beco, J. Lord and S. Quinlivan (eds), *The Right to Inclusive Education in International Human Rights Law* (Cambridge: Cambridge University Press, 2019) 58–92.

de Beco, G., 'The Indivisibility of Human Rights and the Convention on the Rights of Persons with Disabilities' (2019) 68 (1) *International & Comparative Law Quarterly* 141–60.

de Beco, G. and Murray, R., *Commentary on the Paris Principles on National Human Rights Institutions* (Cambridge: Cambridge University Press, 2014).

de Beco, G. and Hoefmans, A., 'National Structures for the Implementation and Monitoring of the UN Convention on the Rights of Persons with Disabilities' in G. de Beco (ed), *Article 33 of the UN Convention on the Rights of Persons with Disabilities: National Structures for the Implementation and Monitoring of the Convention* (Leiden/Boston: Martinus Nijhoff Publishers, 2013) 11–66.

De Bhailís, C. and Flynn, E., 'Recognising Legal Capacity: Commentary and Analysis of Article 12 CRPD' (2017) 13 (1) *International Journal of Law in Context* 6–21.

de Burca, G., Keohane, R. and Sabel, C., 'New Modes of Pluralist Global Governance' (2013) 45 (3) *New York University Journal of International Law & Politics* 723–86.

de Silva de Alwis, R., 'Mining the Intersections: Advancing the Rights of Women and Children with Disabilities within an Interrelated Web of Human Rights' (2009) 18 (1) *Pacific Rim Law & Policy Journal* 293–322.

Degener, T., 'A Human Rights Model of Disability' in P. Blanck and E. Flynn (eds), *Routledge Handbook of Disability Law and Human Rights* (Abingdon: Routledge, 2016) 31–49.

Degener, T., '10 years of Convention on the Rights of Persons with Disabilities' (2017) 35 (3) *Netherlands Quarterly of Human Rights* 152–7.

Dhanda, A., 'Universal Legal Capacity as a Universal Human Right' in M. Dudley, D. Silove and F. Gale (eds), *Mental Health and Human Rights: Vision, Praxis and Courage* (Oxford: Oxford University Press, 2012) 177–94.

Dhanda, A., 'Legal Capacity in the Disability Rights Convention: Stranglehold of the Past or Lodestar for the Future?' (2007) 34 (2) *Syracuse Journal of International Law and Commerce* 429–62.

Dhanda, A., 'Constructing a new Human Rights Lexicon: Convention on the Rights of Persons with Disabilities' (2008) 5 (8) *International Journal on Human Rights* 43–59.

Dodds, S., 'Dependence, Care, and Vulnerability' in C. Mackenzie, W. Rogers and S. Dodds (eds), *Vulnerability New Essays in Ethics and Feminist Philosophy* (Oxford: Oxford University Press, 2014) 181–203.

Donnelly, J., *Universal Human Rights in Theory and Practice* (Ithaca/London: Cornell University Press, 3rd edn, 2013).

Ebersold, S., 'Accessibilité, politiques inclusives et droit à l'éducation: considérations conceptuelles et méthodologiques' (2015) 9 *ALTER European Journal of Disability Research* 22–33.

Elias, N., *What is Sociology?* Transl. S. Mennell and G. Morrissey (New York: Columbia University Press, 1978).

Fiala-Butora, J., Stein, M. and Lord, J., 'The Democratic Life of the Union: Toward Equal Voting Participation for Europeans with Disabilities' (2014) 55 (1) *Harvard International Law Journal* 71–104.

Fineman, M., *The Autonomy Myth: A Theory of Dependency* (New York: The New Press, 2004).

Fineman, M., 'The Vulnerable Subject: Anchoring Equality in the Human Condition' (2008) 20 (1) *Yale Journal of Law & Feminism* 1–23.

Fineman, M., 'The Vulnerable Subject and the Responsive State' (2010) 60 (2) *Emory Law Journal* 251–75, 266–67.

Fineman, M., 'Equality, Autonomy, and the Vulnerable Subject in Law and Politics' in M. Fineman and A. Grear (eds), *Vulnerability: Reflections on a New Ethical Foundation for Law and Politics* (Farnham: Ashgate, 2013) 13–27.

Fineman, M., 'Equality and Difference – The Restrained State' (2015) 66 (3) *Alabama Law Review* 609–26.

Florian, J. and Spratt, J., 'Enacting Inclusion: A Framework for Interrogating Inclusive Practice' (2013) 28 (2) *European Journal of Special Needs Education* 119–35.

Flynn, E. and Arstein-Kerslake, A., 'Legislating Personhood: Realising the Right to Support in Exercising Legal Capacity' (2014) 10 (1) *International Journal of Law in Context* 81–104.

Flynn, E., *Rhetoric to Action. Implementing the UN Convention on the Rights of Persons with Disabilities* (Cambridge: Cambridge University Press, 2011).

Francis, L., 'Understanding Autonomy in Light of Intellectual Disability' in K. Brownlee and A. Cureton (eds), *Disability and Disadvantage* (Oxford: Oxford University Press, 2009) 200–15.

Fraser, N. and Honneth, A., *Redistribution or Recognition? A Political-Philosophical Exchange* (London/New York: Verso, 2003).

Fraser, N., 'Rethinking Recognition' (2000) 3 (3) *New Left Review* 107–20.

Fredman, S., 'Redistribution and Recognition: Reconciling Inequalities' (2007) 23 (2) *South African Journal on Human Rights* 214–34.

Fredman, S., *Discrimination Law* (Oxford: Oxford University Press, 2nd edn, 2011).

Fredman, S., 'Substantive Equality Revisited' (2016) 14 (3) *International Journal of Constitutional Law* 712–38.

Friedlander, H., 'The Exclusion and Murder of the Disabled' in R. Gellately and N. Stoltzfus (eds), *Social Outsiders in Nazi Germany* (Princeton: Princeton University Press, 2001) 145–64.

Garland-Thomson, R., 'Disability, Identity, and Representation' in T. Titchkosky and R. Michalko (eds), *Rethinking Normalcy* (Toronto: Canadian Scholar's Press, 2009) 63–74.

Garland-Thomson, R., 'Misfits: A Feminist Materialist Disability Concept' (2011) 26 (3) *Hypatia* 591–609.

Garland-Thomson, R., 'The Case for Conserving Disability' (2012) 9 (3) *Bioethical Inquiry* 339–55.

Goldschmidt, J., 'New Perspectives on Equality: Towards Transformative Justice through the Disability Convention?' (2017) 35 (1) *Nordic Journal of Human Rights* 1–14.

Gooding, P., *A New Era for Mental Health Law and Policy: Supported Decision-Making and the UN Convention on the Rights of Persons with Disabilities* (Cambridge: Cambridge University Press, 2017).

Gooding, P., 'Supported Decision-Making: A Rights-Based Disability Concept and its Implications for Mental Health Law' (2013) 20 (3) *Psychiatry, Psychology and Law* 431–51.

Gooding, P., 'Navigating the Flashing Amber Lights of the Right to Legal Capacity in the United Nations Convention on the Rights of Persons with Disabilities: Responding to Major Concerns' (2015) 15 (1) *Human Rights Law Review* 45–71.

Goodley, D., *Disability Studies. An Interdisciplinary Approach* (London: SAGE Publications, 2011).

Goodley, D., *Dis/ability Studies: Theorising Disablism and Ableism* (London: Routledge, 2014).

Goonesekere, S., 'Article 15' in M. Freeman, C. Chinkin and B. Rudolf (eds), *The UN Convention on the Elimination of All Forms of Discrimination against Women: A Commentary* (Oxford: Oxford University Press, 2012) 387–407.

Grear, A., "Framing the project' of international human rights law: Reflections on the dysfunctional 'family' of the Universal Declaration' in C. Gearty and C. Douzinas (eds), *The Cambridge Companion to Human Rights Law* (Cambridge: Cambridge University Press, 2013) 17–35.

Griffin, J., *On Human Rights* (Oxford: Oxford University Press, 2008).

Grue, J., 'Inclusive Marginalisation? A Critical Analysis of the Concept of Disability, Its Framings and Their Implications in the United Nations Convention on the Rights of Persons with Disabilities' (2019) 37 (1) *Nordic Journal of Human Rights* 3–17.

Hahn, H., 'The Politics of Physical Differences: Disability and Discrimination' (1988) 44 (1) *Journal of Social Issues* 39–47.

Harnacke, C., 'Disability and Capability: Exploring the Usefulness of Martha Nussbaum's Capabilities Approach for the UN Disability Rights Convention' (2013) 41 (4) *Journal of Law, Medicine and Ethics* 769–80.

Harpur, P., 'Embracing the New Disability Rights Paradigm: The Importance of the Convention on the Rights of Persons with Disabilities' (2012) 27 (1) *Disability & Society* 1–14.

Harpur, P., 'Indigenous Persons with Disabilities and the Convention on the Rights of Persons with Disabilities. An Identity without a Home?' (2018) 7 (2) *International Human Rights Law Review* 165–200.

Harpur, P., *Ableism at Work: Disablement and Hierarchies of Impairment* (Cambridge: Cambridge University Press, 2019).

Hartley, C., 'Justice for the Disabled: A Contractualist Approach' (2009) 40 (1) *Journal of Social Philosophy* 17–36.

Hedge, N. and Mackenzie, A., 'Putting Nussbaum's Capability Approach to Work: Re visiting Inclusion, *Cambridge Journal of Education* (2012) 42 (3) 327–44.

Heikkilä, M., Katsui, H. and Mustaniemi-Laakso, M., 'Disability and Vulnerability: A Human Rights Reading of the Responsive State' (2020) 24 (8) *International Journal of Human Rights* 1180–1200.

Herring, J., 'Forging a Relational Approach: Best Interest or Human Rights?' (2013) 13 (1) *Medical Law International* 32–54.

Herring, J., 'The Disability Critique of Care' (2014) 8 *Elder Law Review* 1–15, 14.

Herring, J., *Vulnerable Adults and The Law* (Oxford: Oxford University Press, 2016).

Herro, A., 'The Pre-negotiation of UN Human Rights Treaties: The Case of the Convention on the Rights of Persons with Disabilities' (2019) 24 (2) *International Negotiation* 240–65.

Heymann, J., Stein, M. and Moreno, G., 'Disability, Employment, and Inclusion Worldwide' in J. Heymann, M. Stein and G. Moreno (eds), *Disability and Equity at Work* (New York: Oxford University Press, 2014) 1–19.

Hirschmann, N., 'Disabling Barriers, Enabling Freedom' in B. Arneil and J. Hirschmann (eds), *Disability and Political Theory* (Cambridge: Cambridge University Press, 2017) 99–122.

Honneth, A., *The Struggle for Recognition. The Moral Grammar of Social Conflicts* (Cambridge: Polity Press, 1995).

Hornby, G., 'Inclusive Special Education: Development of a New Theory for the Education of Children with Special Educational Needs and Disabilities' (2015) 42 (3) *British Journal of Special Education* 234–56.

Hunt, P., 'Configuring the UN Human Rights System in the "Era of Implementation": Mainland and Archipelago' (2017) 39 (3) *Human Rights Quarterly* 489–538.

Johnson, A. and Powell, S., 'Disability and Election Administration in the United States: Barriers and Improvements' (2020) 41 (2–3) *Policy Studies* 249–70.

Johnson, K., 'The UN Convention on the Rights of Persons with Disabilities: A Framework for Ethical and Inclusive Practice?' (2013) 7 (3) *Ethics & Social Welfare* 218–31.

Jones, M. and Basser Marks, L., 'Law and the Social Construction of Disability' in M. Jones and L. Basser Marks (eds), *Disability, Divers-ability and Legal Change* (Leiden/Boston: Martinus Nijhoff Publishers, 1999) 3–24.

Jones, P., 'Collective and Group-Specific: Can the Rights of Ethno-Cultural Minorities be Human Rights?' in G. Pentassuglia (ed), *Ethno-Cultural Diversity and Human Rights. Critiques and Challenges* (Leiden/Boston: Martinus Nijhoff, 2018) 27–58.

Joseph, S. and Castan, M., *The International Covenant on Civil and Political Rights: Cases, Materials and Commentary* (Oxford University Press: Oxford, 3rd edn, 2013).

Kanter, A., *The Development of Disability Rights under International Law. From Charity to Human Rights* (Abingdon: Routledge, 2015).

Kayess, R. and French, P., 'Out of Darkness into Light? Introducing the Convention on the Rights of Persons with Disabilities' (2008) 8 (1) *Human Rights Law Review* 1–34.

Kayess, R. and Green, J., 'Today's Lesson is on Diversity: A Reflection on Inclusive Education' in P. Blanck and E. Flynn (eds), *Routledge Handbook of Disability Law and Human Rights* (London: Routledge, 2016) 53–71.

Kittay, F., *Love's Labor: Essays on Women, Equality and Dependency* (New York/London: Routledge, 1999).

Kittay, F., 'A Feminist Care Ethics, Dependence and Disability' (2007) 6 (2) *Feminism and Philosophy* 3–7.

Kittay, F., 'The Ethics of Care, Dependence and Disability' (2011) 24 (1) *Ratio Juris* 49–58.

Kett, M. et al, 'Disability, Development and the Dawning of a New Convention: A Cause for Optimism?' (2009) 21 (5) *Journal of International Development* 649–61.

Kymlicka, W., *Liberalism, Community and Culture* (Oxford: Oxford University Press Clarendon, 1989).

Lagoutte, S., 'The Role of State Actors within the National Human Rights System' (2019) 37 (3) *Nordic Journal of Human Rights* 177–94.

Liasidou, A., *Inclusive Education, Politics and Policymaking* (London: Continuum, 2012).

Liasidou, A., 'Inclusive Education and Critical Pedagogy at the Intersections of Disability, Race, Gender and Class' (2012) 10 (1) *Journal for Critical Education Policy Studies* 168–84.

Lockwood, E. and Tardi, R., 'The Inclusion of Persons with Disabilities in the Implementation of the 2030 Agenda for Sustainable Development' (2014) 57 (3–4) *Development* 433–7.

Lorion, S., 'A Model for National Human Rights Systems? New Governance and the Convention on the Rights of Persons with Disabilities' (2019) 37 (3) *Nordic Journal of Human Rights* 234–58.

Lord, J., 'Mirror, Mirror on the Wall: Voice Accountability and NGOs in Human Rights Standard Setting' (2004) 5 (2) *Seton Hall Journal of Diplomacy and International Relations* 93–100.

Lord, J., 'Disability Rights and the Human Rights Mainstream: Reluctant Gate-Crashers?' in B. Clifford (ed), *The International Struggle for New Human Rights* (Philadelphia: University of Pennsylvania Press, 2008) 83–92.

Lord, J., 'Persons with Disabilities in International Humanitarian Law – Paternalism, Protectionism or Rights?' in C. Schuland-Vials and M. Gill (eds), *Disability, Human Rights and the Limits of Humanitarianism* (Aldershot: Ashgate, 2014) 155–77.

Lord, J. and Stein, M., 'The Domestic Incorporation of Human Rights Law and the United Nations Convention on the Rights of Persons with Disabilities' (2008) 83 (4) *Washington University Law Review* 449–79.

Lord, J. and Stein, M., 'Future Prospects for the *United Nations Convention on the Rights of Persons with Disabilities*' in O. Arnardóttir and G. Quinn (eds), *The UN Convention on the Rights of Persons with Disabilities. European and Scandinavian Perspectives* (London/Boston: Martinus Nijhoff Publishers, 2009) 17–40.

Lord, J., Stein, M. and Fiala-Butora, J., 'Facilitating an Equal Right to Vote for Persons with Disabilities' (2014) 6 (1) *Journal of Human Rights Practice* 115–39.

Löve, L., Traustadóttir, R. and Rice, J., 'Achieving Disability Equality: Empowering Disabled People to Take the Lead' (2018) 6 (1) *Social Inclusion* 1–8.

Lundy, L., Tobin, J. and Parkes, A., 'Article 12: The Right to Respect for the Views of the Child' in J. Tobin (ed), *The UN Convention on the Rights of the Child. A Commentary* (Oxford: Oxford University Press, 2019) 397–434.

Lynch, S. and Irvine, A., 'Inclusive Education and Best Practice for Children with Autism Spectrum Disorder: An Integrated Approach' (2009) 13 *International Journal of Inclusive Education* 845–59.

Mackenzie, C., 'The Importance of Relational Autonomy and Capabilities for an Ethics of Vulnerability' in C. Mackenzie, W. Rogers and S. Dodds, S. (eds), *Vulnerability New Essays in Ethics and Feminist Philosophy* (Oxford: Oxford University Press, 2014) 30–59.

Mackenzie, C., Rogers, W. and Dodds, S., 'Introduction: What Is Vulnerability and Why Does It Matter for Moral Theory?' in C. Mackenzie, W. Rogers and S. Dodds (eds), *Vulnerability New Essays in Ethics and Feminist Philosophy* (Oxford: Oxford University Press, 2014) 1–29.

Maisley, N., 'The International Right of Rights? Article 25(a) of the ICCPR as a Human Right to Take Part in International Law-Making' (2017) 28 (1) *European Journal of International Law* 89–113.

Malleson, K., 'Equality Law and the Protected Characteristics' (2018) 81 (4) *Modern Law Review* 598–621.

Mallet, R. and Runswick-Cole, K., *Approaching Disability: Critical Issues and Perspectives* (Abington: Taylor Francis, 2014).

Matsubayashi, T. and Ueda, M., '*Disability and Voting*' (2014) 7 (3) *Disability and Health Journal* 285–91.

Mattila, M. and Papageorgiou, A., 'Disability, Perceived Discrimination and Political Participation' (2017) 38 (5) *International Political Science Review* 505–19.

May-Simera, C., 'Reconsidering Sheltered Workshops in Light of the United Nations Convention on the Rights of Persons with Disabilities (2006)' (2018) 7 *Laws*; available at https://www.mdpi.com/2075-471X/7/1/6.

McMurry, M., 'Applying Human Rights to Enable Participation' (2019) 23 (7) *International Journal of Human Rights* 1049–73.

Mégret, F., 'The Disabilities Convention: Human Rights of Persons with Disabilities or Disability Rights' (2008) 30 (2) *Human Rights Quarterly* 494–516.

Mégret, F., 'The Disabilities Convention: Towards a Holistic Concept of Rights' (2008) 12 (2) *International Journal of Human Rights* 261–78.

Mégret, F. and Mspia, D., 'Global Reasonable Accommodation: How the Convention on the Rights of Persons with Disabilities Changes the Way We Think About Equality' (2014) 30 (2) *South African Journal on Human Rights* 251–74.

Minkowitz, T., 'The United Nations Convention on the Rights of Persons with Disabilities and the Right to be Free from Nonconsensual Psychiatric Interventions' (2007) 34 (2) *Syracuse Journal of International and Comparative Law* 405–28.

Minkowitz, T., 'Rethinking Criminal Responsibility from a Critical Disability Perspective: The Abolition of Insanity/Incapacity Acquittals and Unfitness to Plead, and Beyond' (2014) 23 (3) *Griffith Law Review* 434–66.

Minow, M., *Making All the Difference. Inclusion, Exclusion, and American Law* (Ithaca: Cornell University Press, 1990).

Minow, M., 'Universal Design in Education. Remaking All the Difference' in A. Kanter and B. Ferri (eds), *Righting Education Wrongs* (Syracuse: Syracuse University Press, 2013) 38–57.

Mitra, S., 'Employment Challenges and Successes in Low- and Middle-Income Countries' in J. Heymann, M. Stein and G. Moreno (eds), *Disability and Equity at Work* (New York: Oxford University Press, 2014) 267–301.

Moore, M. and Slee, R., 'Disability Studies, Education and Exclusion' in N. Watson, A. Roulstone and C. Thomas (eds), *Routledge Handbook of Disability Studies* (London: Routledge, 2012) 225–39.

Morris, J., 'Impairment and Disability: Constructing an Ethics of Care That Promotes Human Rights' (2001) 16 (1) *Hypatia* 1–46.

Mulligan, D. and Gooding, K., *The Millennium Development Goals and People with Disabilities* (UK: Sightsavers International, 2009).

Murray, J., De Meulder, M. and le Maire, D., 'An Education in Sign Language as a Human Right?: The Sensory Exception in the Legislative History and Ongoing Interpretation of Article 24 of the UN Convention on the Rights of Persons with Disabilities' (2018) 40 (1) *Human Rights Quarterly* 37–60.

Murray, J. et al, 'Intersectional Inclusion for Deaf Learners: Moving beyond General Comment no. 4 on Article 24 of the United Nations Convention on the Rights of Persons with Disabilities' (2018) 24 (7) *International Journal of Inclusive Education* 691–705.

Neill, O., *Towards Justice and Virtue: A Constructive Account of Practical Reasoning* (Cambridge: Cambridge University Press, 1996).

Nussbaum, M., *Frontiers of Justice: Disability, Nationality, Species Membership* (Cambridge, MA: The Belknap Press, 2007).

Nussbaum, M., *Creating Capabilities: The Human Development Approach* (Cambridge, MA: Belknap Press, 2011).

O'Cinneide, C., 'Extracting Protection for the Rights of Persons with Disabilities' in O. Arnardóttir and G. Qunn (eds), *The UN Convention on the Rights of Persons with Disabilities. European and Scandinavian Perspectives* (London/Boston: Martinus Nijhoff Publishers 2009) 163–98.

O'Cinneide, C., 'The Right to Work in International Human Rights Law' in V. Mantouvalou (ed), *The Right to Work. Legal and Philosophical Perspectives* (Oxford: Hart Publishing, 2015) 99–122.

Oliver, M., *Understanding Disability. From Theory to Practice* (New York: Palgrave Macmillan, 2nd edn, 2009).

Otto, D., 'Women's Rights' in D. Moeckli et al (eds), *International Human Rights Law* (Oxford University Press, 3rd edn, 2018) 309–25.

Petman, J., 'The Special Reaching for the Universal: Why a Special Convention for Persons with Disabilities?' in J. Kumpuvuori and M. Scheinin (eds), *United Nations Convention on the Rights of Persons with Disabilities – Multidisciplinary Perspectives* (Helsinki: The Center for Human Rights of Persons with Disabilities in Finland, 2012) 20–33.

Priestley, M. et al, 'The Political Participation of Disabled People in Europe: Rights, Accessibility and Activism' (2016) 42 *Electoral Studies* 1–9.

Quinn, G., *Rethinking Personhood: New Directions in Legal Capacity Law and Policy* (An Ideas Paper), *April 2011, University of British Columbia, Vancouver*; available at: https://www.inclusionireland.ie/sites/default/files/attach/basic-page/846/rethinkingpersonhood-newdirectionsinlegalcapacitylawandpolicy-gerardquinn-april2011.docx.

Quinn, G., 'Disability and Human Rights: A New Field in the United Nations' in K. Krause and M. Scheinin (eds) *International Protection of Human Rights: A Textbook* (Turku: Åbo Akademi University-Institute for Human Rights, 2009) 247–71.

Quinn, G., 'Resisting the "Temptation of Elegance": Can the Convention on the Rights of Persons with Disabilities Socialise States to Right Behaviour?' in O. Arnardóttir and G. Quinn (eds), *The UN Convention on the Rights of Persons with Disabilities. European and Scandinavian Perspectives* (London/Boston: Martinus Nijhoff Publishers, 2009) 215–48.

Quinn, G. and Arstein-Kerslake, A., 'Restoring the 'Human' in 'Human Rights' – Personhood and Doctrinal Innovation in the UN Disability Convention' in C. Gearty and C. Douzinas (eds), *The Cambridge Companion to Human Rights Law* (Cambridge: Cambridge University Press, 2013) 36–55.

Quinn, G. and Degener, T., *The Current Use and Future Potential of United Nations Human Rights Instruments in the Context of Disability* (New York/Geneva: UN, 2002).

Raley, M., 'The Drafting of Article 33 of the Convention on the Rights of Persons with Disabilities: The Creation of a Novel Mechanism' (2016) 20 (1) *The International Journal of Human Rights* 138–52.

Ravet, J., 'Inclusive/Exclusive? Contradictory Perspectives on Autism and Inclusion: The Case for an Integrative Position' (2011) 15 (6) *International Journal of Inclusive Education* 667–82.

Rawls, J., *Political Liberalism* (New York: Columbia University Press, 1993).

Rawls, J., *A Theory of Justice* (Cambridge, MA: Harvard University Press, 2nd rev. edn, 1999).

Rawls, J., *Justice as Fairness: A Restatement* (Cambridge, MA: Harvard University Press, 2001).

Réaume, D., 'Individuals, Groups, and Rights to Public Goods' (1998) 38 (1) *University of Toronto Law Journal* 1–27.

Richardson, H., 'Rawlsian Social-Contract Theory and the Severely Disabled' (2006) 10 (4) *The Journal of Ethics* 419–62.

Rimmerman, A., *Social Inclusion of People with Disabilities. National and International Perspectives* (Cambridge: Cambridge University Press, 2013).

Rimmerman, A., *Family Policy and Disability* (Cambridge: Cambridge University Press, 2015).

Rimmerman, A., *Disability and Community Living Policies* (Cambridge: Cambridge University Press, 2017).

Rioux, M. and Pinto, P., 'A Time for the Universal Right to Education: Back to the Basics' (2010) 31 (5) *British Journal of Sociology of Education* 621–42.

Robeyns, I., 'The Capabilities Approach: A Theoretical Survey' (2005) 6 (1) *Journal of Human Development* 93–114.

Robeyns, I., 'Is Nancy Fraser's Critique of Theories of Distributive Justice Justified?' in K. Olson (ed), *Adding Insult to Injury: Nancy Fraser Debates Her Critics* (London: Verso, 2008) 176–95.

Robeyns, I., 'Justice as Fairness and the Capability Approach' in B. Kaushik and K. Ravi (eds), *Arguments for a Better World: Essays in Honor of Amartya Sen. Volume 1: Ethics, Welfare, and Measurement* (Oxford: Oxford University Press, 2009) 397–413.

Runswick-Cole, K., 'Time to End the Bias Towards Inclusive Education?' (2011) 38 (3) *British Journal of Special Education* 112–19.

Sabatello, M., 'A Short History of the International Disability Rights Movement' in M. Sabatello and M. Schulze (eds), *Human Rights & Disability Advocacy* (Philadelphia: University of Pennsylvania Press, 2013) 13–24.

Sabatello, M., 'The New Diplomacy' in M. Sabatello and M. Schulze (eds), *Human Rights & Disability Advocacy* (Philadelphia: University of Pennsylvania Press, 2013) 238–58.

Saleh, M. and Bruyère, S., 'Leveraging Employer Practices in Global Regulatory Frameworks to Improve Employment Outcomes for People with Disabilities' (2018) 6 (1) *Social Inclusion* 18–28.

Sandel, M., *Liberalism and the Limits of Justice* (Cambridge: Cambridge University Press, 2nd edn, 1998).

Sandland, R., 'A Clash of Conventions? Participation, Power and the Rights of Disabled Children' (2017) 5 (3) *Social Inclusion* 93–103.

Sandland, R., 'Lessons for Children's Rights from Disability Rights' in E. Brems, E. Desmet and W. Vandenhole (eds), *Children's Rights Law in the Global Human Rights Landscape: Isolation, Inspiration, Integration?* (Abingdon: Routledge 2017) 109–28.

Sargeant, A., Radevich-Katsaroumpa, E. and Innesti, A., 'Disability Quotas: Past or Future Policy?' (2018) 39 (3) *Economic and Industrial Democracy* 404–21.

Satz, A., 'Disability, Vulnerability, and the Limits of Antidiscrimination' (2008) 83 (4) *Washington Law Review* 513–68.

Satz, A., 'Disability, Vulnerability, and Fragmented Protections' in A. Kanter and B. Ferri (eds), *Righting Education Wrongs* (Syracuse: Syracuse University Press, 2013) 265–93.

Saul, B., Kinley, D. and Mowbray, J., *The International Covenant on Economic, Social and Cultural Rights. Commentary, Cases, and Materials* (Oxford: Oxford University Press, 2014).

Schur, L., Kruse, D. and Blanck, P., *People with Disabilities. Sidelined or Mainstreamed?* (New York: Cambridge University Press, 2013).

Schur, L., 'Towards Inclusion: Political and Social Participation of People with Disabilities' in P. Blanck and E. Flynn (eds), *Routledge Handbook of Disability Law and Human Rights* (Oxon/New York: Routledge, 2017) 118–33.

Schur, L. and Adya, M., 'Sidelined or Mainstreamed? Political Participation and Attitudes of People with Disabilities in the United States' (2013) 94 (3) *Social Science Quarterly* 811–39.

Sciubba, J., 'Securing Rights in the 21st Century: A Comparison of the Disability and Older Persons' Rights Convention' (2016) 15 (4) *Journal of Human Rights* 533–49.

Scully, J. 'The Convention on the Rights of Persons with. Disabilities and Cultural Understandings of Disability' in J. Anderson and J Philips (eds), *Disability and Universal Human Rights: Legal, Ethical, and Conceptual. Implications of the Convention on the Rights of Persons with Disabilities* (Utrecht: Netherlands Institute of Human Rights, 2012) 71–83.

Scully, J., 'Disability and Vulnerability: On Bodies, Dependence, and Power' in C. Mackenzie, W. Rogers and S. Dodds (eds), *Vulnerability New Essays in Ethics and Feminist Philosophy* (Oxford: Oxford University Press, 2014) 204–21.

Sen, A., *Inequality Re-examined* (Oxford: Clarendon Press, 1992).

Sen, A., *Development as Freedom* (New York: Knopf, 1999).

Series, L., 'Relationships, Autonomy and Legal Capacity: Mental Capacity and Support Paradigms' (2015) 40 *International Journal of Psychiatry* 80–9.

Series, L., 'Disability and Human Rights' in N. Watson and S. Vehmas (eds), *Routledge Handbook of Disability Studies* (London: Routledge, 2nd edn, 2019) 72–88.

Shyman, E., 'Towards a Globally Sensitive Definition of Inclusive Education Based in Social Justice' (2015) 62 (4) *International Journal of Disability, Development and Education* 351–62.

Siebers, T., 'Disability and the Right to Have Rights' (2007) 27 (1–2) *Disability Studies Quarterly*; available at: http://dsq-sds.org/article/view/13/13.

Siebers, T., *Disability Theory* (Ann Arbor: University of Michigan Press, 2008).

Silvers, A., 'A Diverse Theory of Justice for Disability' in K. Brownlee and A. Cureton (eds), *Disability and Disadvantage* (Oxford: Oxford University Press, 2009) 161–99.

Silver, A., 'An Essay on Modeling: The Social Model of Disability' in C. Ralston and J. Ho (eds), *Philosophical Reflections on Disability* (New York: Springer, 2012) 1–36.

Silvers, A. and Francis, L., 'Justice through Trust: Disability and the "Outlier Problem" in Social Contract Theory' (2005) 116 (1) *Ethics* 40–76.

Silvers, A. and Francis, L., 'Thinking About the Good: Reconfiguring Liberal Metaphysics (or Not) for People with Cognitive Disabilities' (2009) 40 (3–4) *Metaphilosophy* 475–99.

Sisson, M. and DeNicola, M., 'Minimal Mutual Advantage: How the Social contract can do Justice to the Disabled (2015) 14 (2) *European Journal of Political Theory* 161–79.

Shaw, B. 'Inclusion or Choice? Securing the Right to Inclusive Education for All' in M. Sabatello and M. Schulze (eds), *Human Rights & Disability Advocacy* (Philadelphia: University of Pennsylvania Press, 2013) 58–69.

Skarstad, K., 'Human Rights through the Lens of Disability' (2018) 36 (1) *Netherlands Quarterly of Human Rights* 24–42.

Skarstad, K. and Stein, M., 'Mainstreaming Disability in the United Nations Treaty Bodies' (2018) 17 (1) *Journal of Human Rights* 1–24.

Stark, C., 'How to Include the Severely Disabled in A Contractarian Theory of Justice' (2007) 15 (2) *The Journal of Political Philosophy* 127–45.

Stein, M., 'Disability Human Rights' (2007) 95 (1) *California Law Review* 75–121.

Stein, M., McClain-Nhlapo, C. and Lord, J., 'Education and HIV/AIDS. Disability Rights and Inclusive Development' in M. Langford, A. Sumner and A.E. Yamin (eds), *Millenium Development Goals and Human Rights* (New York: Cambridge University Press, 2013) 274–94.

Stein, M. and Lord, J., 'Monitoring the Convention on the Rights of Persons with Disabilities: Innovations, Lost Opportunities, and Future Potential' (2010) 32 (3) *Human Rights Quarterly* 689–728.

Stein, M. and Stein, P., 'Disability, Development, and Human Rights: A Mandate and Framework for International Financial Institutions' (2014) 47 (4) *U.C. Davis Law Review* 1231–78.

Stiker, H.-J., *A History of Disability*, Trans. W. Sayers (Ann Arbor: University of Michigan Press, 1999).

Szmukler, G., '"Capacity", "Best Interests", "Will and Preferences" and the UN Convention on the Rights of Persons with Disabilities' (2019) 18 (1) *World Psychiatry* 34–41.

Taylor, C., 'The Politics of Recognition' in A. Gutman (ed), *Multiculturalism: Examining the Politics of Recognition* (Princeton: Princeton University Press, 1994) 25–73.

Terzi, L., 'The Social Model of Disability: A Philosophical Critique' (2004) 21 (2) *Journal of Applied Philosophy* 141–57.

Terzi, L., *Justice and Equality in Education: A Capability Perspective on Disability and Special Educational Needs* (London/New York: Continuum, 2008).

Terzi, L., 'What Metric of Justice for Disabled People? Capability and Disability' in H. Brighouse and I. Robeyns (eds), *Measuring Justice: Primary Goods and Capabilities* (Cambridge: Cambridge University Press, 2010) 150–73.

Thomas, G., 'Inclusive Schools for an Inclusive Society' (1997) 24 (3) *British Journal of Special Education* 103–7.

Tomasevski, T., *Education Denied. Cost and Remedies* (London/New York: Zed Books, 2003).

Tremain, S., 'On the Subject of Impairment' in M. Corker and T. Shakespeare (eds), *Disability/Postmodernity: Embodying Disability Theory* (London: Continuum, 2002) 32–47.

Tremain, S., 'Foucault, Governmentality and Critical Disability Theory' in S. Tremain (ed), *Foucault and the Government of Disability* (Ann Arbor: The University of Michigan Press, 2005) 1–24.

Tromel, S., 'Personal Perspective on the Drafting History of the United Nations Convention on the Rights of Persons with Disabilities' in G. Quinn and L. Waddington (eds), *European Yearbook of Disability Law* (Antwerp: Intersentia, 2009) 115–37.

Vehmas, S. and Mäkelä, P., 'The Ontology of Disability and Impairment: A Discussion of the Natural and Social Features' in K. Kristiansen, S. Vehmas and T. Shakespeare (eds), *Arguing about Disability: Philosophical Perspectives* (London: Routledge, 2009) 42–56.

Venkatapuram, S., 'Mental Disability, Human Rights and the Capabilities Approach: Searching for the Foundations' (2014) 26 (4) *International Review of Psychiatry* 408–14.

Ventegodt Liisberg, M., 'Flexicurity and Employment of Persons with Disability in Europe in a Contemporary Disability Human Rights Perspective' in L. Waddington, G. Quinn and E. Flynn (eds), *European Yearbook of Disability Law* (Antwerp/Portland: Intersentia, 2013) 145–68.

Verheyde, M., *A Commentary on the United Nations Convention on the Rights of the Child. Article 28. The Right to Education* (Leiden/Boston: Martinus Nijhoff, 2006).

Vorhaus, J., 'Disability, Dependency and Indebtedness' (2007) 4 (1) *Journal of Philosophy of Education* 29–44.

Vorhaus, J., 'Capability, Freedom and Profound Disability' (2013) 28 (8) *Disability & Society* 1047–58.

Waddington, L., Priestley, M. and Yalcin, B., 'Equality of Opportunity in Employment? Disability Rights and Active Labour Market Policies' in P. Blanck and E. Flynn (eds), *Routledge Handbook of Disability Law and Human Rights* (Oxon/New York: Routledge, 2017) 72–87.

Wolff, J., 'Disability Among Equals' in K. Brownlee and A. Cureton (eds), *Disability and Disadvantage* (Oxford: Oxford University Press, 2009) 112–37.

Wolff, J., 'Cognitive Disability in a Society of Equals' (2009) 40 (3–4) *Metaphilosophy* 402–15.

Wolff, J., 'Disability, Status Enhancement, Personal Enhancement and Resource Allocation' (2009) 25 (1) *Economics and Philosophy* 49–68.

Wolff, J. and De-Shalit, A., *Disadvantage* (Oxford: Oxford University Press, 2007).

Wong, S., 'Duties of Justice to Citizens with Cognitive Disabilities' (2009) 40 (3–4) *Metaphilosophy* 382–401.

Young, I., *Justice and the Politics of Difference* (Princeton: Princeton University Press, 1990).

Zola, I., 'Toward the Necessary Universalizing of a Disability Policy' (1989) 67 (2) *The Milbank Quarterly* 401–28.

UN Agencies

ILO, *Promoting Diversity and Inclusion through Workplace Adjustments: A Practical Guide* (Geneva: ILO, 2016).

ILO, *Decent Work for Persons with Disabilities: Promoting Rights in the Global Development Agenda* (Geneva: ILO, 2015).

ILO, *Managing Disability in the Workplace: An ILO Code of Practice* (Geneva: ILO, 2015).

OHCHR, *Thematic Study on the Right of Persons with Disabilities to Education*, 18 December 2013, A/HRC/25/29.

OHCHR, *Thematic Study on Work and Employment of Persons with Disabilities*, 17 December 2012, A/HRC/22/25.

OHCHR, *Thematic Study on Participation in Political and Public Life by Persons with Disabilities*, 21 December 2011, A/HRC/19/36.

OHCHR, *Study on International Cooperation to Support National Efforts for the Realization of the Purposes and Objectives of the Convention on the Rights of Persons with Disabilities*, 20 December 2010, A/HRC/16/38.

UNDP Independent Evaluation Office, *Evaluation of Disability-Inclusive Development at UNDP* (New York: UN, 2016).

UNICEF, *The State of the World's Children 2013. Children with disabilities* (New York: UNICEF, 2013).

UNICEF Innocenti Research Centre, *Promoting the Rights of Children with Disabilities* (Florence: UNICEF, 2007).

World Health Organisation (WHO) and World Bank, *World Report on Disability* (Geneva: WHO, 2011).

UN Bodies

Boly Barry, B., *Report of the Special Rapporteur on* the *Right to Education*, 29 September 2017, A/72/496.

CEDAW Committee, *General Recommendation No 23: Political and Public Life*, 13 January 1997, A/52/38.

CEDAW Committee, *General Recommendation No. 18: Disabled Women*, 30 January 1991, A/46/38.

CESCR Committee, *General Comment No 23: The Right to Just and Favourable Conditions of Work*, 27 April 2016, E/C.12/GC/23.

CESCR Committee, *General Comment No 18: The Right to Work*, 6 February 2006, E/C.12/GC/18.

CESCR Committee, *General Comment No. 14: The Right to the Highest Attainable Standard of Health*, 11 August 2000, E/C.12/2000/4.

CESCR Committee, *General Comment No 13: The Right to Education (Art. 13)*, 8 December 1999, E/C.12/1999/10.

CESCR Committee, *General Comment No 11: Plans of Action for Primary Education (Art. 14)*, 10 May 1999, E/C.12/1999/4.

CESCR Committee, *General Comment No. 5: Persons with Disabilities*, 9 December 1994, E/1995/22.

CRC Committee, *General Comment No. 9: The Rights of Children with Disabilities*, 27 February 2007, CRC/C/GC/9.

CRC Committee, *General Comment No 1: The Aims of Education (Art. 29(1)*, 17 April 2001, CRC/GC/2001/1.

CRPD Committee, *General Comment No 7: The Participation of Persons with Disabilities, including Children with Disabilities, through their Representative Organizations, in the Implementation and Monitoring of the Convention*, 9 November 2018, CRPD/C/GC/7.

CRPD Committee, *General Comment No 6: Equality and Non-discrimination*, 26 April 2018, CRPD/C/GC/6.

CRPD Committee, *General Comment No 5. Article 19: Living Independently and Being Included in the Community*, 29 August 2017, CRPD/C/GC/5.

CRPD Committee, *General Comment No 4. Article 24: Right to Inclusive Education*, 2 September 2016, CRPD/C/GC/4.

CRPD Committee, *General Comment No 3. Article 6: Women and Girls with Disabilities*, 2 September 2016, CRPD/C/GC/3.

CRPD Committee, *General Comment No 2. Article 9: Accessibility*, 22 May 2014, CRPD/C/GC/2.

CRPD Committee, *General Comment No 1. Article 12: Equal Recognition Before the Law*, 19 May 2014, CRPD/C/GC/1.

CRPD Committee, *Rules of Procedure. Annex: Guidelines on Independent Monitoring Frameworks and their Participation in the Work of the Committee on the Rights of Persons with Disabilities*, 10 October 2016, CRPD/C/1/Rev.1.

CRPD Committee, *Calleja Loma and Calleja Lucas v Spain*, 30 September 2020, CRPD/C/23/D/41/2017.

CRPD Committee, *Zsolt Bujdosó and five others v Hunguary*, 20 September 2013, CRPD/C/10/D/4/2011.

Devandas Aguilar, C., *Report of the Special Rapporteur on the Rights of Persons with Disabilities*, 12 January 2016, A/HRC/31/62.

GA, *Comprehensive and Integral International Convention to Promote and Protect the Rights and Dignity of Persons with Disabilities*, 26 February 2002, A/RES/56/168.

GA, *Standard Rules for the Equalisation of Opportunities for Persons with Disabilities*, 20 December 1993, A/RES/48/96.

GA, *Principles for Protection of Persons with Mental Illness and the Improvement of Mental Health Care*, 17 December 1991, A/RES/46/119.

GA, *International Decade of Disabled Persons*, 23 November 1984, A/RES/39/26.

GA, *World Programme of Action for Persons with Disabilities*, 3 December 1982, A/RES/37/52.

GA, *International Year of Disabled Persons*, 8 December 1981, A/RES/36/77.

GA, *Declaration on the Rights of Disabled Persons*, 9 December 1975, A/RES/3447 (XXX).

GA, *Declaration on the Rights of Mentally Retarded Persons*, 20 December 1971, A/RES/26/2856.

Human Rights Committee, *General Comment No 25. Article 25: The Right to Participate in Public Affairs, Voting Rights and the Right to Equal Access to Public Service*, 12 July 1996, CCPR/C/21/Rev.1/Add.7.

HRC, *The Right to Education of Persons with Disabilities*, 24 March 2014, A/HRC/25/L.30.

HRC, *The Work and Employment of Persons with Disabilities*, 14 March 2013, A/HRC/22/L.4.

Munoz, V., *The Right to Education of Persons with Disabilities. Report of the Special Rapporteur on the Right to Education*, 19 February 2007, A/HRC/4/29.

World Conference on Human Rights, *Vienna Declaration and Programme of Action*, 25 June 1993, A/Conf.157/23.

World Conference on Special Needs Education: Access and Equality, *Salamanca Statement and Framework for Action on Special Needs Education*, 7–10 June 1994; available at: https://unesdoc.unesco.org/ark:/48223/pf0000098427_eng.

Other

Canadian Human Rights Commission (CHRC) and Global Alliance of National Human Rights Institutions (GANHRI), *Survey. National Human Rights Institutions and the Convention on the Rights of Persons with Disabilities* (Geneva: GANHRI, 2019); available at: https://ganhri.org/wp-content/uploads/2020/08/CHRC_rapport_survey_WEB_fev_2020_final_NEW_-_EN_FINAL-ua.pdf.

FRA, *The Right to Political Participation for Persons with Disabilities: Human Rights Indicators* (Vienna: FRA, 2014).

Global Campaign for Education and Handicap International, *Equal Right, Equal Opportunity. Inclusive Education for Children with Disabilities*; available at: http://www.campaignforeducation.org/docs/reports/Equal%20Right,%20Equal%20Opportunity_WEB.pdf.

Inclusion International, *Better Education for all when we are included too. A Global Report. People with an Intellectual Disability and their Families Speak out on Education for All, Disability and Inclusive Education*, October 2009, available at: http://ii.gmalik.com/pdfs/Better_Education_for_All_Global_Report_October_2009.pdf.

OECD, *Sickness Disability and Work: Breaking the Barriers. A Synthesis of Findings across OECD Countries* (Paris: OECD, 2010).

OSCE Office for Democratic Institutions and Human Rights, *Guidelines on Promoting the Political Participation of Persons with Disabilities* (Warsaw: OSCE, 2019).

Index

For the benefit of digital users, indexed terms that span two pages (e.g., 52–53) may, on occasion, appear on only one of those pages.